Routledge Revivals

Mahatma Gandhi At Work

Mahatma Gandhi At Work

Edited By

C. F. Andrews

First published in 1931 by George Allen & Unwin Ltd.

This edition first published in 2018 by Routledge
2 Park Square, Milton Park, Abingdon, Oxon, OX14 4RN
and by Routledge
52 Vanderbilt Avenue, New York, NY 10017, USA

Routledge is an imprint of the Taylor & Francis Group, an informa business

© 1931 Taylor & Francis

All rights reserved. No part of this book may be reprinted or reproduced or utilised in any form or by any electronic, mechanical, or other means, now known or hereafter invented, including photocopying and recording, or in any information storage or retrieval system, without permission in writing from the publishers.

Publisher's Note
The publisher has gone to great lengths to ensure the quality of this reprint but points out that some imperfections in the original copies may be apparent.

Disclaimer
The publisher has made every effort to trace copyright holders and welcomes correspondence from those they have been unable to contact.
A Library of Congress record exists under ISBN:

ISBN 13: 978-0-367-13695-6 (hbk)
ISBN 13: 978-0-367-13696-3 (pbk)
ISBN 13: 978-0-429-02811-3 (ebk)

MAHATMA GANDHI AT WORK

Edited by C. F. Andrews

MAHATMA GANDHI'S IDEAS
INCLUDING SELECTIONS FROM HIS WRITINGS

Demy 8vo.   Frontispiece.   Second Impression

"It should be studied by all who would try to understand the subtle beauty of the Hindu mind."—*Spectator*

"It throws valuable light on the career of a remarkable personality."—*New Statesman*

"The book is of great value and profound interest."—*Times Literary Supplement*

MAHATMA GANDHI: HIS OWN STORY

Demy 8vo.   With illustrations.   Second Impression

"A self-revelation without a parallel, the record of a personality and a struggle possible only in our age and amid the conditions created by British rule in India. . . . An absorbing book to read. It stands alone in frankness and plain honesty. It reveals a being of profound humanity and of irresistible charm. Its place among the classics of autobiography cannot be in doubt."—*New Statesman*

MAHATMA GANDHI TO-DAY

MAHATMA GANDHI

AT WORK

HIS OWN STORY CONTINUED

EDITED BY

C. F. ANDREWS

LONDON
GEORGE ALLEN & UNWIN LTD
MUSEUM STREET

FIRST PUBLISHED IN 1931

All rights reserved

PRINTED IN GREAT BRITAIN BY
UNWIN BROTHERS LTD., WOKING

DEDICATED

TO THE MEMORY

OF

MAGANLAL K. GANDHI

PREFACE

IN THIS BOOK, which forms the third volume of the series, I have tried to fulfil the promise which I gave in *Mahatma Gandhi: His Own Story*, by relating in his own words the epic struggle in the Transvaal to set right the wrongs which had been done to the Indian Community. There he first proved to the world the practical success of his own original method, called Satyagraha, or Truth Force, whereby the evils of the world may be righted without recourse to the false arbitrament of war. I have also added chapters which complete the picture of his dietetic and fasting experiments, together with certain personal idiosyncrasies that go to make up his complex character. The material for this story is taken from his two books *Satyagraha in South Africa* and *My Experiments with Truth*. A chapter has also been added from *Hind Swaraj*.

"I had long entertained the desire," he declares, "to write a history of that South African struggle. Some things about it I alone could relate. Only the general who conducts the campaign can know the objective of each particular move; and as this was the first attempt to apply the principle of Satyagraha to politics on a large scale, it is necessary that the public should have some idea of its development."

"The beauty," he adds, "of this method is that it comes up to oneself; one has not to go out in search for it. A struggle of Righteousness,[1] in which there are no secrets to be guarded, no scope for cunning, and no

---
[1] He uses the Sanskrit word "Dharma-yudda."

place for untruth, comes unsought; and a man of religion is ever ready for it. A struggle which has to be previously planned is not a righteous struggle. In the latter God Himself plans the campaign and conducts battles. It can be waged only in the name of God. Only when the combatant feels quite helpless—only when he has come to the extreme point of weakness and finds utter darkness all around him, only then God comes to the rescue. God helps, when a man feels himself humbler than the very dust under his feet. Only to the weak and helpless is the divine succour vouchsafed."

This vital principle of moral resistance, or soul force, taking the place of armed revolt, represents in my opinion by far the greatest contribution which Mahatma Gandhi has made to the moral philosophy of our own time. As the passage quoted shows, the movement depends entirely upon God for its accomplishment. It is a religious struggle from first to last; Gandhi is a man of religion, and he cannot think of such a warfare being carried on to success in any other terms. But with this one proviso he believes that what he calls his "experiment with Truth" must succeed wherever this method is sincerely and simply tried. For God is Truth and Goodness.

Here then might be found just that "moral equivalent for war" which the American philosopher William James required. Mahatma Gandhi has shown us by practical experiment how the principle works. For the thoughtful Christian it has a remarkable likeness to the precepts of the Sermon on the Mount. Mr. Gandhi has never failed to acknowledge his debt of gratitude in his own religious life for that sublime teaching. The same principle is deeply embedded as an idea in the ancient

PREFACE

literature of India, going back to Buddhist times and beyond. To the West in its efforts to recover from the disastrous effects of a war, wherein every decency of human life was violated and Truth was trampled in the dust, it offers a way of peace.

At the back of the Disarmament Conference and the Assemblies of the League of Nations there must be some direct method left for suffering mankind to resist intolerable evil. In the past this has nearly always taken the crude form of armed resistance and violent retaliation. Only in the rarest instances, such as the early Christians of the first century, have men sought corporately to overcome evil by the resistance of moral refusal. Powerful as this method has always proved, it has died away again. George Fox has been the latest genius in the West to restore it in an organized manner, and the Society of Friends has nobly carried on his high tradition. In the East, Mohandas Gandhi has revived it in our own times with a wealth of experiment that has made his work take almost the form of the laboratory method of modern science. He has tested every side of it in order to probe its weakness. He has confessed to "Himalayan blunders" in its working. But he has gone steadily forward with the experiment, because he supremely believes the principle itself to be sound. In all kinds of untoward circumstances and impossible conditions, he has met with either partial or complete success. In any other field of scientific investigation even such modified success as he has achieved would have set other investigators at work to carry the principle further and test all its weakest points. Yet this still remains to be done.

There is no reason whatever, as Mr. Gandhi has

shown again and again, why the same principle which he has established in the East should not prove practicable in the West. But it is a force which requires discipline, training and direction. There must be also a religious background combined with a faith that can remove mountains. For the discipline, proceeding from within, implies a sustained courage superior to military fortitude, a bravery more reckless in heroic daring than a forlorn hope in a desperate campaign, a power of suffering greater even than that of the battlefield and the trenches. Mahatma Gandhi believes this force of moral resistance in its purity to be irresistible. For it is a Law of God's Moral Nature, an attribute of God Himself. This is Gandhi's great theory of life which he has tried to bring into line with practical science by repeated experiment.

The epic story contained in this book will go far to confirm Mahatma Gandhi's own belief. We can see here before our eyes, in its dramatic setting, an insignificant body of persecuted and despised men and women transformed into a conquering army. We are not spared any of their weaknesses, though the characters are drawn by the hand of one who loves them. With their loyal support, weak and feeble as they are, Gandhi is able to win in the end a victory for the Truth without a single violent act of retaliation being committed.

I have included, as a kind of interlude at different stages, some of the more intimately personal sections of the autobiography which had been omitted from the previous volume. It would have been a great pleasure to me to have added more of such passages, but the story of the actual struggle, dramatically told, is so simple

PREFACE

that it carries its own inner meaning along with it and the reader almost unconsciously feels the greatness of the issues.

In retracing over again this Transvaal episode for the purpose of editing this book, I had the singular advantage of having been personally present nearly twenty years ago at Durban, Pretoria and Cape Town during some of the most critical events whereby a settlement was reached with General Smuts. It was equally opportune that I should happen to be in South Africa itself, while this volume was being prepared, seeking to the uttermost of my power to prevent new Transvaal legislation from being passed which would have undone by an Act of Parliament much of Mr. Gandhi's laboriously accomplished work. In this connexion, I was able to visit afresh the very place in the centre of Johannesburg where he had his lawyer's office, and also Von Brandis Square where his life was nearly lost at the hands of a Pathan. It was possible for me also to go out to Tolstoy Farm at Lawley, and to see everything there almost unchanged, outwardly, from the time when the passive resisters made it their headquarters. On different occasions I passed outside the jail at Pretoria where he was imprisoned and saw the last resting-place of young Shaporji Sorabji. Along with Valliamma, he was among the noblest of the younger generation of passive resisters, who were ready at all times to lay down their lives for the Truth. For Valiamma's memory in the Transvaal there is still needed some suitable memorial, and my earnest hope is that this will not be forgotten.

Of those who took part in the struggle and are still living, S. B. Medh and Pragjee Desai have been my daily companions in South Africa; Hermann Kallenbach was with me in Johannesburg; Henry and Millie Polak have helped me on my return to London. Others, such as Thambi Naidu and Sonya Schlesin, have been with me from time to time, reviving happy memories of strenuous days in the past. Albert Christopher is now a barrister and a leader of the Indian community in Natal. Haji Habib, who is still living, told me with much detail about his visit to London described in this book.

My deep gratitude is due to Mrs. Gool in Cape Town, whose motherly help made it possible for me to carry through the greater part of this task. In London I received the same care and help from Mrs. Alexander Whyte, and to her the same debt of gratitude is also due. I would wish to add the names of J. S. and Maud Aiman, Horace and Olive Alexander, Agatha Harrison, John Hoyland, along with others too numerous to mention, who have helped me by their sympathy and loving kindness.

To Valji Desai, Indulal Yajnik and S. Ganesan are due my sincerest thanks. It was owing in no little measure to their perseverance that Mahatma Gandhi was able to carry through successfully his original plan of writing and publishing this history. Valjibhai was solely responsible for the translation of the dictated Gujarati narrative into English, and S. Ganesan has published it in its completed form. This translation I have used quite freely, condensing and abbreviating wherever it seemed necessary to do so. In rare instances I have repeated a few lines of the text which had been already used in one or other of the two previous volumes; but this has been

PREFACE

done as sparingly as possible. All that I have thus undertaken has had the full consent of Mahatma Gandhi himself, though it has not received his revision. He has been ready to trust without hesitation my judgment concerning the needs of the English-speaking public in these matters. Dr. Doke has most kindly permitted me to make extracts from his father's book, entitled, *An Indian Patriot in South Africa*, and also from the *Life* of his father, written by W. E. Cursons and published by the Christian Literature Depot, Johannesburg.

The present volume brings to an end at last that work of interpretation of the East to the West which I had contemplated many years ago through the character and work of Mahatma Gandhi. It has been a great happiness to me that the response has been so spontaneous, not only in England and America, but also on the continent of Europe. If health permits, it is still my hope in a further volume to trace out in perspective the historical background of Rabindranath Tagore. These two outstanding personalities—Tagore and Gandhi—are the living examples in our own generation whereby the West may test its capacity to understand the East.

C. F. ANDREWS

CAMBRIDGE

CONTENTS

		PAGE
	PREFACE BY C. F. ANDREWS	7
	A SHORT LIST OF INDIAN WORDS	19
CHAPTER		
I.	THE SOUTH AFRICAN SCENE	23
II.	THE EVILS OF INDENTURE	40
III.	MY FIRST EXPERIENCES	61
IV.	AFTER THE BOER WAR	79
V.	A SIMPLER LIFE	97
VI.	THE PROFESSION OF LAW	112
VII.	THE REGISTRATION ORDINANCE	124
VIII.	THE SATYAGRAHA OATH	142
IX.	IN ENGLAND	160
X.	THE FIRST ENCOUNTER	176
XI.	IMPRISONMENT	195
XII.	THE ATTEMPTED SETTLEMENT	218
XIII.	HELPERS IN THE STRUGGLE	238
XIV.	A BREACH OF FAITH	257
XV.	THE STRUGGLE RENEWED	273
XVI.	GENERAL BOTHA'S OFFER	290
XVII.	'HIND SWARAJ'	308
XVIII.	TOLSTOY FARM	317
XIX.	MR. GOKHALE'S VISIT	336
XX.	THE FAMOUS MARCH (BY C. F. ANDREWS)	349
XXI.	THE END OF THE STRUGGLE	357

APPENDIX		PAGE
I.	FIRST DAYS IN SOUTH AFRICA	371
II.	THE ORIGIN OF SATYAGRAHA	374
III.	PRISON DAYS. MR. DOKE'S DIARY	376
IV.	THE ASSAULT ON MR. GANDHI	378
V.	THOUGHTS ON THE GITA	380
VI.	THE CLOSING EVENTS	388
VII.	MR. POLAK'S VISIT TO INDIA	392
VIII.	THE INDIAN WOMEN'S PART	393
IX.	MR. GANDHI'S FAREWELL	395
	BIBLIOGRAPHY	403
	INDEX	405

ILLUSTRATIONS

MAHATMA GANDHI TO-DAY *Frontispiece*

	FACING PAGE
TOLSTOY FARM	112
MR. GANDHI IN SOUTH AFRICA ABOUT 1900	208
A BAND OF SATYAGRAHIS, WITH MR. GANDHI IN THE CENTRE	320

A SHORT LIST OF COMMON INDIAN WORDS

Titles of Reverence and Respect

Word	Meaning
Mahatma	A title of Gandhi meaning "Great Soul"
Gurudeva	A title of Tagore meaning "Revered Teacher"
Deshbandhu	A title of the late C. R. Das meaning "Friend of the Country"
Lokamanya	A title of the late B. G. Tilak meaning "Beloved by the people"

Religious Institutions

Sabarmati Ashram	The religious institution of Mahatma Gandhi near Ahmedabad
Santiniketan	The religious institution of Rabindranath Tagore near Calcutta
Gurukula	The religious institution founded by Mahatma Munshi Ram near Hardwar

Terms Used in Passive Resistance

Ahimsa	Non-violence
Satya	Truth
Satyagraha	Truth-force or Soul-force
Satyagrahi	One who practises Soul-force
Brahmacharya	The practice of Chastity
Brahmachari	One who practises Chastity

Mahatma Gandhi's Hand-spinning Movement

Charka	The spinning-wheel
Khaddar }	Home-spun cloth
Khadi }	

Muhammadan Religious Terms

Islam	The religion of the Prophet Muhammad
Muslim	Belonging to Islam
Musalman	Follower of Islam
Khilafat	The office of Caliph
Maulvi	Religious Teacher of Islam
Imam	The leader of the prayers

Sacred Sanskrit Books

Vedas	The earliest religious hymns of India
Upanishad . . .	The earliest religious philosophy
Puranas . . .	The sacred Hindu Legends
Gita	The Song of the Divine Lord: a most famous Scripture

Hindu Religion

Dharma . . .	Religion or religious duty
Varnashrama Dharma .	Religion of Caste
Sanatana Dharma . .	Orthodox Hindu religion
Sanatani . . .	An orthodox Hindu

The Four Castes

Brahman . . .	The first Caste (knowledge)
Kshattriya . . .	The second Caste (rule)
Vaishya . . .	The third Caste (trade, agriculture)
Shudra	The fourth Caste (labour)

The Four Religious Stages

Brahmacharya . .	The first stage of the religious life (chastity)
Grihastha . . .	The second stage of the religious life (householder)
Vanaprastha . . .	The third stage of the religious life (gradual retirement)
Sannyas . . .	The fourth stage of the religious life (complete retirement)

The Two Great Epics

Mahabharata . .	The National Epic wherein Krishna is the Divine Hero. The Bhagavad Gita is part of this Epic
Ramayana . . .	The Sacred Epic of North India wherein Rama is the Divine Hero. Tulasidas composed the Hindi form of the original Sanskrit poem

Political Terms

Swadeshi . . .	Belonging to, or made in, one's own country
Swaraj . . .	Self-government
Hind Swaraj . .	Indian Self-government

INDIAN WORDS

Indian Coinage

Anna	Very slightly more than one penny
Rupee	About one shilling and sixpence
Lakh	About seven thousand five hundred pounds sterling
Crore	About seven hundred and fifty thousand pounds sterling

16 annas = 1 rupee

[Note.—The short "a" in Indian languages is frequently pronounced like short "u" in English. For example, Satya is pronounced like Sutya.]

MAHATMA GANDHI AT WORK

CHAPTER I

THE SOUTH AFRICAN SCENE

MY INTENTION IN this book is to tell the story of the Indian struggle in the Transvaal which we ourselves called Satyagraha, or Truth Force—from two Sanskrit words meaning insistence upon Truth. In order to understand what happened, it is necessary to know something about the conditions of life in South Africa and the reasons which led to the settlement of Europeans and Indians in that country. Only a few of the most striking features will be given.

The climate of South Africa is for the most part so healthy and temperate that Europeans can settle there in comfort, while it is nearly impossible for them to reside permanently in India. Even in the warmer parts of South Africa there are lands of great elevation, with important centres of population, where the weather is dry and cold. One of these is Johannesburg, the great mining centre of the Transvaal. Only fifty years ago its site was desolate and covered over with dry grass. But when gold-mines were discovered, houses began to spring up, as if by magic, and to-day there are large substantial buildings everywhere and a great population. The wealthy people of the place have planted many trees which they have obtained from the more fertile tracts of South Africa and from Europe, paying as much as a guinea for a single sapling. This has added to the pleasant character of the surroundings.

The capital of the Transvaal is Pretoria, at a distance of about thirty-six miles from Johannesburg. Pretoria is a comparatively quiet place, while Johannesburg is full of noise and bustle.

Natal is the province on the south-east coast with its fine seaport of Durban and its capital at Maritzburg. The land rises from the Indian Ocean to the high Drakensburg mountain range, which stretches over into the Transvaal.

Travelling farther inland towards the south, we come to the Orange Free State. Its capital is Bloemfontein, a very quiet and small town. There are no mines in this State like those in the Transvaal.

A few hours' journey from Bloemfontein takes us to the boundary of the Cape Province, which covers the whole of the south. Kimberley is its diamond city. Its capital is Cape Town, situated on the beautiful Cape Peninsula. This is the largest seaport in South Africa.

Besides these four provinces, there are several territories under British "protection," inhabited by races which had migrated there before the appearance of Europeans in those areas.

In Natal, oranges and apricots grow in such abundance that thousands of poor people get them in the country for the mere labour of picking them. The Cape Province is the land of grapes and peaches. Hardly any other country in the world grows such fine grapes. During the season they can be had so cheap that even the poorest child can get plenty of them. The Indian settlers planted mango trees in South Africa and consequently mangoes are available. Some varieties of these can certainly compete with the best mangoes of Bombay. Vegetables also are extensively grown in Natal. It may be said that almost all the different vegetables of India are now cultivated by Indians in the Natal Province.

South Africa cannot boast of such mighty rivers as the Ganges or the Indus. The few that are there are neither large nor deep. Furthermore, the water of these rivers cannot reach many places. No canals can be taken up to the highlands; and where large rivers are absent canal irrigation becomes impossible. Wherever there is a deficiency of surface water in South Africa artesian wells are sunk, and the water needed for irrigation of fields is pumped up by windmills and steam-engines. Agriculture receives much encouragement from the Government. As South Africa lies to the south of the Equator, and India to the north, the annual climatic conditions are reversed. For example, while we have summer in India, South Africa is passing through winter.

Among the Bantu races of South Africa, the most handsome are the Zulus. I have deliberately used the word "handsome." A fair complexion and a pointed nose represent our Indian idea of beauty. But if we discard this superstition for the moment, we feel that the Creator did not spare Himself in fashioning the Zulu to perfection. Men and women among them are tall and broad-chested in proportion to their height. Their muscles are strong and well set. Their legs and arms are always well shaped. You will scarcely find a man or woman walking with a stoop. The lips are certainly large and thick, but they are in perfect symmetry with the entire physique, and I for one would not say that they are unsightly. Their eyes are round and bright. The nose is flat and large, such as would become a broad face, and the curled hair on the head sets off to advantage the Zulu's skin, which is black and shining like ebony.

If we asked a Zulu to which of the various races he would award the palm for beauty, he would unhesitatingly decide in favour of his own people; and in this I for one would not see any want of judgment on his part. For the physique of the Zulu, as I have shown, is magnificent. It is a natural law that the skins of those races which have lived in the past near the Equator should be dark. And if we believe that there must be beauty in everything fashioned by God, we not only avoid all narrow and one-sided conceptions of beauty, but we in India would become free from any improper sense of shame and dislike which we might feel for our own complexions if they are anything but fair.

The Bantus live in round huts built of wattle and daub. These huts have a single round wall and are thatched with hay. A pillar inside supports the roof. A low entrance is the only opening for the passage of air. The Bantus plaster the wall and the floor with animal dung. It is said that they cannot make anything square in shape. They have trained their eyes to see and make round things only. We never find Nature drawing straight lines, and these innocent children of Nature derive all their knowledge from their own experience. The furniture of the hut is in keeping with the simplicity of the people. There is no room for tables, chairs, boxes, and these things are rarely found in a Bantu hut.

Before the advent of European civilization, the Bantus

THE SOUTH AFRICAN SCENE

used to wear animal skins, which also served them for other purposes. Nowadays they use blankets. Before the British rule, men as well as women moved about almost in a state of nudity. Even now many do the same in the country. But let not anyone infer from this that these people cannot control their senses. Where a large society follows a particular custom, it is quite possible that the custom is quite harmless even if it seems highly improper to the members of another society. These primitive people have no time to be staring at one another.

The law requires Zulu women to cover themselves from the chest to the knees when they go into town. They are thus obliged to wrap a piece of cloth round their body. Consequently cotton pieces of that size command a large sale in South Africa, and thousands of blankets and sheets are imported from Europe every year. The men are similarly required to cover themselves from the waist to the knees. Many, therefore, have taken to the practice of wearing second-hand clothing from Europe. Others wear a sort of knickers with a fastening of tape. All these clothes are imported from Europe.

The staple food of the Zulus is maize, but they take meat also when available. Fortunately they know nothing about spices or condiments. If they find hot spices in their food they dislike them. Those among them who are looked upon as quite uncivilized will not so much as touch food with spices. It is no uncommon thing for a Zulu to take, at a time, one pound of boiled maize with a little salt. He is quite content to live upon porridge made from crushed mealies, boiled in water. Whenever he can get meat, he eats it, raw or cooked, boiled or roasted, with salt only. He will not mind taking the flesh of any animal.

The Bantu languages are named after the various tribes. The art of writing was recently introduced by Europeans. There is nothing like a special Bantu alphabet, but the Bible and other books have now been printed in Roman characters. The Zulu language is very sweet. Most of the words end with the sound of a broad "a"; therefore it sounds soft and pleasing to the ear. I have read in books that there is poetry in the words themselves. Judging from the few words which I have happened to pick up, I think this statement is true. To most of the places in Zululand they have given poetical names.

According to the missionaries, the Bantus had no religion when the white man came among them. But taking the word "religion" in a wide sense, they do believe in and worship a supreme Being beyond human comprehension. They also fear this Power. They are dimly conscious of the fact that the dissolution of the body does not mean utter annihilation. If we acknowledge morality as the basis of religion, the Bantus being moral may be held to be religious. They have an admirable grasp of the distinction between falsehood and truth. It is doubtful whether Europeans or Indians practise truthfulness to the same extent as they do in their primitive state. They have no temples or anything else of that kind. There are many superstitions among them as among other races.

This Zulu race, which is second to none in the world in physical strength, is so timid in mind to-day that even the sight of a European child brings fear. If someone aims a revolver, they will either flee or else will be too stupefied to have the power even of flight. There is certainly a reason for this. They had never seen a rifle before and had never fired a gun. This was magic to them. Nothing more had to be done beyond moving a finger, and yet a small tube all at once emits a sound, a flash is seen, and a bullet causes death in an instant. This was something the Bantu could not understand. So he stands in mortal terror of those who wield such a weapon. He and his forefathers before him have seen how such bullets have taken the lives of many helpless and innocent people. Many even to-day do not know how this happens.

"Civilization" is gradually making headway among them. Pious missionaries deliver the message of Christ, as they have understood it. They open schools for them, and teach them how to read and write. But many, who in their primitive state were free from vices, have now become corrupt. Hardly any Bantu who has come in contact with "civilization" has escaped the evil of drink. When his powerful physique is under the influence of liquor, he becomes quite insane and commits all manner of crimes. That "civilization" must lead to a multiplication of wants is as certain as that two and two make four. In order to increase the Zulu's wants, or to teach him the value of labour, a poll-tax and a hut-tax have been imposed upon him. If these were not levied, this race, attached to the soil, would not enter mines, hundreds of feet deep, in order to extract gold or diamonds; and if their labour were not available for the mines, then gold and diamonds would remain in the depths of the earth. Likewise, the Europeans would find it difficult to get any servants. The result has been that thousands of Bantu miners now suffer from "miners' phthisis" in order that gold may be obtained. This is a fatal disease. Those who fall into its clutches rarely recover.

One can easily imagine how difficult moral restraint becomes when thousands of men are living in mines away from their families. They consequently fall easy victims to venereal disease. Thoughtful Europeans of South Africa are alive to this very serious question. Some of them definitely hold that civilization has failed to exercise a wholesome influence upon them. As for the evil effects, he who runs may read.

About four hundred years ago the Dutch founded a settlement in South Africa which was then inhabited by such a simple and unsophisticated dark race as I have described. The Dutch kept slaves. Some of the Dutchmen from Java, with their Malay slaves, entered that part of the country which we now call the Cape Province. These Malays are Musalmans. They have Dutch blood in their veins and inherit some of the qualities of the Dutch. They are found scattered throughout South Africa, but Cape Town is their stronghold. Some of them to-day are in the service of Europeans, while others follow their own pursuits. Malay women are very industrious and intelligent. They are generally cleanly in their ways of living. In laundry work and sewing they are experts. The men carry on some petty trade. Many drive horses and carriages. Some have received higher English education. One of them is the well-known Doctor Abdurrahman of Cape Town, who was a member of the old Colonial Legislature; but under the new constitution the right of any coloured person becoming a member of the Union Parliament has been denied.

The Dutch have been as skilful cultivators as they have been brave soldiers. They saw that the country around them was admirably suited for agriculture. They also saw that the natives easily maintained themselves by working for only a short time during the year. Why should they not force these people to labour for them? The Dutch had guns and knew the methods of warfare. They also knew how to tame human beings like other animals, and they believed that their Christian religion did not object to this. They therefore commenced agriculture with the slave labour of the Hottentot and Bantu people without having a doubt as to the morality of their action.

As the Dutch were in search of good land for their own expansion, so were the English, who had also gradually arrived on the scene. The English and the Dutch were cousins. Their characters and ambitions were the same. Pots from the same pottery are often likely to clash against one another. So these two nations, while gradually advancing their respective claims, came into collision. There were disputes, and then battles between them.

When the first collision occurred many of the Dutch were unwilling to remain even under the nominal authority of the British, and therefore "trekked" into the unknown interior of South Africa. This was the origin of the settlement of the Transvaal and the Orange Free State. At a later date the English suffered a defeat at Majuba Hill. Majuba left a soreness which came to a head in the Boer War. When General Cronje surrendered, Lord Roberts could at last cable to Queen Victoria that Majuba had been avenged.

These Dutch came to be known as Boers in South Africa. They have preserved their language by clinging to it as a child clings to its mother. They have a vivid perception of the close relation between their language and their national freedom. Therefore in spite of many attacks they have preserved their mother tongue intact. But the language has now assumed a new form suited to the genius of the Boers. As they could not keep up a very close relationship with Holland, they began to speak a dialect, derived from Dutch, and they have given this a permanent shape called Afrikaans. Their books are written in Afrikaans, their children are educated through it, and Boer members of the Union Parliament make it a point to deliver their speeches in it. Since the formation of the South African Union, Afrikaans and English have been officially treated on a footing of equality throughout the whole country, so much so that the Government Gazette and records of Parliament must be published in both languages.

The Boers are simple, frank and religious. They settle on extensive farms. We in India can hardly have any idea of the size of these farms; for in India a farm means generally an acre or two, and sometimes even less. In South Africa, a single farmer has hundreds or even thousands of acres of land. He is not anxious to put all this under cultivation at once; and if anyone argues with him he takes no notice. "Let it lie fallow," he will say. "Lands which now lie fallow will be cultivated by our children."

Every Boer is a good fighter. However the Boers might quarrel among themselves, their liberty is so dear to them that when it is in danger, all get ready and fight as one man. They do not need elaborate drilling, because fighting with rifles is a characteristic of the whole nation. Generals Botha, Smuts, De Wet and Hertzog have been great lawyers, great farmers and also great soldiers. General Botha had one farm of nine thousand acres. He was a first-rate farmer. When he went to Europe, in connection with negotiations for peace, it was said of him that there was hardly anyone in Europe who was as good a judge of sheep as he was.

General Botha succeeded the late President Kruger. His knowledge of English was excellent; nevertheless, when he met the King of England and his Ministers he always preferred to talk in his own mother tongue, Afrikaans. Who would dare to say that this was not the proper thing to do? Why should he run the risk of committing a mistake in order to display his knowledge of English before the King? Why should he allow his train of thought to be disturbed in the search for the right English word? The British ministers might quite unintentionally employ some unfamiliar English idiom, and owing to misunderstanding he might be led into giving the wrong reply and get confused; and thus his cause would suffer. Why should he risk committing such a serious blunder as that?

Boer women are as brave and simple as the men. If the Boers shed their blood in the Boer War, they were able to offer this sacrifice owing to the wonderful courage of their women-folk and the inspiration they received from them. The women were not afraid of widowhood and refused to waste a thought upon the future.

The Boers, both men and women, are religiously-minded Christians. Yet it cannot be said that they believe in the New Testament. As a matter of fact, Europe itself does not believe in it. But in Europe they do claim to respect it, although only a few observe in action Christ's own religion of peace. But the Boers know the New Testament merely by name. They read the Old Testament with devotion and know by heart the descriptions of battles which it contains. They fully accept the Old Testament doctrine of an "eye for an eye and a tooth for a tooth," and they act accordingly.

Boer women have always understood that their religion required them to suffer in order to preserve their independence, and therefore they patiently and cheerfully endured all hardships. Lord Kitchener left no stone unturned in order to break their spirit. He confined them in separate concentration camps, where they had to undergo indescribable sufferings. They were short of food and suffered from piercing cold as well as scorching heat. Still the brave Boer women did not flinch. At last, King Edward wrote to Lord Kitchener, saying that he could not tolerate such things any longer; if this was the only means of reducing the Boers to submission, he would prefer any sort of peace rather than the continuance of war carried on in that fashion. He asked the General to bring the war to a speedy end.

When this cry of anguish reached the English people they were very deeply pained. They were still full of admiration for the bravery of the Boers. The fact that such a small nationality should sustain a conflict with their world-wide empire was rankling in their minds. So when the cry of agony raised by the women in the concentration camps was heard, not through themselves nor through the Boer men, who then were fighting valiantly on the battlefield, but through a few high-souled Englishmen and women, the English people began at last to relent. Sir Henry Campbell-Bannerman read the mind of the British nation, and raised his voice against the war. Mr. W. T. Stead publicly prayed, and invited others to pray, that God might decree even a defeat to his own countrymen in such an unjust war. This was a remarkable sight. Real suffering, bravely borne, melts even the heart of stone. Such is its spiritual power. There lies the key to the Satyagraha Movement.[1]

In the end, the Peace of Vereeniging was concluded, and eventually all the four colonies of South Africa were united under one Government. There are a few facts connected with this peace which are not within the knowledge of many. The Act of Union did not immediately follow the Peace of Vereeniging, but each colony had its own legislature for the time being. The ministry was not fully responsible to the legislature. The Transvaal and the Free State were governed on Crown Colony lines. General Botha and General Smuts were not the men to be satisfied with such restricted freedom. They flatly refused to have anything to do with the Transvaal Legislative Council. They non-co-operated and kept aloof altogether from the Government. Lord Milner made a pungent speech, in the course of which he said that General Botha need not have attached so much importance to himself. The country's Government could well be carried on without him. Lord Milner thus decided to stage *Hamlet* without the Prince of Denmark.

[1] Satyagraha means literally "Truth Force." It implies moral resistance without the use of physical force.

I have written in unstinted praise of the bravery, the love of liberty, and the self-sacrifice of the Boers. But I did not intend to convey the impression that there were not differences of opinion among them during their days of trial, or that there were not weak-kneed persons among them. Lord Milner succeeded in setting up a party among the Boers who were not difficult to satisfy, and persuaded himself into the belief that he could make a success of the Transvaal Legislature with their assistance. But even a stage play cannot be managed without a hero: and an administrator in this matter-of-fact world who expects to succeed, while ignoring all the while the central figure in the situation, can only be described as insane.

Such, indeed, was the fate of Lord Milner. It was said that though he indulged in bluff, he found it so difficult to govern the Transvaal and the Free State without the assistance of General Botha, that he was often seen in his garden in an anxious and disturbed state of mind. General Botha distinctly affirmed that by the Treaty of Vereeniging, as he understood it, the Boers were immediately entitled to complete internal autonomy. He added that if this had not been the case he would never have signed the treaty at all. Lord Kitchener declared in reply that he had given no such pledge to General Botha. The Boers would only be gradually granted full self-government as they proved their loyalty. Now, who was to judge between these two? How could one expect General Botha to agree if arbitration were suggested?

The decision arrived at in the end by the Imperial Government of those days was very creditable to them. They conceded that the stronger party should accept the interpretation of the agreement put upon it by the weaker. According to the principles of justice and truth that is the correct canon of interpretation. For though I may have meant to say something different, nevertheless I must concede that my speech or writing conveyed the meaning ascribed to it by my hearer or reader. We often break this golden rule in our lives. Hence arise many of our disputes; and a half-truth, which is worse than untruth, is made to do duty for truth itself.

Thus when truth—in the present case, General Botha—had fully triumphed, he set to work. All the colonies were eventually united, and South Africa obtained full self-government. It is no exaggeration to say that South Africa is to-day completely independent. The British Empire cannot receive a single farthing from South Africa without its own consent. Still further, the British Ministers have conceded that if South Africa wishes to remove the Union Jack and to be independent even in name, there is nothing to prevent it from doing so. If as a matter of fact the Boers have so far not taken this step, there are strong reasons for it. For one thing, the Boer leaders are shrewd and sagacious men. They see nothing improper in maintaining within the British Empire a partnership in which they have nothing to lose. But there is another very practical reason. In Natal the British predominate; in the Cape Province the British are numerous also, though they do not there outnumber the Boers; in Johannesburg itself the British element is predominant, though the Boers are in a large majority in the rest of the Transvaal. This being the case, if the Boers were to seek to establish an independent Republic in South Africa, the result would be internecine strife and possibly a civil war. South Africa, therefore, continues to rank as a Dominion of the British Empire.

The way in which the Constitution of the South African Union was framed is worthy of note. A National Convention, composed of delegates representative of all parties appointed by the Colonial legislatures, unanimously prepared a Draft Constitution and the British Parliament had to approve of it in its entirety. A member of the House of Commons drew the attention of the House to a grammatical error, and suggested that it should be rectified before the Draft Constitution was passed. Sir Henry Campbell-Bannerman, while rejecting the suggestion, observed that faultless grammar was not essential to carrying on a government; that this Draft Constitution had been framed as a result of negotiations between the British Cabinet and the Ministers of South Africa, and that they did not reserve to the British Parliament even the right of correcting a grammatical error. The Constitution, therefore, recast in the form of an Imperial Bill, passed through both Houses of the British Parliament just as it was, without the slightest alteration.

There is one more circumstance worthy of notice in this connexion. There are some provisions in the Act of Union which would appear meaningless to the lay reader. They have led to a great increase in expenditure. This had not escaped the notice of the framers of the Constitution; but their object was not to attain perfection, but by compromise to arrive at an understanding and to make the Constitution a success. That is why the Union still has four capitals, no colony being prepared to part with its own capital. Similarly, although the old colonial legislatures were abolished, Provincial Councils with subordinate and delegated functions were set up. And though Governorships were abolished, Administrators corresponding in rank to Governors were appointed for each province. Everyone knows that four legislatures, four capitals, and four Governors are unnecessary and serve merely for display. But the shrewd statesmen of South Africa did not mind this. A South African Union was desirable, and therefore the politicians did what they thought fit, regardless of outside criticism. Afterwards they got everything approved of by the British Parliament without a single addition or alteration.

CHAPTER II

THE EVILS OF INDENTURE

THE BRITISH HAD settled in Natal, where they obtained at first some concessions from the Zulus. They noticed that excellent sugar-cane, tea and coffee could be grown there. Thousands of labourers would be needed to produce such crops on a scale far beyond the working capacity of a handful of colonists from England. Therefore, they first offered inducements and then threats to the Zulus in order to make them work, but in vain. Slavery had already been abolished, and the Zulu is not used to hard agricultural labour. He can easily maintain himself by working six months in the year. Why, then, should he bind himself to an employer for a longer term? The English settlers could not get on at all with their plantations in the absence of a stable labour force. They therefore opened negotiations with the Government of India, which was in the complete control of Great Britain. They requested its help in order to obtain a steady supply of labour. The Government of India complied with their request. The first batch of indentured labourers from Calcutta and Madras reached Natal on November 16, 1860, truly an ominous date for India itself. For if these indentured labourers had not arrived, there would have been no Indians in South Africa and therefore no Satyagraha.

In my humble opinion, the Government of India was not well advised in taking the action it did. The British officials in India, consciously or unconsciously, were

THE EVILS OF INDENTURE

partial to the British settlers in Natal. It is true that, wherever possible, conditions purporting to safeguard the labourers' interests were entered upon the indentures. Arrangements were also made for their lodging. But no adequate consideration was given to the method by which these illiterate labourers, who had gone out to a distant land, should seek redress if they had any grievances against the British settlers. Not a thought was given also to their religious needs, or to the preservation of their morality. The British officials in India did not realize that, although slavery had been abolished by law, the employers had not yet got rid of the desire to make slaves of their employees, and that therefore the Indian labourers, who went out under indenture to Natal, would virtually become slaves on the estates for the whole term of their indenture.

Sir W. W. Hunter, the great Indian historian, who had studied very closely indeed these indentured labour conditions, once used a remarkable phrase about them. Writing about the Indian labourers in Natal, he said that theirs was a "state of semi-slavery." On another occasion, in the course of a letter, he described their condition as "bordering on slavery." Mr. Harry Escombe, the most prominent European in Natal at the end of last century, while tendering his evidence before an Industrial Commission in Natal on indentured labour, practically admitted as much. Testimony to the same effect can readily be gathered from the statements of leading Europeans in South Africa which were incorporated in the memorials on the subject submitted to the Government of India. But the fates had to run their course; and the steamer which carried those first Indian labourers to Natal carried with them the seed of the great Satyagraha movement.

I have not the space to relate the whole sordid story of Indian indenture in detail—how the labourers were fraudulently inveigled to come out by Indian recruiting agents connected with Natal; how under this delusion as illiterates they left the mother country; how their eyes were opened on reaching Natal; how all the restraints of religion and morality gave way at last, until the very distinction between a married woman and a concubine ceased to exist among these unfortunate people.

Many years before this, thousands of Indians, under the same indenture system, had already settled in Mauritius. When therefore the news reached Mauritius that indentured labourers were going to Natal in great numbers, some Indian traders, who had already done business with such indentured emigrants, were induced to follow these new labourers to Natal in order to trade with them. Sheth Abubakar Amod[1] of Mauritius, a Muhammadan Meman, first thought of opening a shop in Natal. The British in Natal had then no idea of the ability of these Gujarati Indian traders, nor did they much care about it. They had been able to raise very profitable crops of sugar-cane with the assistance of Indian labour, and in a surprisingly short time they had been able to supply South Africa with their manufactured sugar. They made so much money out of these plantations that they were able to build mansions for themselves and to turn the coastal belt of Natal from a wilderness into a garden. In such circumstances, they

---

[1] Sheth is a title of respect, meaning a banker or a large merchant. A Meman is a special class of Muhammadan traders.

THE EVILS OF INDENTURE

naturally did not mind an honest and plucky trader like Abubakar Sheth settling in their midst. So he peacefully carried on trade and purchased land, and in due time the story of his prosperity reached Porbandar, his native place in India.[1] Other Memans consequently reached Natal. Borahs from Surat followed them.[2] These Muhammadan traders needed accountants, and Hindu accountants accompanied them. Thus two different classes of Indians settled in Natal; first of all there were the free traders and their free servants chiefly from Gujarat, and secondly there were the ex-indentured labourers who had been recruited chiefly from Madras Presidency in the early days of the indenture.

In course of time children were born to these Indian labourers under indenture. Although not bound to labour, these children were affected by several stringent provisions of the indenture law of Natal. How can the offspring of slaves altogether escape slavery? The Indian labourers had gone to Natal under no obligation to labour on the plantations after the five years' period of indenture was over. They were entitled to settle in Natal if they wished. Some elected to do so, while others returned home. Those who remained in Natal came to be known as "free Indians." They were not, however, admitted to all the privileges enjoyed by the entirely free Indians who had come out as traders. For instance, those who had been indentured, even after their release, were required to obtain a pass if they wanted to go from one

[1] Porbandar is a seaport in Kathiawar on the west coast of India. A group of Indian Muhammadan merchants, called Memans, live there. Mahatma Gandhi was himself born at Porbandar and his father was Prime Minister of the State.
[2] Surat is a town on the sea border, north of Bombay. The Borahs are another special class of Muslim traders.

place to another. If they married and desired that the marriage should be legal they were required to register it with an official known as the Protector of Indian Immigrants. They were also subject to other restrictions which distinguished them as a class by themselves.

The Indian traders saw that they could trade not only with the indentured labourers and these "free Indians," but also with the Zulus. Indeed, these Indian traders became a source of great convenience to the Zulus, who were afraid of the European traders. The European traders might desire to sell goods to the Zulus, but it would be too much for the latter to expect courtesy at European hands. They might think it a great good fortune if they were given full consideration for their money. Some of the Zulus had the bitter experience that they purchased an article worth four shillings, then placed a sovereign on the counter, and received four shillings as a balance instead of sixteen, and sometimes even nothing at all. If the Zulu asked for the balance, or showed how the amount paid him was less than his due, the reply would only be gross abuse.

On the other hand, Indian traders had usually an easy way of trading with the Zulus. The latter would like to enter the shop and handle and examine any goods they wanted to purchase without hindrance. Indian traders permitted all this, because it was in their own interest. The Indian also did not miss an opportunity of cheating his Zulu customers; but all the same his general courtesy made him popular with them. Moreover, the Zulus never had any fear of the Indian traders. On the contrary, cases occurred in which the Indian tried to cheat them and in consequence was roughly handled by the Zulus.

More often still, Zulu customers have been heard to abuse Indian traders. Thus it was the Indian who feared the Zulu, rather than the Zulu who feared the Indian. The result was that trade with the Zulus proved very profitable to Indian merchants and they came over from India in order to make wealth.

In the Transvaal and the Orange Free State there were Boer Republics during the latter half of last century. In these Boer Republics the Bantu races had no power at all. The European has remained all-powerful. Indian traders had heard that they could also trade with the Boers, who, being simple, frank and unassuming, would not think it below their dignity to deal with them. Several Indian traders, therefore, proceeded to the Transvaal and the Orange Free State and opened shops there. As there were no railways these traders earned large profits. Their expectations were generally fulfilled, and they carried on considerable trade both with the Boers and the Bantus. In the same way, several Indian traders went to Cape Colony and began to prosper there also.

Thus the Indians became gradually distributed as traders in all four colonies; but the indentured labourers, who had come over from India in large numbers owing to recruiting, were all confined to Natal. At the present time, after more than seventy years, there are about 150,000 Indians in Natal, 15,000 in the Transvaal, and 6,000 in the Cape Province. The Orange Free State has evicted all Indians, with the exception of a few hotel waiters.

The European planters, however, could not afford to have Indian labourers who, after serving their term, were free to compete with them. No doubt the indentured Indians had gone to Natal because they had not been very successful in agriculture or other pursuits in India. Still it is not to be supposed that they had no knowledge of agriculture, or that they did not understand the value of cultivating the soil. They found that even if they grew only vegetables in Natal they could earn a good income, and that their earnings would be still better if they owned a small piece of land. Many, therefore, on the termination of their indentures began to purchase land for market gardening, and thus made a fair income, especially in the country district round Durban.

This was, on the whole, advantageous to the settlers in Natal. Various kinds of vegetables, which had never been grown before for want of a competent class of market gardeners, became now available. Other kinds, which had been grown in small quantities before, could now be had in abundance. The result was a fall in the price of vegetables.

But the European planters as a whole did not relish this new development. They began to realize that they had possible competitors in the field where they believed they had a monopoly. A movement was therefore set on foot against these ex-indentured immigrants. While, on the one hand, the Europeans demanded more and more labourers and easily took in as many of them as came over direct from India, on the other hand they started an agitation to harass the free Indians in a variety of ways in order to drive them back to India.

The movement assumed many forms. Some people demanded that the labourers who had already completed their indentures should be sent back to India at once,

THE EVILS OF INDENTURE

and that all fresh labourers arriving in Natal should have a new clause entered in their indentures, providing for their compulsory repatriation at the end of the five years' indenture. A second set advocated the imposition of a heavy annual capitation tax on the labourers at the end of the first period of five years in order to force them back under indenture. Both parties desired one thing, to make it impossible for ex-indentured labourers to live as free men in Natal.

This European agitation attained such serious dimensions that the Government of Natal at last appointed a Commission of Enquiry. Since the presence of the ex-indentured Indian labourers was clearly beneficial to the Natal population from an economic point of view, the independent evidence recorded by the Commission was against the European agitators, who thus failed to achieve any tangible result for the time being. But just as fire, although extinguished, leaves a trail behind it, so this European movement against the Indians made its impression on the Government of Natal.

How could it be otherwise? The Government of Natal was naturally friendly to the European planters. Therefore, at last, it corresponded at length with the Government of India on the subject. But the Government of India could not all at once accept proposals which would reduce indentured labourers to perpetual slavery. One main justification for sending the Indian labourers to such a far-off land under indenture had been that the labourers, after completing their indentures, would become free to develop their powers, and consequently improve their economic status. As Natal was still a Crown Colony, the Colonial Office was fully responsible for the control of its administration. Natal planters, therefore, could not look for help from that quarter in satisfying their unjust demands. For this and similar reasons a movement was set on foot to attain responsible government, which was eventually conferred on Natal in 1893.

Natal now began to feel her own strength. The Colonial Office no longer found it difficult to adopt whatever demands she might choose to make. Delegates from the new responsible Government of Natal came to India to confer with the Government of India. They proposed the imposition of an annual tax of twenty-five pounds, or three hundred and seventy-five rupees, on every Indian who had been freed from indenture.

No Indian labourer could pay such an exorbitant tax and live in Natal as a free man. Lord Elgin, the Governor-General of India, considered the amount excessive, but ultimately he accepted an annual poll tax of three pounds. This was equivalent to nearly six months' earnings under indenture. The tax was levied, not only on the labourer himself, but also upon his wife, together with his daughters over thirteen years and his sons over sixteen years of age. There was hardly any labourer who had not a wife and a couple of children. Thus, as a general rule, every labourer in Natal was required to pay an annual tax, averaging twelve pounds, after he had been released from indenture.

Only those who actually were obliged to undergo these hardships could fully realize their injustice and misery, and only those who witnessed the sufferings of the ex-indentured Indians could have some idea of their meaning. The Indian Community carried on a powerful agitation against this action of the Government of Natal.

Memorials were submitted to the Imperial Government and the Government of India, but to no purpose apart from the reduction in the amount of the tax which I have mentioned. What could the illiterate labourers do or understand in this matter? The agitation on their behalf was carried on by the Indian traders, actuated by motives either of patriotism or philanthropy, but they had no political training.

Free Indians fared no better. The European traders of Natal carried on a similar agitation against them for mainly the same reason. Indian traders were well established. They had acquired land in good localities. As the number of freed labourers began to increase there was a larger and larger demand for the class of goods required by them. Bags of rice were imported from India in their thousands and sold at a good profit. Naturally this trade was largely in the hands of Indians, who had besides a fair share of the trade with the Zulus. Thus they became an eyesore to the European traders on account of the profits they made.

Again, some Englishmen pointed out to the Indian traders that according to the law they were entitled to vote in the elections for the Legislative Council of Natal, and to stand as candidates for the same. Some Indians, therefore, got their names entered on the electoral roll. This made the European politicians of Natal join ranks with the anti-Indians. They doubted whether the Europeans could stand in competition with Indians if the Indian prestige increased, and if their position was consolidated.

The first step, therefore, taken by the responsible Government of Natal in relation to the free Indians was to enact a law disfranchising all Asiatics save those who were at the time already on the voters' list. A Bill to that effect was first introduced into the Legislative Assembly of Natal in 1894. This was based on the principle of excluding Indians, as Indians, from the franchise. It was the first piece of legislation in Natal directly affecting them in which racial distinctions were made. Therefore Indians resisted this measure, a memorial was hastily prepared and four hundred signatures were appended to it. When the memorial was submitted to the Legislative Council of Natal that body was startled. But the Bill was passed all the same. A memorial bearing ten thousand Indian signatures was then submitted to Lord Ripon, who was Secretary of State for the Colonies. Ten thousand signatures meant almost the total population at the time of adult free Indians in Natal. Lord Ripon disallowed the Bill and declared that the British Empire could not agree to the establishment of a colour bar in its legislation. The reader will be in a position later on to appreciate how great was this victory for the Indian cause.

The Natal Government, therefore, brought forward another Bill removing racial distinctions, but indirectly disqualifying Indians on other grounds. A strong protest was made against this as well, but without any success. The new Bill was ambiguous in meaning. Indians were in a position to carry it finally to the Privy Council to obtain its correct interpretation; but they did not think it advisable to do so. I still think that they did the right thing in avoiding this endless litigation. It was no small thing that the Colour Bar was not allowed to be set up against them in the Bill when it became law.

THE EVILS OF INDENTURE

But the planters and the Government of Natal were not likely to stop there. To nip the political power of the Indians in the bud was for them the indispensable first step; but the real point of their attack was Indian trade and free Indian immigration. They were uneasy at the thought of the Europeans in Natal being swamped if India with its teeming millions invaded Natal. The approximate population of Natal at the time was 400,000 Zulus and 40,000 Europeans, as against 60,000 indentured, 10,000 ex-indentured and 10,000 free Indians. The Europeans had no solid grounds for apprehension, but it is impossible to convince by arguments men who have been seized with vague terrors. As they were ignorant of the helpless condition of India and of the manners and customs of the Indian people, they were under the impression that the Indians were as adventurous and resourceful as themselves.

The result of successful opposition to the disfranchising Bill was that in two other laws passed by the Natal Legislature it was obliged to avoid racial distinction and to attain its end in an indirect manner. The position, therefore, was not as bad as it might have been. On this occasion too, Indians offered a strenuous resistance, but the laws were enacted in spite of their opposition. One of these imposed severe restrictions on Indian trade and the other on Indian Immigration in Natal. The substance of the first Act was that no one could trade without a licence issued by an official appointed in accordance with its provisions. In practice, any European could get a licence without any difficulty, while the Indian had to face every difficulty in the matter. He had to engage a lawyer and incur other expenditure.

Those who could not afford it had to go without the licence.

The chief provision of the Immigration Act was that only such immigrants as were able to pass the education test in a European language could enter the colony. This closed the doors of Natal against scores of Indians. Lest I might inadvertently do the Government of Natal an injustice, I must state that the Act further provided that an Indian resident in Natal for three years before the passing of that Act could obtain a certificate of domicile enabling him to leave the colony and return at any time with his wife and minor children without being required to pass an education test.

The indentured and free Indians in Natal were and still are subject to other disabilities, both legal and extra-legal, in addition to those already described above. But it is not necessary to tax the reader with a recital of them. Only such details will be given here as are essential to a clear understanding of the story.

As in Natal, so in the other Colonies anti-Indian prejudice had more or less begun to develop even before 1880. Except in Cape Colony, the general European opinion was that as labourers the Indians were unobjectionable, but it had become an axiom with many Europeans that the immigration of free Indians was purely a disadvantage to South Africa. The Transvaal was a Republic. For Indians to declare their British citizenship before its President was only to invite ridicule. If they had any grievance, all they could do was to bring it to the notice of the British Agent at Pretoria. But the outrageous thing was that when the Transvaal came under the British flag there was none from whom the

THE EVILS OF INDENTURE

Indians could expect even such assistance as the Agent rendered when the Transvaal was independent.

Lord Morley was Secretary of State for India when a deputation on behalf of the Indians waited upon him. He declared in so many words that, as the members of the deputation were aware, the Imperial Government could exercise but little control over self-governing Dominions. They could not dictate to them; they could plead, they could argue, they could press for the application of their principles. Indeed, in some instances they could more effectively remonstrate with foreign Powers—as they had remonstrated with the Boer Republic—than with their own people in the Dominions. The relations between the Mother Country and the Dominions were in the nature of a silken thread which would snap with the slightest tension. Since force was out of the question, he assured the Deputation that he would do all he could by negotiation. When war had been declared on the Transvaal, Lord Lansdowne, Lord Selborne and other British statesmen declared that the scandalous treatment accorded to the Indians by the South African Republic had been one of the causes which led to the war.

Let us now see what sort of treatment this was. Indians first entered the Transvaal in 1881. The late Sheth Abubakar opened a shop in Pretoria and purchased land in one of the principal streets of the city. Other traders followed. Their great success excited the jealousy of European traders, who commenced an anti-Indian campaign in the newspapers and submitted petitions to the Boer Volksraad, or Parliament, praying that Indians should be expelled and their trade stopped.

The Europeans in this newly opened-up country had

boundless hunger for riches. They were nearly strangers to the dictates of morality. Here are some statements in their petitions: "These Indians have no sense of human decency. They suffer from loathsome diseases. They consider every woman as their prey. They believe that women have no souls." These four statements contain four lies. It would be easy to multiply such specimens. As were the Europeans, so were their representatives. Little did the Indian traders know what a sinister and unjust movement was being carried on against them. They did not read the newspapers. Yet in the end the Press campaign and the petitions had the desired effect, and a Bill was introduced against the Indians into the Volksraad. The leading Indians were taken aback when they came to know how events had shaped themselves. They went to see President Kruger, who did not so much as admit them to his house, but made them stand in the courtyard.

After hearing them for awhile, President Kruger said: "You are the descendants of Ishmael, and therefore from your very birth you are bound to slavery. As you are the descendants of Esau and Ishmael we cannot admit you to rights placing you on an equality with ourselves. You must remain content with the rights we grant you." It cannot be said that this reply from the President was inspired by any malice or anger. President Kruger had been taught from his childhood the stories of the Old Testament, and he believed them to be true. How can we blame a man who gives candid expression to his opinions, such as they are? Ignorance, however, is bound to do harm even when associated with candour, and the result was that in 1885 a very drastic law was

THE EVILS OF INDENTURE

rushed through the Volksraad, as if thousands of Indians were on the point of flooding the Transvaal.

The British Agent was at last obliged to move in the matter. The question was finally carried to the Secretary of State for the Colonies. In terms of this Law 3 of 1885, every Indian settling in the Republic for the purpose of carrying on trade was required to register at a cost of twenty-five pounds, subject to heavy penalties. No Indian could hold an inch of land or enjoy the rights of citizenship. All this was so manifestly unjust that the Transvaal Government could not defend it in argument. There was a treaty in existence between the Boers and the British known as the London Convention, Article 14 of which secured the rights of British subjects. The British Government objected to this anti-Indian law as being in contravention of that Article. The Boers urged in reply that the British Government had previously given their consent, whether express or implied, to the law in question.

A dispute thus arose between the British and the Boer Governments, and the matter was referred to arbitration. The arbitrator's award was unsatisfactory. He tried to please both parties. The Indians were therefore the losers. The only advantage they reaped, if advantage it can be called, was that they did not lose so much money as they might otherwise have done. The Law was amended in 1886 in accordance with the arbitrator's award. The registration fee was reduced from twenty-five pounds to three pounds. The clause which completely debarred Indians from holding landed property was removed. But it was provided instead that Indians could acquire fixed property only in such locations, wards and streets as were specially set apart for their residence by the Transvaal Government. This Government did not honestly carry out the terms of the amendment clause, and withheld from Indians the right to purchase freehold land even in the locations. In all townships where Indians had already entered these locations were selected in dirty places, situated far away from the towns, with no water supply, no lighting arrangements, and no sanitary conveniences.

Thus the Indians became the "untouchables" of the Transvaal; for it can be truly said that there is no difference between these locations and the untouchables' quarters in India. Just as the Hindus believe that the touch of the Dheds,[1] or residence in their neighbourhood, leads to pollution of high caste people, so did the Europeans in the Transvaal believe for all practical purposes that physical contact with the Indians would defile them.

In Christian Europe the Jews were once its "untouchables," and the quarters that were assigned to them had the offensive name of "ghettoes." The ancient Jews regarded themselves as the chosen people of God, to the exclusion of all others, with the result that their descendants were visited with a strange and even unjust retribution. Almost in a similar way the Hindus have considered themselves "Aryas" or civilized, and a section of their own kith and kin as "Anaryas" or untouchables, with the result that a strange, if unjust, nemesis is being visited not only upon the Hindus in South Africa, but also upon the Musalmans and Parsis as well, inasmuch as they belong to the same country and have the same colour as their Hindu brethren.

[1] A lower caste in India whose work is that of scavenging.

THE EVILS OF INDENTURE

In South Africa we have acquired the odious name of "coolies." It has a contemptuous connotation. It means what a pariah or an untouchable means to us, and the quarters assigned to the "coolies" are known as "coolie locations." People were densely packed in these ghettoes, the area of which never increased with the increase in population. Beyond arranging to clean the latrines in a haphazard way, the Municipality did nothing to provide any sanitary facilities, much less good roads or lights. It was hardly likely that it would safeguard its sanitation, when it was indifferent to the welfare of the people. The Indians living there were too ignorant of the rules of municipal hygiene to do without the supervision of the Municipality. Usually people migrate abroad in search of wealth, and the bulk of the Indians who went to South Africa were ignorant agriculturists who needed all the care and protection that could be given them in these matters. The traders and educated Indians who followed them were very few in number.

The Transvaal Government interpreted Law 3 of 1885 to mean that the Indians had only trading rights in the locations. The matter was put to arbitration. The arbitrator had decided that the interpretation of the Law rested with the ordinary tribunals of the Transvaal. The Indian traders were therefore in a very precarious position. Nevertheless, they managed somehow to maintain themselves fairly well by carrying on negotiations in one place, by having recourse to law courts in another, and by exerting what little influence they possessed to get relief in a third. Such was the miserable and almost intolerable position of the Indians in the Transvaal at the outbreak of the Boer War.

In the Orange Free State matters were carried to an even greater length of injustice and unfair treatment. Hardly a dozen Indians had opened shops there when the Europeans started a powerful agitation against them. The Volksraad passed a stringent law and expelled Indian traders from the Free State altogether, awarding them a merely nominal compensation. This law provided that no Indian could on any account hold fixed property, or carry on mercantile or farming business, or enjoy franchise rights in the Orange Free State. With special permission an Indian could reside as a labourer or as a hotel waiter. But the authorities were not obliged to grant even this precious permission in every case. The result was that a respectable Indian could not live in the Free State even for a couple of days without great difficulty. At the time of the Boer War there were no Indians in the Free State except a few hotel waiters.

In Cape Colony, too, there was some newspaper agitation against Indians, and the treatment to which they were subjected was not free from humiliating features. For example, Indian children could not attend public schools. Indian travellers could hardly secure hotel accommodation. But there were no restrictions as to trade and the purchase of land for a long time.

There were special reasons for this different attitude in Cape Colony. As we have already seen, there was a fair proportion of Malays in the Cape population. Since the Malays are Musalmans, they soon came into contact with their Indian co-religionists, and consequently with other Indians later on. How could the Government of Cape Colony legislate against the Malay? The Cape was their mother-land and Dutch was their mother tongue. They had been living with the Dutch from the very beginning and therefore had largely imitated them in their ways of life. Cape Colony, therefore, had been the least affected by the colour prejudice.

Again, as Cape Colony was the oldest settlement and the chief centre of culture in South Africa, it produced sober, gentlemanly and large-hearted Europeans. In my opinion there is no place on earth and no people which are incapable of producing the finest types of humanity, given suitable opportunities and education. It has been my good fortune to come across such men and women in South Africa. In Cape Colony, however, the proportion was very much larger than elsewhere. Perhaps the best known and the most learned among them was Mr. J. X. Merriman, who was a member of the first and subsequent ministries that came into power after the grant of responsible government in 1872. He was again the Premier of the last ministry when the Union was established in 1910, and was known as the Gladstone of South Africa.

Then there were the Moltenos and the Schreiners. Sir John Molteno was the first Premier of the Colony in 1872. Mr. W. P. Schreiner was a well-known advocate, for some time Attorney-General, and later on Premier. His sister, Olive Schreiner, was a gifted woman, popular in South Africa and well known wherever the English language is spoken. Her love for mankind was altogether unbounded. Love was written in her eyes and in her face. Although she belonged to a distinguished family and was a learned lady, she was so simple in her habits that she cleaned the utensils in her house herself. Mr. J. X. Merriman, the Moltenos and the Schreiners had always espoused the cause of the Bantus and coloured people. They had a kindly feeling for the Indians as well, though they made a certain distinction.

Their argument was that as the Hottentots and other races had been the inhabitants of South Africa long before the European settlers, the latter could not deprive them of their natural rights. But as for the Indians, it would not be unfair if laws calculated to remove the danger of their undue competition were enacted. Nevertheless, these noble people always had a warm corner in their hearts for Indians. When Mr. G. K. Gokhale went to South Africa, Mr. Schreiner presided over the Town Hall meeting in Cape Town, where he was accorded his first public reception in that country. Mr. J. X. Merriman also treated him with the greatest courtesy and expressed his sympathy with the Indian cause. There were other Europeans of the type of Mr. Merriman. I have only mentioned these well-known names as typical of their class. The newspapers also in Cape Town were less hostile to Indians than those in other parts of South Africa.

It can be said that the door into South Africa, which was formerly wide open, had thus been almost closed against the Indians at the time of the Boer War. In the Transvaal there was no restriction on immigration except the registration fee of three pounds. When, however, Natal and Cape Colony closed their ports to Indians, the latter had great difficulty in reaching the Transvaal, which was in the interior. They could reach it via Delagoa Bay, a Portuguese port, but the Portuguese had more or less imitated the British, and it became almost impossible to enter from that direction.

CHAPTER III

MY FIRST EXPERIENCES

UP TO the year 1893 there were hardly any free Indians in South Africa capable of doing public work on behalf of the Indian community. Those who were educated were, for the most part, clerks, whose knowledge of English was not sufficient for the skilled drafting of petitions and protests which had to be sent to the Administration. They were also obliged to give up all their time to their employers. A second group, who had received a smattering of education, were the descendants of indentured Indian labourers; but these, if at all qualified for public work, were usually in Government service, as interpreters in the law courts, and therefore not in a position to help the Indian cause beyond expressing their fellow-feeling in private.

The Indian community itself was held in the lowest esteem by Europeans throughout the country on account of colour prejudice. All indentured labourers were called 'coolies.' This word means literally a porter or a carrier of a burden. But it was used so extensively in Natal that the Indian indentured labourers themselves began to describe themselves as 'coolies.' Many Europeans called the Indian lawyers and Indian traders 'coolie' lawyers and 'coolie' traders. There were some who could not believe that this name implied an insult, while many used it as a term of deliberate contempt. Free Indians, therefore, tried to draw a distinction between themselves and the indentured labourers. No direct attempt was made to seek their co-operation in the common cause. Probably it did not strike any one of the traders to enlist their support. If the idea did suggest itself to some of them they felt the risk of making their own position worse by allowing them to join the movement. Since the Indian traders were the first target of attack, the measures for defence were limited to that class. They were thus seriously handicapped by having no knowledge of English and no experience of public work in India. They sought the help of European barristers, had petitions prepared at considerable cost, waited in deputation, and did what they could to mend matters. This was the state of things up to the year 1893.

It will be helpful at this point to keep some important dates in mind. Before the year 1893 Indians had been banished from the Orange Free State by unscrupulous methods. In the Transvaal, Law No. 3 of 1885 was in force with all its obnoxious clauses. In Natal, measures were under contemplation as early as 1892, whose direct object was to allow only indentured labourers to reside in the Colony and to turn out the rest. Everywhere, except in Cape Colony, the very existence of the community was being threatened.

I left India for South Africa in April 1893, on a purely professional visit, without any knowledge of the conditions out there.[1] A well-known firm of Porbandar Memans carried on trade in Durban under the name of Dada Abdulla. An equally well-known and rival firm at Pretoria traded under the name of Tyeb Haji Mahomed. Unfortunately, an important law-suit was pending between the rivals. A partner of the firm of Dada Abdulla

[1] See *Mahatma Gandhi: His Own Story*, p. 92.

MY FIRST EXPERIENCES

in Porbandar thought that it might help their case if they engaged me and sent me to South Africa. I had only recently been called to the Bar and was quite a novice in the profession. But he had no fear of my mishandling the law-suit, as he did not want me to conduct the case in court but only to instruct the able European lawyers whom they had retained. I was fond of novel experiences. It was disgusting to me in India to have to give commissions to those who brought me work. The atmosphere of political intrigue in Kathiawar was choking me. The engagement was only for one year, and there seemed no objection against my acceptance of the offer.[1]

There was nothing to lose, because the firm of Dada Abdulla had expressed their willingness to pay all my expenses on the voyage and also in South Africa, and a fee of one hundred and five pounds besides. This arrangement was made through my eldest brother, now deceased, who had been like a father to me. His will was a command to me. He liked the idea of my going to South Africa. So I reached Durban in May 1893.

Being a barrister-at-law, I was well dressed according to my lights when I landed at Durban; and no doubt I had a due sense of my own importance. But I was soon disillusioned by what happened. The partner of Dada Abdulla who had engaged me had already given me an account of things that happened to Indians in Natal. But what I saw there with my own eyes was quite different from the picture he had drawn. There was no blame, however, on his part. He was a frank, simple man, ignorant of the real state of affairs. He had no true idea

[1] The whole account of this is told in detail in *Mahatma Gandhi: His Own Story*, pp. 97–103.

of the hardships to which Indians were subjected. Conditions which implied grave insult had not appeared to him in that light at all. On the very first day after landing I observed that the Europeans meted out most insulting treatment to Indians as a matter of course on different occasions.

I have recorded elsewhere my bitter experience in the courts within a fortnight of my arrival, the hardships I encountered on railway trains, the thrashings I received on the way, and the practical impossibility of securing accommodation in any of the hotels.[1] I had gone there for a single law-suit, prompted by self-interest and curiosity without any political motive; but all these things entered like iron into my soul.

During the first year, therefore, I was merely the witness and the victim of these wrongs. From the standpoint of self-interest in my legal profession South Africa was no good to me. Not only had I no desire, but on the contrary there was a positive disgust in my mind at the very thought of earning money or sojourning in a country where I was insulted every day. Thus I was between the horns of a dilemma.

Two courses were clearly open to me. I might, on the one hand, free myself from my contract with Dada Abdulla on the ground that circumstances had come to my knowledge on my arrival which had not been disclosed to me before. In that case I could run back to India. On the other hand I might bear all the hardships and fulfil my engagement.

While I was still undecided I was pushed out of the

[1] Special instances of these things are given in *Mahatma Gandhi: His Own Story*, pp. 102-105.

MY FIRST EXPERIENCES

train one night by a European police constable at Maritzburg. The train having departed I was left behind sitting in the waiting-room, shivering in the bitter cold. I did not know where my luggage was, nor did I dare enquire of anybody, lest I might be insulted and assaulted over again. Sleep was out of the question. Doubt took possession of my mind.

Late that night I came to the conclusion that to run away back to India would be a cowardly affair. I must accomplish what I had undertaken. This meant that I must reach Pretoria at all costs, without minding insults and even assaults. Pretoria was my goal. This resolution which I made somewhat pacified and strengthened me, but I did not get any sleep that night.

Next morning I sent a telegram to the firm of Dada Abdulla and to the General Manager of the Railway. Replies were received from both. Dada Abdulla and his partner, Sheth Abdulla Haji Adam, at once took strong measures. They wired to their Indian Agents in various places to look after me, and also to the General Manager of the State Railway. The Indian traders at Maritzburg came to see me in response to the telegram received by the local agent. They tried to comfort me, and told me that all of them had met with the same bitter experiences which had pained them greatly at first. But they had at last become used to these things and therefore took little notice of them. Trade and sensitiveness could ill go together. They had therefore made it a rule to pocket insults just as they might pocket cash. They told me how Indians could not enter the railway station by the main entrance, and how difficult it was for them even to purchase tickets. I left for Pretoria the same night.

God, who is the Almighty Searcher of all hearts, soon put my determination to a full test. I suffered further insults and received more beatings on my journey. But all this only confirmed me in my determination to stay in South Africa.

Thus in 1893 I had gained full experience of Indian conditions in Natal and the Transvaal. But I did nothing at the time beyond occasionally talking over the subject with my Indian companions in Pretoria. It appeared to me that to look after the firm's lawsuit and also to take up at the same time the political question of Indian grievances was impossible.

Early in the year 1894 I went back to Durban and booked my passage for India. At the farewell entertainment held by Dada Abdulla in my honour, someone put a copy of the *Natal Mercury* into my hands. I read it and found that the detailed report of the proceedings of the Natal Legislative Council contained a few lines on "Indian Franchise." The local Government was about to introduce a Bill to disfranchise Indians. This could only be the beginning of the end of what little rights they were enjoying. The speeches made in the Council left no doubt about the intention of the Government. I read out the report to the traders and others present and explained the situation as well as I could, suggesting that the Indians should strenuously resist this attack on their rights.

They agreed, but declared that they could not fight the battle themselves and therefore urged me to stay on. So I consented to stay a month or so longer, by which time the struggle would be fought out. The same night I drew up a petition to be presented to the Legislative

Council. A telegram was sent to the Government requesting them to delay the proceedings. A Committee was appointed, with Sheth Abdulla Haji Adam as chairman, and the telegram was sent in his name. The further reading of the Bill was postponed for two days. That petition was the first ever sent by the Indians to a South African Legislature. It was the South African Indians' first experience of such a mode of procedure and a new thrill of enthusiasm passed through the community. Meetings were held every day and more and more persons attended them. The requisite funds were soon oversubscribed. Many volunteers helped in preparing copies, securing signatures and similar work without any remuneration. There were others who both worked and also subscribed to the funds. The colonial-born descendants of the ex-indentured Indians joined in the movement with alacrity. They knew English and wrote a good hand. They did copying and other work ungrudgingly night and day alike. Within a month a memorial with ten thousand signatures was forwarded to Lord Ripon, and the immediate task I had set before myself was accomplished.

Then I asked leave to return to India. But the agitation had roused such keen interest among the Indians that they would not let me go.

"You yourself," they said, "have explained to us that this is the first step taken with a view to our ultimate extinction. Who knows whether the Colonial Secretary will return a favourable reply to our memorial? You have now witnessed our enthusiasm. We are willing to work and we have funds. But for want of a guide, what little has been already done will go to nothing. We therefore regard it to be your duty to stay on."

I also felt it would be well if a permanent organization was formed to watch our Indian interests. But where was I to live, and how? They offered me a regular salary for public work, but I expressly declined. It is not right to receive a large salary for public work. Besides, I was a pioneer. According to my notions at the time, I thought I ought to live in a style usual for barristers, and that would mean great expense. It would be improper to depend for my maintenance upon a body whose activities would necessitate a public appeal for funds. My powers of work would thereby be crippled. For this and similar reasons I flatly refused to accept remuneration for public work. But I suggested that I was prepared to stay if the principal traders among them could see their way to offer me legal work and give me retaining fees for it beforehand. The retainers might be for one year. We might deal with each other for that period, examine the results, and then continue the arrangement if both parties were satisfied. This suggestion was cordially accepted by all.

Then I applied for admission as an Advocate of the Supreme Court of Natal. The Natal Law Society opposed my application on the sole ground that the law did not contemplate having coloured barristers on the roll. The late Mr. Escombe, the famous advocate, who was afterwards Attorney-General and also Premier of Natal, was my Counsel. The prevailing practice for a long time was that the leading barrister should present such applications, without any fees, and Mr. Escombe advocated my cause accordingly. He was also Senior Counsel for my employers. The Supreme Court upheld the application. Thus the Law Society's opposition brought me

MY FIRST EXPERIENCES

into further public prominence. The newspapers of South Africa ridiculed the Law Society and some of them even congratulated me.

The temporary committee was now placed on a permanent footing. I had never attended a session of the Indian National Congress, but had often read about it. Dadabhai, the Grand Old Man of India, had always been before my mind as a model of a patriotic Indian leader. I had very greatly admired him and was therefore already a National Congress enthusiast, and wished to popularize the name. So I advised the Indians to call their organization the Natal Indian Congress. I laid before them very imperfectly what meagre knowledge I had of Indian National Congress affairs.

Anyhow, the Natal Indian Congress was founded about May 1894. There was this difference between the Indian and the Natal Congress, that the latter organization worked throughout the year and only those who paid annual subscriptions of at least three pounds were admitted to membership. Amounts exceeding that sum were gratefully received. Endeavours were made to obtain the maximum from each member. There were about half a dozen members who paid twenty-four pounds a year. There was a considerable number of those paying twelve pounds. About three hundred members were enrolled every month. They included Hindus, Musalmans, Parsis, and Christians, and came from all Indian Provinces that were represented in Natal. The work proceeded with great vigour throughout the first year. Indian merchants went to distant townships where Indians resided, in their own conveyances, enrolling new members and collecting subscriptions. Everybody did not pay for the mere asking. Some required to be persuaded. This persuasion was a political training, and made people acquainted with all the facts of the situation.

Again, a meeting of the Congress was held at least once a month, when detailed accounts were presented and adopted. Current events were explained and recorded in the minute-books. Members asked various questions. Fresh subjects were considered. The advantage of all this was that those who never spoke at such meetings got accustomed to the art of speaking. The speeches, again, had to be in proper form. All this was a novel experience. In the meanwhile, the welcome news came that Lord Ripon had disallowed the Disfranchising Bill, and this redoubled our zeal and self-confidence.

Along with the external agitation, the question of internal improvement was also taken up. The Europeans throughout South Africa had been agitating against the Indians on the ground of their ways of life. They always argued that the Indians were very dirty and close-fisted. They were said to live in the same place where they traded, and to spend nothing on their own comforts. How, then, could cleanly open-handed Europeans compete in trade with such parsimonious and dirty people? Lectures were delivered, debates held, and suggestions made at Congress meetings on subjects such as domestic sanitation, personal hygiene, the necessity of having separate buildings for houses and shops. The proceedings were conducted in Gujarati.

It is easy to see what an amount of practical and political education the Indians thus received. Under the auspices of the Natal Indian Congress a new society

MY FIRST EXPERIENCES

called the Natal Educational Association was formed for the benefit of the young Indians, who, being the children of ex-indentured labourers, were born in Natal and spoke English. Its members paid a nominal fee. The chief objects of the Association were to provide a meeting-place for these youths, to create in them a love for the mother country, India, and to give them general information about it. It was also intended to impress upon them that free Indians considered them to be their own kith and kin. The funds of the Congress were large enough to leave a surplus after defraying all its expenses. This surplus was devoted to the purchase of land, which yields an income even up to the present day.

I have deliberately entered into all these details, because without them it is not possible to understand how Satyagraha spontaneously sprang into existence. I am compelled to omit the remarkable subsequent story of the Congress, how it was confronted with difficulties, how Government officials attacked it, and how it escaped without serious injury from these attacks. But one important fact must be placed on record. Steps were at once taken to save the Indian community from the habit of exaggeration. Attempts were always made to draw their attention to their own shortcomings. Whatever force there was in the arguments of the European was duly acknowledged. Every occasion when it was possible to co-operate with Europeans on terms of equality was heartily made use of. The newspapers were supplied with as much information about the Indian Community as they could publish, and whenever Indians were unfairly attacked in the Press replies were sent to the newspapers concerned.

There was an association in the Transvaal similar to the Natal Indian Congress. A similar body was formed in Cape Town also with a constitution different from that of the Natal Indian Congress and the Transvaal Indian Association. Still the activities of all three bodies were nearly identical.

Thus the Natal Indian Congress was placed on a permanent footing. I spent nearly two years and a half in Natal, doing for the most part political work. Then I saw clearly that if I was still to prolong my stay in South Africa I must bring over my family from India. It seemed also advisable for me to make a brief stay in India, as far as time allowed, acquainting the political leaders there with South African conditions and seeking their active assistance. The Congress allowed me leave of absence for six months. Sheth Adamji Miankhan, the well-known merchant of Natal, was appointed Secretary in my stead. He discharged his duties with great ability. He had a fair knowledge of English and had studied Gujarati in the ordinary course. As he had mercantile dealings all day long with the Zulus, he had acquired an intimate knowledge of the Zulu language and was well conversant with their manners and customs. He was a man of very quiet disposition who was not given to much speech. Fidelity, patience, firmness, presence of mind, courage and common sense are far more essential qualifications for holding responsible positions than a knowledge of English. Where these qualities are absent, the best literary attainments are of little use in public work.

It was May 1896 when I reached India. Since steamers from Natal were then more easily available for

Calcutta than Bombay, I travelled on board one of them as an ordinary passenger.

While proceeding from Calcutta to Bombay, I missed my train on the way and had to stop at Allahabad for a day. But this materially helped the work I had come to perform. For I saw Mr. Chesney of the *Pioneer*, and he talked with me courteously, making full enquiries into Indian conditions in South Africa. In the end, he told me frankly that his sympathies were with the colonials. He promised, however, that if ever I wrote anything he would read it and notice it in his paper. This was good enough for me.

It was during this visit that I had the privilege of seeing the great Indian Congress leaders and others, Sir Pherozeshah Mehta, Justice Badruddin Tyabji, Justice Ranade in Bombay, Lokamanya Tilak and his circle, Professor Bhandarkar and Gopal Krishna Gokhale in Poona.

I cannot resist the temptation of describing here a sacred reminiscence of Poona, although it is not entirely relevant to the subject. The Sarvajanik Sabha was controlled by Lokamanya Tilak, while Mr. Gokhale was connected with the Deccan Sabha. First I saw Tilak Maharaj.[1] When I spoke to him about my intention of holding a meeting in Poona, he asked me if I had seen "Gopalrao." I did not understand at first whom he meant. He therefore asked me if I had seen Gopalrao Krishna Gokhale and if I knew him at all well.

"I have not seen him," said I; "I know him only by name and mean to see him."

---

[1] Maharaj is sometimes added as a title of respect for one who is a Brahman.

"You do not seem to be familiar with Indian politics," said Tilak Maharaj.

"After my return from England," I replied, "I only stayed in India for a short time. I had not then applied myself to the political question because I thought it beyond my capacity."

"In that case," said Lokamanya Tilak, "I must give you some information. There are two parties in Poona, one represented by the Sarvajanik Sabha and the other by the Deccan Sabha."

"I know nothing about this matter," I replied.

"It is quite easy to hold meetings here," said Lokamanya Tilak. "But it seemed to me that you wish to lay your case before all parties. Now, I like your idea and wish to help you. But if a member of the Sarvajanik Sabha is selected to preside over your meeting in Poona, no member of the Deccan Sabha will attend it, and *vice versa*. You should therefore find out a non-partisan as a chairman. I can only offer my own suggestion. Do you know Professor Bhandarkar? He is considered by everyone to be a neutral. He does not take part in politics, but perhaps you can induce him to preside over your meeting because it is of a non-party character. Speak to Gopalrao Krishna Gokhale about this and seek his advice. If a man of Professor Bhandarkar's position consents to preside, then I am certain that both parties will join in the meeting and make it a success. At any rate, you can count upon our fullest help in the matter."

Gokhale at once saw me. I have told the story elsewhere how I fell in love with him at very first sight. Gokhale liked the advice which Lokamanya had given me. Accordingly I paid my respects to the venerable

Professor Bhandarkar. He heard attentively the whole history of the Indian wrongs in Natal and the Transvaal.

"You see," he said at the end of my story, "I rarely take part in public affairs. Besides, I am getting old. But what you have told me has stirred me very deeply indeed. I like your idea of seeking the co-operation of all parties. You are young and ignorant of the political conditions in Poona. Please tell the members of both parties that I have complied with your request."

Thus a successful meeting was held in Poona. The leaders of both parties attended and spoke in support of the cause.

It now remains also to note what further steps were taken to enlist support from England itself. It was essential, in the first place, to establish relations with the British Committee of the Indian National Congress, which was then a powerful body in London. Weekly letters, full of particulars, were therefore written to Dadabhai Naoroji, the Grand Old Man of India, and to Sir William Wedderburn, the Chairman of the Committee. Whenever there was an occasion to send copies of representations, a sum of at least ten pounds was remitted as a contribution towards the postal charges and general expenditure of the British Committee.

There still remains in my mind a striking recollection of Dadabhai Naoroji. He was not the Chairman of the Committee. But it seemed to us that the proper course was to send money to him, in the first instance, so that he might then forward it himself to the Chairman. But Dadabhai returned the very first instalment and suggested that we should remit the money intended for the British Committee directly to Sir William

Wedderburn. The prestige of the Committee, he wrote, would increase if we approached it through Sir William Wedderburn direct.

Dadabhai, though far advanced in age, was very regular in his correspondence. Even when he had nothing particular to write about he would acknowledge the receipt of letters by return of post with a word of encouragement thrown in. These letters he used to write personally, and kept copies of them in his tissue-paper book.

Although we had called our organization the "Natal Indian Congress" we never intended to make our grievances a mere party question. We therefore corresponded with gentlemen belonging to other political views in England as well, with the full knowledge of Dadabhai. The most prominent among them were Sir Muncherjee Bhownaggree and Sir W. W. Hunter. Sir Muncherjee was then himself a Member of Parliament. His assistance was valuable, and he used to favour us with important suggestions. But if there was anyone who realized the importance of the Indian question in South Africa, even before the Indians themselves, it was Sir W. W. Hunter. He was the editor of the Indian section of *The Times*, wherein, ever since we first addressed him, he continually discussed our question in its true perspective, thus rendering us inestimable assistance. He wrote personal letters to several gentlemen in full support of our cause. Almost every week, when some important question was being decided, he used to write to us the fullest information available about it.

I have his very first letter still with me. "I am sorry," he wrote, "to read of the situation in Natal. You have been conducting your struggle courteously, peacefully and without exaggeration. My sympathies are entirely with you. I will do my best publicly as well as privately to see that justice is done to you. I am certain that we cannot yield even an inch of ground further. Your demand being so reasonable, no impartial person would even suggest that you should moderate it."

This was the purport of Sir William Hunter's letter, and he reproduced it almost word for word in the first article that he wrote for *The Times* on the question. His attitude remained the same throughout, and Lady Hunter wrote to me that shortly before his death he had prepared an outline of a series of articles which he had planned for *The Times* on the Indian question in South Africa.

I have mentioned already the name of Mansukhlal Nazar. This Indian gentleman was deputed to England on behalf of the Indian Community at a later date in order to explain the situation in detail. He was instructed to work with members of all parties, and during his stay in England he kept in touch with Sir W. W. Hunter, Sir Muncherjee Bhownaggree and also with the British Committee of the Indian National Congress. He was likewise in touch with several retired officers of the Indian Civil Service, with the India Office, and with the Colonial Office. Thus our endeavours to gain helpers in Great Britain were directed in all possible quarters. The result was the condition of Indians overseas became at last a question of first-rate importance in the eyes of the Imperial Government.

After this, I thought that my work in South Africa was now over. I had stayed there six years instead of one, as originally intended. The outline of the work before us was fairly fixed. Still, I could not leave South Africa without the willing consent of the Indian community.

At last, after thinking the matter over, I informed my colleagues that I intended taking up public work in India. I had learnt in South Africa the lesson of service instead of self-interest, and was longing for opportunities of such work in India. Mansukhlal Nazar was there and so was Advocate Khan, who were both able to carry on the work. Some Indian youths had also returned from England as barristers. In such circumstances it would not be improper if I returned to India.

When I urged all these arguments, I was permitted to return only on one condition: that if an unexpected situation arose in South Africa requiring my presence, the community might recall me any day and I should come back at once.

In such a contingency they undertook to pay my travelling expenses and whatever amount was incurred on my behalf during my stay in South Africa. To this arrangement I agreed, and returned to India.

I decided to practise in Bombay as a barrister, primarily with a view to public work under the advice and guidance of Gokhale. In the second place I wished to make a living for myself side by side with active participation in public work. So I rented chambers in Bombay and began to get some practice as a lawyer. Thanks to my close connexion with South Africa, clients who had returned from that country gave me work which more than sufficed for my needs.

CHAPTER IV

AFTER THE BOER WAR

PEACE WAS NEVER to be my portion in this life. Hardly had I been in Bombay for three or four months when I received an urgent cable from South Africa stating that the situation there was very serious, that Mr. Chamberlain was expected shortly, and that my presence was necessary.

I wound up my office in Bombay immediately and started for South Africa by the first available steamer. This was near the end of 1902. The cablegram did not contail full details. I guessed that there was trouble in the Transvaal. But I went out to South Africa hurriedly without my family; for I thought I would be able to return to India in five or six months. When I reached Durban and heard what had happened, I was amazed.

Many of us had hoped that the position of Indians throughout South Africa would improve after the Boer War. At any rate, we did not anticipate trouble in the Transvaal and the Free State; for Lord Lansdowne and Lord Selborne and other high functionaries had declared, when the war broke out, that the treatment accorded the Indians by the Boers was one of the causes of the war. The British Agent at Pretoria had often told me that if the Transvaal became a British Colony, all the grievances under which the Indians laboured would be instantly redressed. The Europeans, too, believed that as the Transvaal was now under the British flag, the old laws of the Boer Republic directed against the Indians could not be enforced. This principle was so widely accepted that the auctioneers who before the war were not ready to accept offers from Indians for the purchase of land, now openly accepted them. Many Indians thus purchased lands at public auctions; but when they tendered the deeds of transfer to the revenue officer for registration the officer in charge refused to register the deeds, quoting Law No. 3 of 1885.

All this I learnt on landing at Durban. The leaders said that Mr. Chamberlain would first come to Durban, and we must there acquaint him with the situation in Natal. When this was done, I was to follow him to the Transvaal.

A deputation waited upon Mr. Chamberlain in Natal. He gave it a courteous hearing and promised to confer with the Natal Government on the subject of its representations. Personally I did not expect that the laws which had been promulgated in Natal before the war would be modified very soon.

Before the Boer War, any Indian could at any time enter the Transvaal. I observed that this was not the case any longer. The restrictions, however, equally applied to all—Europeans as well as Indians. The condition of the country was such that if a large number of people entered the Transvaal all at once there would not be sufficient food and clothing to go round, as all the shops had not reopened since the war. The goods stocked in the shops had been unceremoniously appropriated by the late Boer Government. I thought, therefore, that if the restrictions were merely temporary, there was no reason for apprehension.

But then there was a difference in the procedure by

which a European and an Indian could obtain a permit, and this afforded ground for misgiving and alarm. Permit offices were opened in the various parts of South Africa. For all practical purposes a European could obtain a permit for the mere asking, while an Asiatic Department was created in the Transvaal for dealing with Indians. The creation of this special department was a new departure. Indians were required to apply to the Head of that department in the first instance. After he had granted their application, they would generally obtain permits at Durban or any other port.

If I had to go through all these formalities there was no hope of my getting a permit before Mr. Chamberlain left the Transvaal. The Indians in the Transvaal could not procure a permit for me. They had, therefore, relied upon my connections in Durban. I did not know the Permit Officer personally; but as I knew the Police Superintendent of Durban I asked him to accompany me to the permit office. He consented and gave the necessary assurances. I obtained a permit on the strength of the fact that I had stayed in the Transvaal for a year in 1893, and thus reached Pretoria.

The atmosphere in Pretoria was decidedly ominous. I could see that the Asiatic Department was merely a frightful engine of oppression for the Indian. The officers in charge were some of the adventurers who had accompanied the army from India to South Africa during the war, and had settled there in order to try their luck. Some of them were corrupt. Two officers were even prosecuted for bribery. The jury declared them not guilty. But since really there was no doubt entertained about their guilt they were subsequently dismissed from service. Partiality was the order of the day. When a separate department is thus created and the restriction of existing rights is the sole reason for its existence, officers are naturally inclined to devise fresh restrictions from time to time in order to justify their own occupation. This is exactly what happened in the Transvaal.

I saw that I had to begin all my work over again from the very start. The Asiatic Department could not at once discover how I managed to enter the Transvaal. They did not venture to ask me directly. I imagine they thought me too open in my conduct to get smuggled into the country. A deputation from Pretoria prepared to wait upon Mr. Chamberlain. I drafted the memorial for submission to him, but the Asiatic Department excluded me from the deputation. Though I had succeeded in entering the Transvaal, they could still successfully prevent me from waiting on Mr. Chamberlain.

So the community was asked by the department to submit the names of the representatives who were to form the deputation. Colour prejudice was, of course, in evidence everywhere in South Africa, but I was not prepared to find here the miserable underhand dealing among officials that I was familiar with in India. In South Africa the public departments were maintained for the good of the people, and were responsible to public opinion. Hence officials in charge had a certain courtesy of manner and humility about them, and coloured people also got the benefit of it more or less. With the coming of these officers from Asia, however, came also its autocracy, and the habits that the autocrats had imbibed there. In South Africa there was a kind of responsible Government, whereas the commodity imported from Asia was autocracy pure and simple; for the Indian people had no responsible Government, there being a foreign Power governing them. In South Africa the Europeans were settled emigrants. They had become South African citizens and had control over the department officers. But the autocrats from Asia now appeared on the scene, and the Indians in consequence found themselves between the devil and the deep sea.

I had a fair taste of this autocracy. First of all I was summoned to see the chief of the department, an officer from Ceylon. Lest I should appear to exaggerate when I say that I was "summoned" to see the chief, I would make myself clear. No written order was sent to me at all. Indian leaders often had to visit the Asiatic Department. Among these was Sheth Tyeb Haji Khan Mahomed. The chief of the office asked who I was and why I had come there.

"He is our adviser," said Tyeb Sheth, "and he has come here at our request."

"Then what are *we* here for? Have *we* not been appointed to protect you?" asked the autocrat. "What can Gandhi know of the conditions here?"

Tyeb Sheth answered the charge as best he could: "Of course you are here," he said politely; "but Gandhi is our man. He knows our language and understands us. You are, after all, officials."

The Sahib ordered Tyeb Sheth to fetch me before him. I went to the Sahib in company with him and others. No seats were offered, we were all kept standing.

"What brings you here?" said the Sahib, addressing me.

"I have come here at the request of my fellow-countrymen to help them with my advice," I replied.

"But don't you know," he asked, "that you have no right to come here? The permit you hold was given you by mistake. You must go back. You shall not wait on Mr. Chamberlain. It is for the protection of the Indians here that the Asiatic Department has been especially created. Well, you may go."

With this he dismissed me, giving me no opportunity to make any reply. But he detained my companions. He gave them a sound scolding, and advised them to send me away. They returned thoroughly chagrined. We were now confronted with a quite unexpected situation.

I smarted under the insult, but as I had pocketed many such in the past I had become fairly inured to them. Therefore I decided to forget this latest one, and take what course a dispassionate view of the case might suggest.

We received a letter from the Chief of the Asiatic Department to the effect that as I had seen Mr. Chamberlain in Durban, it had been found necessary to omit my name from the Transvaal deputation.

The letter was more than my co-workers could endure. They proposed to drop the idea of a deputation altogether. I pointed out to them the awkward situation in which this would leave them.

"If you do not represent your case before Mr. Chamberlain," said I, "it will be presumed that you have no case at all. After all, the representation has to be made in writing and we have got it ready. It does not matter in the least whether I read it or someone else reads it. Mr. Chamberlain is not going to argue the matter out with us. I am afraid we must swallow the insult."

I had scarcely finished speaking when Tyeb Sheth

cried out: "Does not an insult to you amount to an insult to the community? How can we forget that you are our representative?"

"That is perfectly true," said I. "But even the community will have to pocket insults like these. Have you any alternative to offer?"

"Come what may," asked Tyeb Sheth, "why should we swallow a fresh insult? Nothing worse can possibly happen to us. Have we many rights to lose?"

I liked the spirited reply he made to me, but I also knew that the spirit was of no avail. Therefore I pacified my friends and advised them to appoint in my place Mr. George Godfrey, an Indian barrister.

So Mr. Godfrey led the deputation. Mr. Chamberlain referred in his reply to my exclusion. "Rather than hear," he said, "the same representative over and over again, is it not better to have someone new?" Thus he tried to heal the wound, but only increased it.

Mr. Chamberlain spoke as he had been tutored by the Asiatic Department, which in this way sought to import into the Transvaal the atmosphere which pervades India.

Little did Mr. Chamberlain know that I had lived in the Transvaal, and even if I had not I was fully conversant with the Indian situation there. There was only one pertinent question: Who possessed the best knowledge of the situation in the Transvaal? The Indians had already answered for themselves that question by asking me to come all the way from India. But it is no new experience to find that arguments based on reason do not always appeal to men in authority. Mr. Chamberlain was then so much under the influence of the men on the spot and so anxious to humour the Europeans that there was little hope of his doing justice. Nevertheless, the deputation waited on him, in order that no legitimate step for obtaining redress might be omitted, whether by oversight or through a sense of wounded self-respect.

I was now confronted by a dilemma even more difficult than that which faced me in 1894. From one standpoint it seemed I could return to India as soon as Mr. Chamberlain left South Africa. On the other hand I could clearly see that if I returned with the vain idea of serving on a larger field in India while I knew well the danger which stared the South African Indians in the face, the spirit of service which I had acquired would be stultified. I thought that even if I should not have to live altogether in South Africa I must remain there at least until the gathering clouds were dispersed.

With this in my mind I soon applied for admission to practise law in the Transvaal. There was some apprehension that the Law Society would here also oppose my application, but it proved groundless. I was thus enrolled as an attorney of the Supreme Court, and opened an office in Johannesburg. I had given up all hope of returning to India in the near future. Yet I had promised my wife that I would return home within a year. The year was gone without any prospect of my going back, and I decided to send for her and the children.

On the boat bringing them to South Africa, Ramdas, my third son, had injured his arm while playing with the ship's captain. The captain had looked after him as well as he could and had him attended to by the ship's doctor. Ramdas therefore landed with his arm in a sling. The doctor had advised that as soon as we reached home the wound should be dressed by a qualified surgeon. But this was the time when I was full of faith in my experiments in earth treatment as a cure. I had even succeeded in persuading some of my clients who had faith in my quackery to try the earth-and-water treatment.

What, then, was I to do for Ramdas? He was just eight years old. I asked him if he would mind my dressing his wound. With a smile he said that he did not mind at all. It was not possible for him at that age to decide what was the best thing for him, but he knew my habit of home treatment and had faith enough to trust himself to me. In fear and trembling I undid the bandage, washed the wound, applied a clean earth poultice, and tied the arm up again. This sort of dressing went on daily for about a month until the wound was completely healed. There was no hitch, and the wound took no more time to heal than the ship's doctor had said it would under the usual treatment.

This, and other experiments, enhanced my faith in such household remedies, and I now proceeded to practise them with more self-confidence. I widened the sphere of their application, trying earth and water and fasting treatment in cases of wounds, fevers, dyspepsia, jaundice, and other complaints, with success on most occasions. But nowadays I have not the confidence which I had in South Africa, and experience has even shown me that these experiments involve obvious risks.

The reference here, therefore, to these experiments is not meant to demonstrate their success. I cannot claim complete success for any experiments. Even medical men can make no such claim about their experiments. My object is only to show that he who would go in for novel experiments must begin with himself. That leads to a quicker discovery of truth, and God is always protecting the honest experimenter.

The risks involved while making experiments in cultivating intimate personal contacts with Europeans were always as grave as those in the nature of trying to make physical healing of disease—only those risks were of a different kind. But in cultivating these contacts I never so much as thought of the risks involved.

I invited Polak to come and stay with me, and we began to live like blood brothers. Mrs. Polak and he had been engaged to be married for some time, but the marriage had been postponed for a propitious moment. I have an impression that Polak wanted to put some money by before he settled down to a married life. He knew Ruskin much better than I did, but his Western surroundings were a bar against his translating Ruskin's teachings immediately into practice.

"When there is a heart union, as in your case," I pleaded with him, "it is hardly right to postpone marriage merely for financial considerations. If poverty is a bar, poor men can never marry. And then you are now staying with me. There is no question of household expenses in your case. I think that you should get married as soon as possible."

I had never to argue a thing twice with Polak. He appreciated the force of my argument and immediately opened correspondence with his fiancée on the subject. She gladly accepted the proposal and in a few months reached Johannesburg. Any expense over the wedding was out of the question. Not even a special dress was thought necessary. They needed no religious rites to seal the bond. Mrs. Polak was a Christian by birth and Mr. Polak was a Jew. Their common religion was the religion of higher humanity.

I may mention in passing an amusing incident in connection with this wedding. The Registrar of European marriages in the Transvaal could not register marriages between black or coloured people. In the wedding in question I acted as the best man. It would have been easy to get a European friend for the purpose, but Polak would not for a moment listen to the suggestion. So we three went to the Registrar of Marriages together. The poor man was puzzled. How could he be sure that the parties to a marriage in which I acted as best man were whites? He proposed, therefore, to postpone registration pending enquiries.

The next day was a Sunday. The day following that was New Year's Day—a public holiday. To postpone the date of the solemnly arranged wedding on such a flimsy pretext was more than I could put up with. I happened to know the Chief Magistrate, who was head of the Registration Department. So I appeared before him with the couple. He laughed and gave me a note to the Registrar, and the marriage was duly registered.

Up to now the Europeans living with us had been more or less known to me before. But now an English lady who was an utter stranger to us had entered our family. I do not remember ever having a difference with the newly married couple, but even if this had occurred it would have been no more than what happened in the best regulated homogeneous families. And let it be remembered that mine would be considered an essentially heterogeneous family, where people of all kinds and temperaments were freely admitted. Indeed, the distinction between heterogeneous and homogeneous, when analysed, is discovered to be merely imaginary. We are all one human family.

I introduced as much simplicity as was possible in a barrister's house. It was impossible to do without a certain amount of furniture. The change was internal more than external. The liking for doing personally all the physical labour increased. Therefore I began to bring children also under that discipline.

Instead of buying baker's bread we began to prepare unleavened wholemeal bread at home according to the recipe of Kuhne. Common mill flour was no good for this, and the use of hand-ground flour, it was thought, would ensure more simplicity, health and economy. So I purchased a hand-mill for £7. The iron wheel was too heavy to be tackled by one man, but it was easy for two. Polak and I and the children usually worked it. Mrs. Polak now joined us on her arrival. The grinding proved very beneficial exercise for the children. Neither this nor any other work was ever imposed upon them, but it was a pastime to them to come and lend a hand, and they were at liberty to break off whenever tired. But the children, including those whom I shall have occasion to introduce later, as a rule never failed me. Not that there were no laggards at all, but most did their work cheerfully enough. I can recall few youngsters in those days fighting shy of work or pleading fatigue. We were a happy family together.

Although I had furnished the house with care, yet it failed to have any hold on me. Therefore no sooner had I launched forth on this new form of life than I began to cut down expenses. The washerman's bill was heavy, and since also he was by no means noted for his punctuality, even two to three dozen shirts and collars proved insufficient for me. Collars had to be changed daily, and shirts, if not daily, at least every alternate day. This meant double expense, which appeared to me unnecessary. So I equipped myself with a washing oufit in order to economize. Then I bought a book on washing and studied the art very carefully indeed. This no doubt added to my work, but its novelty made it a pleasure, and it became a hobby in my spare time.

I shall never forget the first collar that I washed for myself. I had used more starch than was necessary; the iron had not been hot enough, and for fear of burning the collar I had not pressed it sufficiently. The result was that although the collar was fairly stiff the superfluous starch continually dropped off. I went to the law court with this collar on, thus inviting the ridicule of my brother practitioners; but even in those days I could be impervious to ridicule, and in these matters I was quite hardened.

"Hallo," said one of them, "what has happened to your collar?"

"Well," said I, "this is my first experiment at washing my own collars, and hence the loose starch. But it does not trouble me a bit, and then there is the advantage of providing you with so much fun."

"But surely," asked my friend, "there is no lack of laundries here?"

"The laundry bill is very heavy," said I. "The charge for washing a collar is almost as much as its price, and even then there is the eternal dependence on the washerman. I prefer by far to wash my things with my own hands."

But I could not make my friends appreciate the beauty of self-help. In course of time I became an expert washerman so far as my own work went, and my washing at last became in no way inferior to the laundry washing. My collars were no less stiff or shiny than others that had come from the laundry.

When Gokhale came to South Africa, he had with him a scarf which was a gift from Mahadeo Govind Ranade. He treasured this memento with the utmost care and used it only on very special occasions. One such occasion was the banquet given in his honour by the Johannesburg Indians. The scarf was creased and it needed ironing. It was not possible to send it to the laundry and get it back in time. I offered to try my art.

"I can trust to your capacity as a lawyer," said Gokhale, "but not as a washerman. What if you should soil it? Do you realize what it means to me?"

He then narrated to me with evident pleasure the story of the gift. I still insisted, guaranteed good work, got his permission to iron it, and won his certificate. After that I did not mind if the rest of the world refused me its certificate as a washerman, for I had Gokhale's.

In the same way that I freed myself from the slavery of the washerman I threw off dependence on the barber. All Indians who go to England learn there at least the art of shaving; but none, to my knowledge, learn to cut their own hair. I had to learn that too. I once went to an English haircutter in Pretoria. He contemptuously refused to cut my hair. I certainly felt hurt, but immediately purchased a pair of clippers and cut my hair before the mirror. I succeeded more or less in cutting the front hair, but I must confess that I spoiled the back. My barrister friends in court shook their sides with laughter when they saw the result of my experiment. "Hallo!" they cried. "Why! What's wrong with your hair, Gandhi? Have the rats been at it?"

"No," said I, enjoying the joke. "The white barber would not condescend to touch my hair, so I preferred to cut it myself, no matter how badly I did it."

This reply did not surprise my friends, who by this time had begun to understand my idiosyncrasies and account for them. The barber was not at fault in having refused to cut my hair, and I did not blame him for it, in my own mind, at the time. For there was every chance of his losing his custom if he should serve coloured men. In India itself we do not allow our barbers to serve our untouchable brethren. I got this reward in South Africa not once, but many times, and the conviction that it was the punishment for our sins saved me from becoming angry.

The peculiar and varied forms in which my passion for self-help and extreme simplicity ultimately expressed itself will duly appear in the course of this present narrative. I shall tell later on the story of Tolstoy Farm. The seed had long been sown. It only needed careful and continuous watering to take root, to blossom and bear fruit. The watering came in due course.

We had engaged a servant to look after the house. He lived with us as a member of the family, and the children used to help him with his work. The municipal sweeper removed the nightsoil, but we personally attended to the cleaning of the closet instead of asking or expecting the servant to do it. This proved a good training for the children. The result was that none of my sons developed any aversion for scavenger's work, and they naturally got a good grounding in general sanitation. There was hardly any illness in the home in Johannesburg, but whenever there was any, the nursing was willingly done by the children. I will not say that I was indifferent to their literary education, but I certainly did not hesitate to sacrifice it in these higher interests, as I regarded them. My sons have therefore some reason for grievance against me. Indeed, they have occasionally given expression to it, and I must plead guilty to a certain extent.

The desire to give them a literary education was always there. I even endeavoured to give it to them myself, but every now and then there was some hitch or other. As I had made no other arrangement for their private tuition, I used to get them to walk with me daily to the office and back home, a distance of about five miles in all. This gave them a fair amount of exercise during these walks. I tried to instruct them by conversation, if there was no one else claiming my attention. All my children, excepting the eldest, Harilal, who had stayed away in India, were brought up in Johannesburg in this manner. Had I been able to devote at least one hour to their literary education, with strict regularity, I should have given them, in my opinion, an ideal education. But it has been my regret that I failed to ensure for them enough training in that direction.

My eldest son has often given vent to his distress privately before me and publicly in the Press; my other sons have generously forgiven the failure as unavoidable. I am not heartbroken over it, and the regret, if any, is that I did not prove an ideal father. But I hold that I sacrificed their literary training to what I genuinely believed to be a service to the Indian community. At the same time I am quite clear that I have not been negligent in fulfilling whatever was needful for building up their characters, and I believe it is the bounden duty of every parent to provide for this properly. Whenever, in spite of my endeavour, my sons have been found wanting in character, it is my certain conviction that they have reflected, not want of care on my part only, but the effects of both their parents. For children inherit the qualities of their parents no less than their physical features. Environment does play an important part, but the original capital on which the child starts in life is inherited from its ancestors. I have also seen children successfully surmounting the effects of an evil inheritance. That is due to inner purity being an inherent attribute of the soul.

Polak and I had often very heated discussions about the desirability or otherwise of giving the children an English education. It has always been my conviction that Indian parents who train their children to think and talk in English from their infancy, betray their children and their country. They deprive them of the spiritual and social heritage of the nation and render them to that extent unfit for the service of the country. Having these convictions, I made a point of always talking to my children in Gujarati. Polak never liked this. He thought that I was spoiling their future. He contended, with all the vigour and love at his command, that if children were to learn a universal language, like English, from their infancy, they would easily gain a considerable advance over others in the race of life. He failed to convince me. I do not remember, on the other hand, whether I convinced him as to the correctness of my attitude or whether he gave me up as too obstinate.

This all happened about twenty years ago, and my convictions have only deepened with my experiences. Even though my sons have suffered for want of a full literary education, the knowledge of the vernacular that they naturally acquired has been all to the good, inasmuch as they do not appear when in India to be the foreigners they would otherwise have seemed to be. They naturally became bilingual, speaking and writing English with fair ease, because of daily contact with a large circle of English friends and because of their stay in a country where English is the chief language spoken.

CHAPTER V

A SIMPLER LIFE

THE PROBLEM OF further simplifying my life and of doing some concrete act of service to my fellow-men had been constantly agitating me, when a leper came to my door. I had not got the heart to dismiss him merely with a meal. So I offered him shelter, dressed his wound, and began to look after him. But I could not go on like that indefinitely. I could not afford to keep him always with me, and I lacked the will to do so. So I sent him to the Government Hospital.

Nevertheless, I was ill at ease, and I longed for some humanitarian work of a permanent nature. So I found time to serve in the small hospital. This meant two hours every morning, including the time taken in going to and from the hospital. This work brought me some peace of mind. The special duty consisted in ascertaining the patients' complaints, laying the facts before the doctor and dispensing the prescriptions. It brought me in close touch with the suffering Indians.

The question of the rearing of children had been ever before me. I had two sons born in South Africa, and my service in the hospital was very useful to me in solving the question of their upbringing. My independent spirit was a constant source of trial to me. My wife and I had decided to have the best medical aid at the time of her delivery; but if the doctor and the nurse were to leave us in the lurch at the critical moment, what was I to do? Besides, the nurse had to be an Indian. And the difficulty of getting a trained Indian nurse in South Africa can be easily imagined from the similar difficulty in India. So I studied the things necessary for safe delivery. I read Dr. Tribhuvandas' book, *Ma-ne Shikhaman*—"Advice to a Mother"—and I nursed both my children according to the instructions given in the book, tempered here and there by such experience as I had gained elsewhere.

The birth of the last child put me to the severest test of all. The travail came on quite suddenly. The doctor was not immediately available, and some time was lost in fetching the midwife. Even if one had been on the spot, she could not have helped delivery. I had to see through the safe delivery of the baby myself. My careful study of the subject in Dr. Tribhuvandas' work was of inestimable help. I was not nervous.

I am convinced that for the proper upbringing of children the parents ought to have a general knowledge of the care and nursing of babies. At every step I have seen the advantages of a thorough study of the subject. My children would not have enjoyed the general good health that they possess to-day had I not studied the subject and turned my knowledge to account. We labour under a sort of superstition, that the child has nothing to learn during the first five years of its life. On the contrary, the fact is that the child never learns in afterlife what it does in its first five years. The education of the child begins with conception. The physical and mental conceptions are reproduced in the baby. Then during the period of pregnancy it continues to be affected by the mother's moods, desires and temperament, as also by her ways of life. After birth the child imitates the

A SIMPLER LIFE

parents, and for a considerable number of years entirely depends on them for its growth.

I had been devoted to a monogamous ideal ever since my marriage. Faithfulness to my wife was a part of my love of Truth. But it was in South Africa that I came to realize the importance of observing Brahmacharya, even with respect to my wife. I cannot definitely say what circumstances, or what book it was, that set my thoughts in that direction, but I have a recollection that the predominant factor was the influence of Raychandbhai, of whom I have already written.[1] I can still recall a conversation that I had with him. On one occasion I spoke to him in high praise of Mrs. Gladstone's devotion to her husband. I had read somewhere that Mrs. Gladstone insisted on preparing tea for Mr. Gladstone, even in the House of Commons, and that this had become a rule in the life of this illustrious couple, whose actions were governed by regularity. I spoke of this to the poet Raychandbhai and incidentally eulogized conjugal love.

"Which of the two do you prize more," asked Raychandbhai, "the love of Mrs. Gladstone for her husband as his wife or her devoted service irrespective of her relation to Mr. Gladstone? Supposing she had been his sister, or his devoted servant, and had administered to him with the same attention, what would you have said? Do we not have instances of such devoted sisters or servants? Supposing you had found the same loving devotion in a male servant, would you have been pleased in the same way as in Mrs. Gladstone's case? I would like you to examine the viewpoint suggested by me."

[1] See *Mahatma Gandhi: His Own Story*, pp. 80, 81 and 122.

Raychandbhai was himself married. I have an impression that at the moment his words sounded harsh, but they gripped me irresistibly. The devotion of a servant was, I felt, a thousand times more praiseworthy than that of a wife to her husband because it was entirely unselfish. There was nothing surprising in the wife's devotion to her husband, as there was an indissoluble bond between them. The devotion was perfectly natural. But it required a special effort to cultivate equal devotion between master and servant. The poet's point of view began gradually to grow upon me and to gain ground in my own mind.

What, then, I asked myself, should be my relation to my wife? Did my faithfulness consist in making my wife an instrument of my passion? So long as I was the slave of passion, my faithfulness was worth nothing. To be fair to my wife I must say that she never was the temptress. It was therefore the easiest thing for me to take the vow of Brahmacharya (Chastity), if only I willed it. It was my weak will or lustful attachment that was the obstacle.

Even after my conscience had been roused in the matter I failed twice. I failed, because the motive that actuated the effort was none of the highest. My main object was to escape having more children. Seeing, therefore, that I did not desire more children I began to strive after self-control. There was endless difficulty in the task. I decided to retire to bed only after the day's work had left me completely exhausted. All these efforts did not seem to bear much fruit; but when I look back upon the past I feel that the final resolution was the cumulative effect of these unsuccessful strivings.

The final resolution could only be made as late as 1906.

A SIMPLER LIFE

The Satyagraha campaign had not then been started. I had not the least notion even of its coming. I was practising at the Bar in Johannesburg at the time of the Zulu "Rebellion" in Natal, which came soon after the Boer War. On that occasion I felt that I must offer my services to the Natal Government. The offer was accepted.[1] But the work set me furiously thinking in the direction of self-control, and according to my wont I discussed my thoughts with my co-workers. It became my conviction that to have more children and be responsible for their care and upbringing would be inconsistent with public service. I had to break up my household at Johannesburg in order to be able to serve during the "Rebellion." Within one month of offering my services I had to give up the house which I had so carefully furnished. Then I took my wife and children to Phœnix. After that I led the Indian Ambulance Corps attached to the Natal forces. During the difficult marches that had to be performed in Zululand the idea flashed upon me that if I wanted to devote myself to the service of the community in this manner I must relinquish the desire for children and wealth, and must live the life of a Vanaprastha—of one retired from household cares.

At this time the importance of vows grew upon me more clearly than ever before. I discovered when making my experiments with Truth that a vow, far from closing the door to real freedom, opened it wider. Up to this time I had not met with success because the will had been lacking, because I had no faith in myself and no faith in the grace of God, and therefore my mind had been tossed on the boisterous sea of doubt. I realized

[1] See *Mahatma Gandhi: His Own Story*, p. 142.

that in refusing to take a vow man was drawn into temptation, and that to be bound by a vow was like a passage from libertinism to a real monogamous marriage.

When a man says to himself, "I believe in effort, I do not want to bind myself with vows," it is really the mentality of weakness that makes the excuse. He betrays in those very words a subtle desire for the thing to be avoided. Otherwise, where can be the difficulty in making a final decision? I take a vow to flee from the serpent which I know will bite me; I do not simply make an effort to flee from him. I know that mere effort means ignorance of the certain fact that the serpent is bound to kill me. The fact, therefore, that I could rest content with an effort only means that I have not yet clearly realized the necessity of definite action.

"But supposing my views are changed in the future, how can I bind myself by a vow?" Such a doubt often deters us. But that doubt also betrays a lack of a clear perception, that a particular thing must be renounced. That is why Nishkulanand has sung:

> Renunciation without aversion is not lasting.

Where, therefore, the desire is gone, a vow of renunciation is the natural and inevitable fruit.

After full discussion and mature deliberation I took the vow in 1906. I had not shared my thoughts with my wife until then. I only consulted her at the time of taking the vow. She had no objection. But I was hard put to it in making the final resolve. I had not the necessary strength. How was I to control my passions? The elimination of carnal passion seemed then a strange thing. But I launched forth in the sustaining power of God.

A SIMPLER LIFE

As I look back upon the twenty years of the vow, I am filled with happiness and wonderment. The more or less successful practice of self-control had been going on since 1906. But the freedom and joy that came to me after taking the vow had never been experienced until that date. Before the vow had been taken I had been open to temptation at any moment. Now the vow was a sure shield against temptation. The great potentiality of Brahmacharya became daily more and more patent to me. As though unknown to me, the vow had been preparing me for Satyagraha. It has not been a preconceived plan. It came to me spontaneously, without my having willed it. But I could see now that all my previous steps had led on to that goal. I had cut down my heavy household expenses at Johannesburg and gone to Phœnix in order to take, as it were, the Brahmacharya vow.

I did not owe to a study of the Scriptures the knowledge that a perfect observance of my vow meant realization of Brahman.[1] It slowly grew upon me with experience. The scriptural texts on the subject I read only later in life. Every day of the vow has taken me nearer the knowledge that in Brahmacharya lies the protection of the body, the mind and the soul. For it was now no process of hard penance, it was rather a matter of consolation and joy. Every day revealed a fresh beauty in it.

But if it was a matter of ever-increasing joy, let no one believe that it was an easy thing for me. Even now that I have grown old I realize how hard a thing it is. Every

[1] The Hindu name for God in His infinitude. The word Brahmacharya has this divine name as its affix.

day I realize more and more that it is like walking on the sword's edge, and I see every moment the necessity for eternal vigilance.

Control of the palate is the first essential in the observance of this vow. I found that complete control of the palate made the observance very easy, and so I now pursued my dietetic experiments not only from the vegetarians' but also from the Brahmachari's point of view. As the result of these experiments I saw that the food eaten should be limited, simple, spiceless, and, if possible, uncooked.

Six years of experiment have shown me that the Brahmachari's ideal food is fresh fruit and nuts. The immunity from passion that I enjoyed when I lived on this food was unknown to me after I changed that diet. Brahmacharya needed no effort on my part in South Africa when I lived on fruits and nuts alone. It has been a matter of very great effort ever since I began to take milk again. I have not the least doubt that milk diet makes the Brahmacharya vow difficult to observe. Let no one deduce from this that all Brahmacharis must give up milk. The effect of different kinds of food can be determined only after numerous experiments. I have yet to find a substitute for milk which is an equally good muscle-builder and as easily digestible. The doctors, Eastern and Western, have alike failed to enlighten me. Therefore, though I know milk to be partly a stimulant, I cannot for the time being advise anyone to give it up.

As an external aid, fasting is as necessary as selection and restriction in diet. So overpowering are the senses that they are completely hedged in on all sides, from

A SIMPLER LIFE

above and from beneath. It is common knowledge that the senses are powerless without food, and so fasting undertaken with a view to control the senses is no doubt very helpful. With some, fasting is of no avail, because assuming that mechanical fasting alone will make them immune, they keep their bodies without God. But the possibilities of renunciation are unlimited even as there is no limit to those of Brahmacharya. It is impossible of attainment by limited effort. For many, it must remain only as an ideal. An aspirant will always be conscious of his own shortcomings. He will seek out the passions lingering in the innermost recesses of his own heart and will incessantly strive to get rid of them. So long as the inner thoughts are not under complete control of the will, Brahmacharya in all its fullness is absent. Involuntary thought is an affection of the mind. The complete curbing of thought, therefore, means curbing of the mind, which is even more difficult to restrain than the body. Nevertheless, the existence of God within makes even control of the mind possible. For He can do what no human being can perform. Let no one think that it is impossible to control the inner thoughts simply because it is so difficult. It is the highest goal, and it is no wonder that the highest effort should be necessary to attain it.

But in my own case it was only after coming back to India that I realized that such Brahmacharya in the inmost heart was impossible to attain by mere human effort and apart from divine aid. Until then I had been labouring under the delusion that a change to fruit diet alone would enable me to eradicate all passions, and I had flattered myself with the belief that I had nothing more to do than thus to regulate my external life and its appetites. But I found that mere human effort always failed. Without God's help nothing was lasting.

Meanwhile, let me make it clear that those who desire to observe Brahmacharya with a view to realizing God through inner purity of heart need not despair, provided only their faith in God goes side by side with their confidence in their own effort.

"The sense-objects turn away from an abstemious soul, leaving the relish behind. The relish also disappears with the realization of the Highest."[1] Therefore His name and His grace are the last resources of the aspirant after spiritual freedom. This truth only came to me in full after my return to India and at a much later period in my life.

Fasting and restrictions in diet now began to play a much more important part in my experiments with Truth. Passion in man is generally co-existent with a hankering after the pleasure of the palate. And so it was continually with me. I have encountered many difficulties in trying to control passion as well as taste, and I cannot claim even now that I have brought them under complete control. I have considered myself naturally to be a heavy eater. What friends have thought to be my restraint has never appeared to me in that light. If I had failed to develop restraint I should have descended lower than the beasts and met my doom long ago. However, as I had adequately realized my shortcomings, I made a great effort to get rid of them. Thanks to this daily endeavour, I have managed to pull on with my body all these years and put in with it my share of work.

Being conscious of my own weakness and imper-

[1] *The Bhagavad Gita*, 2–59.

A SIMPLER LIFE

fection, and unexpectedly coming in contact with congenial company, I began to take an exclusive fruit diet or to fast on different suitable occasions. My first effort was with a fruit diet, but from the standpoint of restraint I did not find much to choose between a fruit diet and a diet of food grains. I observed that the same indulgence of taste was possible with the former as with the latter, and even more, when one got accustomed to it. Therefore I came to attach greater importance to fasting or having only one meal a day on holidays. And if there was some occasion for penance I gladly utilized it also for the purpose of fasting.

But I saw, further, that the body being now trained more effectively the food yielded greater relish and the appetite grew keener. It dawned upon me that fasting could be made as powerful a weapon of indulgence as restraint. Many similar later experiences of mine as well as of others can be adduced in evidence of this startling fact. I wanted to improve and train my body; but as my chief object was to achieve restraint and conquest of the palate, I selected first one food and then another, and at the same time restricted the amount. But the relish, as it were, always pursued me. As I gave up one thing and took up another, this latter afforded me a fresher and greater relish than its predecessor.

In making these experiments I had several companions, the chief of whom was Hermann Kallenbach. Mr. Kallenbach was always with me whether in fasting or in dietetic changes. I lived with him at his place when the Satyagraha struggle was at its height. We discussed our changes of food and derived more pleasure from the new diet than from the old. Conversation about food of this nature sounded more pleasant in those days, and did not strike me as at all improper. Experience has taught me, however, that it was wrong to have dwelt upon the relish of food. We should eat not in order to please the palate but just to keep the body going. When each organ of sense subserves the body and through the body the soul, the special relish disappears and then alone does it begin to function in the way nature intended it to do.

Any number of experiments is too small and no sacrifice is too great for attaining this symphony with nature. But unfortunately the current in these days is flowing strongly in the opposite direction. We are not ashamed to sacrifice a multitude of other lives in order merely to decorate the perishable body. We try also to prolong its existence for a few fleeting moments, with the result that we kill ourselves, body and soul. In trying to cure one old disease we give rise to a hundred new ones. In seeking to enjoy the pleasures of sense we lose in the end even our capacity for enjoyment. All this is going on before our eyes, but there are none so blind as those who will not see.

Just about this time when I gave up milk and cereals, and started on the experiment of the fruit diet, I commenced fasting as a means of self-restraint. In this Kallenbach also joined me. I had been used to fasting now and again, but for purely health reasons. It was from a friend that I learnt that fasting was necessary for self-restraint. Having been born in a Vaishnava family and of a mother who was given to keeping all sorts of hard vows, I had observed while in India the Ekadashi[1]

---

[1] A fast on the eleventh day practised specially by widows in Hindu India.

A SIMPLER LIFE

and other fasts, but in doing so I had merely copied my mother and sought to please my parents.

At that time I did not understand, nor did I believe in the efficacy of fasting. But seeing that the friend I have mentioned was observing a fast with benefit, I followed his example and began keeping the Ekadashi fast. As a rule Hindus allow themselves milk and fruit on a day of fasting, but such a fast I had been keeping already. So now I began a complete fast, allowing myself only water.

When I entered on this experiment the Hindu month of Shravan and the Muhammadan month of Ramazan happened to coincide. The Gandhis used to observe not only the Vaishnava[1] but also the Shaivite vows, and visited the Vaishnava as also the Shaivite temples. Some of the members of the family used to observe the pradosha[2] in the whole of the month of Shravan. I decided to do likewise.

These important experiments were undertaken at a later date while we were at Tolstoy Farm, where Kallenbach and I were staying with a few of the Satyagrahi families, including young people and children. Among them were four or five Musalmans. I always helped and encouraged them in keeping all their religious observances. I took care to see that they offered their daily prayers. There were Christians and Parsis too, whom I considered it my duty to encourage to follow their respective religious observances.

During the month of Ramazan,[3] therefore, I persuaded

---
[1] Vishnu is the name for the Supreme God among one section of Hindus; Shiva is the name for the Supreme God among another section. The former are called Vaishnavas, the latter are called Shaivites.
[2] Fasting until the evening.
[3] During the month of Ramazan, orthodox Musalmans only take food and water before sunrise and after sunset.

the Musalman youngsters to observe the fast. I had, of course, decided to observe the pradosha myself, but I now asked the Hindu, Parsi and Christian youngsters to join me. I explained to them that it was always a good thing to participate with others in any matter of self-denial. Many of the Farm inmates welcomed my proposal. The Hindu and the Parsi youngsters did not copy the Musalmans in every detail; it was not necessary. The Musalmans had to wait for their breakfast until sunset, whereas the others did not do so, and were thus able to prepare delicacies for the Musalman friends and serve them. Nor had the Hindu and other youngsters to keep the Musalmans company when they had their last meal before sunrise the next morning, and of course all except the Musalmans allowed themselves water.

The result was that everyone was convinced of the value of fasting, and a splendid loyalty to one another grew up among them.

We were all vegetarians on that occasion, thanks, I must gratefully confess, to the readiness of all to respect my feelings. The Musalman youngsters must have missed their meat during the Ramazan month, but none of them ever let me know that they did so. They took delight in the relish of a vegetarian diet, and the Hindu youngsters often prepared vegetarian delicacies for them, in keeping with the simplicity of the Farm.

Thus the atmosphere of self-restraint naturally sprang up amongst us. All the inmates now began to join us in keeping partial and complete fasts, which I am sure was entirely to the good. I cannot definitely say how far this self-denial touched their hearts and helped them in their striving to conquer the flesh. For my part, however,

A SIMPLER LIFE

I am convinced that I greatly benefited by it both physically and morally. Yet I know that it does not necessarily follow that fasting and similar discipline would have the same effect on all.

Fasting can help to curb animal passion only if it is undertaken with a view to self-restraint. Some of my friends have actually found their animal passions and palate stimulated as an after-effect of fasts. That is to say, fasting is futile unless it is accompanied by an incessant longing for self-restraint. The famous verse from the second chapter of the Bhagavad Gita is worth noting in this connection:

For a man who is fasting his senses outwardly, the sense-objects disappear, leaving the yearning behind; but when he has seen the Highest, even the yearning disappears.

Fasting is therefore one of the means to attain the end of self-restraint, but it is not all; and if physical fasting is not accompanied by mental fasting, it is bound to end in hypocrisy and consequent disaster.

CHAPTER VI

THE PROFESSION OF LAW

AS A STUDENT I had heard that the lawyer's profession made lying a necessity. But this did not deter me or influence me against it; for I had no intention of earning either position or money by lying.

My principle of honesty was put to the test many times over in South Africa. Often I would know that my opponents had tutored their witnesses, and if only I encouraged my client or his witness to lie, we should certainly win the case. But I always resisted the temptation. I remember only one occasion when, after having won a case, I suspected that my client had deceived me. In my heart of hearts I only wished that I should win if my client's case was right and just. In fixing my fees I do not recall ever having made them conditional on my winning the case. Whether my client won or lost I expected nothing more or less than my fee.

I warned every new client at the outset that he should not expect me to take up a false case or to coach the witnesses, with the result that I built up such a reputation that no false cases used to come to me; and indeed some of my clients would keep their clean cases for me and take the doubtful ones elsewhere.

There was one law-suit which proved a severe trial to me. It was brought to me by one of my best clients. It was a case of highly complicated accounts and had been a prolonged one.

It had been heard in parts before several Courts. Ulti-

TOLSTOY FARM

mately the book-keeping portion of it was entrusted by the Court to the arbitration of some qualified accountants. The award was entirely in favour of my client, but the arbitrators had inadvertently committed an error in calculation which, however small, was serious, inasmuch as an entry that ought to have been made on the debit side was put down to the credit side. The opponents had opposed the award on other grounds. I was acting as junior counsel for my client. When the senior counsel became aware of the error in the calculation he was of opinion that our client was not bound to admit it. No counsel, he thought, was bound to admit anything that went against his client's interests. I said we ought to admit the error.

"In that case," the senior counsel contended, "there is every likelihood of the court cancelling the whole award; and no sane counsel would imperil his client's case to that extent. At any rate, I personally would be the last man to take any such risk. If the case were to be sent up for a fresh hearing, one could never tell what expenses might have to be incurred and what the ultimate result might be."

The client himself was present when this conversation took place.

"Personally," I said, "I feel that both we and our client ought to run the risk. Where is the certainty of the Court upholding a wrong award, simply because we do not admit an error? And supposing the admission were to bring the client to grief, what harm is there?"

"But why should we make the admission at all?" asked the senior counsel.

"Where is the certainty," I replied, "that the Court

will not detect the error, or that our opponent will not discover it?"

"Well, then, you had better argue the case," replied the senior counsel. "I am not prepared to be responsible for it on your terms."

"If you will not take it up," I replied humbly, "then I am prepared to do so, if our client so desires. But I shall have nothing to do with the case if the error is not admitted."

With this I looked at my client. He was a little embarrassed. I had been engaged in the case from the very first. The client fully trusted me, and knew me through and through. "Very well," he said at last. "You will argue the case and admit the error. We shall lose, if that is to be our lot. May God defend the right."

I was delighted. I had expected nothing less from him. The senior counsel again warned me and pitied me for my obduracy, but congratulated me all the same.

I had no doubt about the soundness of my advice, but I doubted very much my fitness for doing full justice to the case. I felt it would be a most hazardous undertaking to argue such a difficult case before the Supreme Court, and therefore when I appeared before the Bench I was in fear and trembling.

As soon as I referred personally to the error in the accounts, one of the judges said:

"Is not this sharp practice, Mr. Gandhi?"

I boiled within to hear this charge. It was intolerable to be accused of sharp practice when there was not the slightest warrant for it.

"With the judge prejudiced from the start like this,"

I said to myself, "there is little chance of success." But I composed my thoughts.

"I am surprised," I answered, "that your Lordship should suspect sharp practice without hearing me out."

"I make no charge against you," said the judge. "It is a mere suggestion."

"The suggestion," I replied, "seems to me to amount to a charge. I would ask your Lordship to hear me out, and then arraign me if there is any occasion for it."

"I am sorry to have interrupted you," replied the judge. "Pray do go on with your explanation of the discrepancy."

I had enough material in support of my explanation. Thanks to the judge having raised this question, I was able to rivet the Court's attention on my argument from the very start. I felt much encouraged and took the opportunity of entering into a long detailed explanation. The Court gave me a patient hearing and I was able to convince the judges that the discrepancy was due entirely to inadvertence. They therefore did not feel disposed to cancel the whole award.

The opposing counsel seemed to feel secure in the belief that not much argument on his side would be needed after the error had been admitted. But the judges continued to interrupt him, as they were convinced that the error was a slip which could be easily rectified. The counsel laboured hard to attack the award; but the judge, who had originally started with the suspicion, had now come round definitely to my side.

"Supposing Mr. Gandhi had not admitted the error," he asked, "what would you have done?"

"It was impossible," the counsel replied, "for us to

secure the services of a more competent and honest expert accountant than the one appointed by us."

"The Court must presume," said the judge, "that you know your case best. If you cannot point out anything beyond the slip, which any expert accountant is liable to commit, the Court will be loath to compel the parties to go in for fresh litigation and fresh expenses because of a patent mistake. We may not order a fresh hearing when such an error can be easily corrected."

And so the counsel's objection was overruled. The Court either confirmed the award, with the error rectified, or else ordered the arbitrator to rectify the error.

I was delighted. So were my client and senior counsel; and I was confirmed in my conviction that it was not impossible to practise law without compromising truth. Let the reader, however, remember that even truthfulness in the practice of the profession cannot cure it of the fundamental defect that vitiates it.

On one occasion while I was conducting a case before a magistrate in Johannesburg I discovered that my client had deceived me. I saw him completely break down in the witness-box. So without argument I asked the magistrate to dismiss the case. The opposing counsel was astonished and the magistrate was pleased. I rebuked the client for bringing a false case to me. He knew that I never accepted false cases, and when I brought the thing home to his conscience he admitted his mistake; and I have an impression that he was not angry with me for having asked the magistrate to decide against him. At any rate, my conduct in this case did not affect my practice for the worse; indeed, it made my work easier. I also saw that my devotion to truth enhanced my reputation amongst the members of the profession. In spite of the handicap of colour, I was able in some cases to win even their affection.

During my professional work it was also my habit never to disguise my ignorance from my clients or my colleagues. Wherever I felt myself at sea I would advise my client to consult some other counsel, or, if he preferred to stick to me, I would ask him to let me seek the assistance of a senior counsel. This frankness earned me the unbounded affection and trust of my clients. They were always willing to pay the fee whenever consultation with senior counsel was necessary. This affection and trust served me in good stead in my public work.

I have indicated in the foregoing chapters that my object in practising in South Africa was the service of the community. Even for this purpose winning the confidence of the people was an indispensable condition. The large-hearted Indians magnified into service professional work done for money, and when I advised them to suffer the hardships of imprisonment for the sake of their rights, many of them cheerfully accepted the advice, not so much because they had reasoned out the correctness of the course, as because of their confidence in and affection for me.

As I write this, many happy reminiscences come to my mind. Hundreds of clients became friends and real co-workers in public service, and their association sweetened a life that was otherwise full of difficulties and dangers.

Parsi Rustomji was one who became at once my client and co-worker. I won his confidence to such an extent that he sought and followed my advice also in private and domestic matters. Even when he was ill he would seek my aid, and though there was much difference between our ways of living he did not hesitate to accept my medical treatment.

This friend once got into a very bad scrape. Though he kept me informed of most of his affairs, he had studiously kept back one thing. He was a large importer of goods from Bombay and Calcutta and it turned out that not infrequently he resorted to smuggling. But as he was on the best of terms with the Customs officials no one was inclined to suspect him. In charging duty they used to take his invoice on trust. Some may even have connived at the smuggling.

But to use the telling simile of the Gujarati poet Akho, theft, like quicksilver, won't be suppressed, and Parsi Rustomji proved no exception. The good friend ran posthaste to me, the tears rolling down his cheeks as he said: "Bhai, I have deceived you. My guilt has been discovered to-day. I have smuggled and I am doomed. I must go to jail and be ruined. You alone can save me from this predicament. I have kept back nothing else from you, but I had thought I ought not to bother you with such tricks of the trade, and so I had never told you about this smuggling. But now, how deeply I repent it!"

I calmed him and said: "To save or not to save you is in His hands. As for me, you know my way; I can but try to save you by means of a confession."

The good Parsi felt deeply mortified.

"But is not my confession before you enough?" he asked.

"You have wronged not me but the Government. How will the confession made before me avail you?" I replied gently.

"Of course I will do just as you advise, but will you

not consult with my old counsel, Mr. A——? He is a friend too," said Parsi Rustomji.

Enquiry revealed that the smuggling had been going on for a long time, but the actual offence detected involved a trifling sum. We went to his counsel. He perused the papers, and said: "The case will be tried by a jury, and a Natal jury will be the last to acquit an Indian. But I will not give up hope."

I did not know this counsel intimately. Parsi Rustomji intercepted—"I thank you," he said, "but I should like to be guided by Mr. Gandhi's advice in this case. He knows me intimately. Of course you will advise me whenever necessary."

Having thus shelved the counsel's question, we went to Parsi Rustomji's shop.

And now explaining my view, I said to him: "I don't think this case should be taken to court at all. It rests with the Customs Officer to prosecute you or to let you go, and he in turn will have to be guided by the Attorney-General. I am prepared to meet both. I propose that you should offer to pay the penalty they fix, and the odds are that they will be agreeable. But if they are not, you must be prepared to go to jail. I am of opinion that the shame lies not so much in going to jail as in committing the offence. The deed of shame has already been done. Imprisonment you should regard as a penance. The real penance lies in resolving never to smuggle again."

I cannot say that Parsi Rustomji took all this quite well. He was a brave man, but his courage failed him for the moment. His name and fame were at stake, and where would he be if the edifice he had reared with such care and labour should go to pieces?

"Well, I have told you," he said, "that I am entirely in your hands. You may do just as you like."

I brought to bear on this case all my powers of persuasion. I met the Customs Officer and fearlessly apprised him of the whole affair. I also promised to place all the books at his disposal and told him how penitent Parsi Rustomji was feeling. The Customs Officer said: "I like the old Parsi. I am sorry he has made a fool of himself. You know where my duty lies. I must be guided by the Attorney-General and so I would advise you to use all your persuasion with him."

"I should be thankful," said I, "if you do not insist on dragging him into court."

Having got him to promise this, I entered into correspondence with the Attorney-General, whom I also met. I am glad to say that he appreciated my complete frankness and was convinced that I had kept back nothing.

I now forget whether it was in connexion with this or with some other case that my persistence and frankness extorted from him this remark: "I see you will never take 'no' for an answer."

The case against Parsi Rustomji was compromised. He was to pay a penalty equal to twice the amount he had confessed to having smuggled. Rustomji reduced to writing the facts of the whole case, got the paper framed and hung it up in his office to serve as a perpetual reminder to his heirs and fellow merchants.

These friends of Rustomji warned me not to be taken in by this transitory contrition. When I told Rustomji about this warning he said: "What would be my fate if I deceived you?"

Johannesburg was the stronghold of the Asiatic

Department. I had been observing that far from protecting the Indians, Chinese and others, these officers of the Department were grinding them down. Every day I had complaints like this: "The rightful ones are not admitted, while those who have no right are smuggled in on payment of £100. If you will not remedy this state of things, who will?"

I shared the feeling. If I did not succeed in stamping out this evil, I should be living in the Transvaal in vain. So I began to collect evidence, and as soon as I had gathered a fair amount I approached the Police Commissioner. He appeared to be a just man. Far from giving me the cold shoulder, he listened to me patiently and asked me to show him all the evidence in my possession. He examined the witnesses himself and was satisfied, but he knew as well as I that it was difficult in South Africa to get a white jury to convict a white offender against a coloured man.

"But," said he, "let us at any rate try. It is not proper, either, to let these criminals go scot-free, for fear of the jury acquitting them. I must get them arrested. I assure you that I shall not leave a stone unturned."

I did not need the assurance. I suspected quite a number of officers, but as I had no unchallengeable evidence against them all, warrants of arrest were issued against the two about whose guilt I had not the slightest doubt.

My movements could never be kept secret. Many knew that I was going to the Police Commissioner practically daily. The two officers, against whom warrants had been issued, had spies—more or less efficient. They used to patrol my office and report my movements to the officers. I must admit, however, that these officers were so bad that they could not have had many spies. Had the Indians and Chinese not helped me, they would never have been arrested.

One of them absconded. The Police Commissioner obtained an extradition warrant against him and got him arrested and brought to the Transvaal. They were tried, and although there was strong evidence against them, and in spite of the fact that the jury had evidence of one of them having absconded, both were declared not guilty and acquitted.

I was sorely disappointed. The Police Commissioner was also very sorry. I got disgusted with the legal profession. The very intellect became an abomination to me, inasmuch as it could be prostituted for screening crimes.

However, the guilt of both these officers was so patent that in spite of their acquittal the Government could not harbour them. Both were cashiered and the Asiatic Department became comparatively clean, and the Indian community was somewhat reassured.

The event enhanced my prestige and brought me more business. The bulk, though not all, of the hundreds of pounds that the community was monthly squandering in peculation was saved. All could not be saved, for the dishonest still plied their trade. But it was now possible for an honest man to preserve his honesty.

Though these officers were so bad, I had nothing against them personally. They were aware of this themselves, and when in their straits they approached me, I helped them too. They had a chance of getting employment by the Johannesburg Municipality in case I did not oppose the proposal. A friend of theirs saw me in this connexion and I agreed not to thwart them, and they succeeded.

This attitude of mine put the officials with whom I came in contact perfectly at ease, and though I had often to fight with their department and use strong language, they remained quite friendly with me. I was not then quite conscious that such behaviour was a part of my nature. I learnt that it was an essential part of Satyagraha, and an attribute of Ahimsa.

Man and his deed are two distinct things. Whereas a good deed should call forth approbation and a wicked deed disapprobation, the doer of the deed, whether good or wicked, always deserves respect or pity as the case may be. "Hate the sin and not the sinner" is a precept which, though easy enough to understand, is rarely practised, and that is why the poison of hatred spreads over the world.

This love is the basis of the search for Truth. That is why Ahimsa and Satya always go together. I am realizing every day that the search for truth is vain unless it is founded on Love. It is quite proper to resist and attack a system, but to resist and attack its author is tantamount to resisting and attacking oneself. For we are all subject to the same weakness and are children of one and the same Father; and as such the divine powers within us are infinite. To injure a single human being is to injure those divine powers within us, and thus the harm reaches not only that one human being, but with him the whole world.

CHAPTER VII

THE REGISTRATION ORDINANCE

BITTER EXPERIENCE OF the corruptness of the Asiatic Department was reaching me every day in Johannesburg. The best efforts of the Transvaal British Indian Association were directed to finding a remedy for this disease. The repeal of Act 3 of 1885 now receded into the background as a distant objective. The immediate aim was limited to saving ourselves from the onrushing flood of this Asiatic Department. Indian deputations waited on Lord Milner, Lord Selborne, Sir Arthur Lawley and also on officers of lesser dignity. I used often to see Government officers. We obtained some slight relief here and there, but it was all patch-work, pure and simple. We used only to receive such satisfaction as is experienced by a man who has been deprived of everything by robbers and then induces them by entreaty to return something of very small value.

It was in consequence of our own agitation that the officers, whose dismissal I have already referred to, were prosecuted. Our misgivings as regards the restrictions on Indian immigration proved correct. Permits were no longer required from Europeans, while they continued to be demanded from Indians. The late Boer Government never strictly enforced their drastic anti-Asiatic legislation, not because they were generous, but because their administration was lax.

The British Constitution is old and stereotyped, and officers under it have to work like machines. Their

THE REGISTRATION ORDINANCE

liberty of action is restricted by a system of progressive checks. Under the British Constitution, therefore, if the policy of the Government is liberal, the subject receives the utmost advantage of its liberality. On the other hand, if their policy is oppressive and niggardly, the subjects feel the maximum weight of their heavy hand.

The reverse is the case under constitutions such as that of the late Boer Republic. Whether or not the subjects reap full advantage from the liberal laws largely depends upon the officers who are in charge of its administration. Thus, when British power was established in the Transvaal, all laws adversely affecting the Indians began to be more strictly enforced. Loopholes, wherever they existed, were carefully closed. The Asiatic Department was bound to be harsh in its operations. The repeal of the old laws was therefore out of the question. It only remained for the Indians to see how their rigours might be mitigated in practice.

Soon after the establishment of British rule in the Transvaal and the Free State, Lord Milner appointed a Committee whose terms of reference were to prepare a list of those old laws of both the Republics which placed restrictions on the liberty of the subject or were opposed to the spirit of the British Constitution. The anti-Indian laws could clearly have been included in this description. But Lord Milner's object in appointing the Committee was not to redress the grievances of the Indians but those of the British. The Committee submitted their report in a very short time, and many acts, large and small, which already affected the British were repealed merely by a stroke of the pen.

The same Committee prepared a list of anti-Indian

Acts. These were published in the form of a book which served as a handy manual for the Asiatic Department.

Now, if the anti-Indian laws had not mentioned the Indians by name and had not thus been made expressly applicable to them alone, the object of the legislators might have been achieved; and yet the laws would have remained general laws instead of racial laws. None would have felt insulted by their enactment; and when the existing bitterness was softened by time, there would have been no need to modify the laws, but simply to exercise a more liberal administration of them.

To take one instance from the laws which already were in force. The first disfranchising Act which was enacted in Natal, but was subsequently disallowed by the Imperial Government, provided for the disqualification as voters of all Asiatics as such. Now if the laws were to be altered, public opinion would have to be so far educated that the majority would be not only not hostile but actually friendly to Asiatics. The colour bar, if set up, could only be removed when feelings of cordiality were established between the races. This is an illustration of racial or class legislation.

The Act referred to was withdrawn and a second Act enacted in its place which nearly achieved an identical object yet was of a general nature, the sting of racial distinction being removed. The substance of one of its clauses stated that no person could be placed on the voters' roll in Natal who belonged to a country which had not hitherto possessed elective and representative institutions based on the parliamentary franchise. No reference was made here to Indians or Asiatics. The opinions of counsel could differ as to whether India

THE REGISTRATION ORDINANCE

possessed representative institutions based on the parliamentary franchise or not. But assuming for the sake of argument that India did not, in 1894, enjoy the parliamentary franchise, no one could say off-hand that the officer in charge of voters' lists in Natal had done an illegal thing if he included the names of Indians in the lists.

There is always a general presumption in favour of the rights of the subject. So long, therefore, as the government of the day does not become positively hostile, the names of Indians and others could be included in the electoral roll, the above law notwithstanding. Then, if the dislike for Indians became less marked and if the local Government was unwilling to injure the Indians, their names could be entered in the voters' lists without any modification of the law.

This is the advantage of a general law. The wise policy, therefore, would be to enact as little class legislation as possible, and it would be wiser still to avoid it altogether. Once a law is enacted, many difficulties must be encountered before it can be reversed. It is only when public opinion is highly educated that the laws in force in a country can be repealed. A constitution under which laws are continually being modified or repealed cannot be said to be stable or well organized.

We can now better appreciate the poison which was present in anti-Asiatic laws in the Transvaal. They were not general laws at all but racial in character. The Asiatics as such could not vote; nor could they own land outside the locations set apart for them by the Government. The administrators could do nothing for the Indians so long as these laws remained on the statute-book. Lord Milner's

Committee could make a list of such laws only as were not general in character. Had they been general laws, not expressly directed against Asiatics, they might have been repealed along with the rest. The officers in charge could never have argued their helplessness and said that they had no alternative but to enforce the law.

The local officials clearly observed that the anti-Asiatic laws enacted by the late Boer Government were neither adequately severe nor systematic. If the Indians could enter the Transvaal at will and carry on trade wherever they chose, then British traders would suffer. This argument carried great weight with the Europeans and their representatives in the Ministry. They were all out to amass the maximum of wealth in the minimum of time; how could they endure the Indians becoming co-sharers with them? Hypocrisy pressed political theory into service in order to make out a plausible case. A barefaced selfish or mercantile argument would not satisfy the intelligent Europeans of South Africa. The human intellect delights in inventing specious arguments in order to support injustice, and the South African Europeans were no exception to this general rule.

The arguments used by General Smuts and others deserve special notice. They would lay stress on the fact that South Africa was a representative of Western civilization while India was a centre of Oriental culture. Thinkers of the present generation hold that these two civilizations cannot go together. If nations representing these rival cultures met even in small groups, the result would only be an explosion. The West has become opposed to simplicity while the East considers this virtue to be of primary importance. How can these opposite

THE REGISTRATION ORDINANCE

views be reconciled? It is not the business of statesmen who are practical men to adjudicate upon the relative merits of each. Western civilization may or may not be good, but Westerners wish to stick to it. They have made tireless endeavours to save that civilization. They have shed rivers of blood for its sake. They have suffered great hardships on its behalf. It was therefore too late for them now to chalk out a new path for themselves.

Thus considered, the Indian question could hardly be resolved into one of trade jealousy or race hatred, as if these were the only factors. The problem was rather one of preserving one's own civilization, that is, of enjoying the supreme right of self-preservation and discharging the corresponding duty. Some public speakers might like to inflame the Europeans by finding fault with the Indians, but political thinkers believed that the very qualities of Indians count for defects in South Africa. The Indians were disliked in South Africa for their simplicity, patience, perseverance, frugality and other-worldliness. Westerners were enterprising, impatient, engrossed in multiplying their material wants and in satisfying them, fond of good cheer, anxious to save physical labour and prodigal in their habits. They were therefore afraid that if thousands of Orientals settled in South Africa, the Westerners would have to go to the wall. They were not prepared to commit suicide, and their leaders would never permit them to be reduced to such straits.

I believe I have impartially recapitulated the arguments urged by men of the highest character among Europeans. I have characterized their arguments as pseudo-philosophic, but I do not thereby wish to suggest that they are groundless. From the standpoint of immediate self-interest they have much force. But from the philosophical point of view they tend to hypocrisy. In my humble opinion, no impartial person could accept such conclusions and no reformer would place his civilization in such a position of helplessness. So far as I am aware no Eastern thinkers fear that if Western nations came into free contact with the East, the culture of the East would be swept away like sand by the onrushing tide of Western civilization. So far as I have a grasp of Eastern thought it seems to me that its civilization not only does not fear but would positively welcome free contact with the West. If contrary instances can be met with in the East, they do not affect the principle I have laid down; for a number of illustrations can be cited in its support.

However that may be, Western thinkers claim that the foundation of their civilization is the predominance of might over right. Therefore the protagonists of that civilization devote most of their time to the conservation of brute force. These thinkers likewise assert that the nations which do not increase their material wants are doomed to destruction. It is in pursuance of these principles that Western nations have settled in South Africa and subdued the numerically overwhelmingly superior races of South Africa. It is absurd to imagine that they would fear the harmless population of India. The best proof of the statement that the Europeans have nothing to fear from Asiatics is provided by the fact that if the Indians had continued to work in South Africa for all time as mere labourers, no agitation would have been started against the Indian immigration.

The only remaining factors are trade and colour.

THE REGISTRATION ORDINANCE

Thousands of Europeans have admitted that trade by Indians hits retail European trade hard, and that dislike of them has at present become part and parcel of the mentality of Europeans. Even in the United States of America, where the principle of statutory equality has been established, a man like Booker T. Washington, who is a Christian of high character and has fully assimilated Western civilization, was not considered fit for admission to the court of President Roosevelt, and probably would not be so considered even to-day. The negroes of the United States have accepted Western civilization. They have embraced Christianity. But the black pigment of their skins constitutes their crime, and while in the Northern States they are socially despised, they are lynched in the Southern States on the suspicion of wrongdoing.

This seems to point to the fact that there is not substance in the "philosophical" arguments. But all those who urge them do not necessarily do so in a hypocritical spirit. Many of them honestly hold these views to be sound. It is possible that if we were placed in their position, we too might advance similar arguments. We have a saying in India that as is a man's conduct, such is his understanding. Our arguments are but a reflection of our mentality. If they do not commend themselves to others, we become dissatisfied, impatient and even indignant.

I have deliberately discussed this question with much minuteness, because I wish the different points of view to be understood. Magnanimity and patience are essential to the understanding of Satyagraha and, above all, to the practice of that principle. My object in writing is to show clearly how Satyagraha, for which I live and for which I believe I am equally prepared to die, originated and how it was practised on a large scale.

Thus the British administrators had decided to prevent fresh Indian immigrants from entering the Transvaal, and to render the position of the old Indian settlers so uncomfortable that they would feel compelled to leave the country in sheer disgust, and even if they did not leave it, they would be reduced to a state bordering on serfdom. Some men, looked upon as great statesmen in South Africa, had declared more than once that they could afford to keep the Indians only as hewers of wood and drawers of water. On the staff of the Asiatic Department was Mr. Lionel Curtis, who has since become known to fame as an ambassador for Dyarchy in India. He enjoyed the confidence of Lord Milner and claimed to do everything according to scientific methods; but he was capable of committing serious blunders. He suggested that if fresh Indian immigration was to be stopped, the first step to be taken was the effective registration of the old Indian residents. That done, no one could smuggle himself into the country by practising evasion, and if any one did, he could be easily detected.

The permits, which were issued to Indians after the establishment of British rule in the Transvaal, contained the signature of the holder, or his thumb impression if he was illiterate. Later on some one suggested the inclusion of a photograph of the holder, and this suggestion was carried out by administrative action, legislation being unnecessary. The Indian leaders, therefore, did not come to know of this innovation at once. When, in course of time, these novel features came to their notice, they sent

THE REGISTRATION ORDINANCE

memorials to the authorities, and waited upon them in deputations on behalf of the community. The officials' argument was that Government could not permit Indians to enter the country without regulation of some sort, and that therefore all Indians should provide themselves with uniform permits containing such details as might render it impossible for any one but the rightful holders to enter the country. It was my opinion that although we were not bound by law to take out such permits, the Government could insist on requiring them so long as the Peace Preservation Ordinance in South Africa was in force. But just as the Defence of India Act was kept on the Statute Book in India longer than necessary in order to harass the people, so was this Ordinance allowed to remain in force long after the necessity for it had passed. As for the Europeans, it was as a dead letter for all practical purposes. Now if permits must be taken out they should contain some mark of identification. There was nothing wrong, therefore, that those who were illiterate should allow their thumb impressions to be taken. I did not at all like the inclusion of photographs in the permits. Musalmans have religious objections to such a course.

The final upshot of the negotiations between the Indians and the authorities was that the Indian community consented to change their permits and agreed that fresh Indian immigrants should take out permits in the new form. Although the Indians were not bound in law, they voluntarily agreed to re-register so that it might be clear to all concerned that the Indians did not wish to bring in fresh immigrants by unfair means, and the Peace Preservation Ordinance might no longer be used to harass newcomers. Almost all Indians thus changed their old permits for new ones.

This was no small thing. Like one man, the community completed with the greatest promptitude this re-registration, which they were legally bound to carry out. This was a proof of their sincerity, large-mindedness, commonsense and humility. It also showed that the community had no desire to violate in any way any law in force in the Transvaal. The Indians believed that if they behaved towards the Government with such courtesy, it would treat them well.

The year 1906 was advancing when this re-registration was completed. I had re-entered the Transvaal in 1903 and opened my office in Johannesburg about the middle of that year. Two years had thus passed in merely resisting the inroads of the Asiatic Department. We all expected now that re-registration would satisfy the Government, and confidently looked forward to a period of comparative peace for the community.

But this was not to be. Mr. Lionel Curtis held that the Europeans had not attained their object merely because the Indians had changed their old permits for new certificates of registration. It was not enough in his eyes that great good had been achieved by mutual understanding. He was of opinion that these certificates should have the force of law behind them, and that thus only could the principles underlying them be secured. He would not carry Indian opinion with him, but would frighten us into submission to external restrictions backed up by rigorous legal sanctions.

He therefore drafted an Asiatic Bill and advised the Government that until his Bill was passed, there was no

THE REGISTRATION ORDINANCE

provision in the laws already in force to prevent the Indians from secretly entering the Transvaal. Mr. Curtis's argument met with a ready response from the Government, and a draft Asiatic Law Amendment Ordinance was published in the Transvaal Government Gazette.

Before dealing with this Ordinance in detail, it would be well to dispose of an important event in a few words. As I was the author of the Satyagraha movement, it is necessary to enable the reader fully to understand some events of my life. The Zulu "rebellion" broke out in Natal just while attempts were thus being made to impose further disabilities upon the Indians in the Transvaal. I doubted then, and doubt even now, if the outbreak could be described as a rebellion, but it had always been thus described in Natal. Now, as in the Boer War, many Europeans resident in Natal joined the army as volunteers. As I too was considered resident in Natal, I thought I must do what I could. With the Community's permission, therefore, I made an offer to the Government to raise a Stretcher-bearer Corps for service with the troops. The offer was accepted. I therefore broke up my Johannesburg home and sent my family to Phoenix in Natal, where my co-workers had settled and from where *Indian Opinion* was published. I did not close the office, as I knew that I should not be away long.

I joined the army with a small corps of twenty-five men. Most of the provinces of India were represented even on this small body of men. The Corps was on active service for a month.

I have always been thankful to God for the work which then fell to our lot. We found that the wounded Zulus would have been left uncared for unless we had attended them. No Europeans would help to dress their wounds. Dr. Savage, who was in charge of the ambulance, was himself a very humane person. It was no part of our duty to nurse the wounded after we had taken them to the hospital. But we had joined the war with a desire to do all we could, no matter whether it did or did not fall within the scope of our work. The good Doctor told us that he could not induce any of the Europeans to nurse the Zulus, that it was beyond him to compel them. He would therefore feel obliged if we undertook this mission of mercy. We were only too glad to do this. We had to cleanse the wounds of several Zulus which had not been attended to for as many as five or six days and were therefore stinking horribly.

We liked the work. The Zulus could not talk to us, but from their gestures and the expression in their eyes they seemed to feel as if God had sent us to their succour. The work for which we had enlisted was also fairly heavy; for sometimes during the month we had to perform a march of as many as forty miles a day.

The Corps was disbanded in a month. Its work was mentioned in dispatches. Each member of the Corps was awarded a medal especially struck for the occasion. The Government wrote a letter of thanks. The three sergeants of the Corps were Gujaratis, Messrs. Shelat, Medh and Joshi. All three had a fine physique and worked very hard. I cannot just now recall the names of the other Indians, but I well remember that one of these was a Pathan, who used to express his astonishment on finding us carrying as large a load as himself.

While I was working with the Corps, two ideas which had long been floating in my mind became firmly fixed.

THE REGISTRATION ORDINANCE

First, an aspirant after a life exclusively devoted to service must lead a life of celibacy. Secondly, he must accept poverty as a constant companion through life. He may not take up any occupation which would prevent him or make him shrink from undertaking the lowliest duties or the largest risks.

Letters and telegrams, asking me to proceed to the Transvaal at once, had poured in, even while I was serving with the Corps. On return from the war, therefore, I just met the friends at Phoenix and then at once went to Johannesburg.

There I read the draft Ordinance referred to above. The Transvaal Government Gazette Extraordinary of August 22, 1906, in which the Ordinance was published, was waiting for me in the office. I went up the hill near the house with a friend and began to translate the draft Ordinance into Gujarati for *Indian Opinion*. As I read the sections one after another I was first alarmed and then horror-stricken. I saw nothing in it except hatred of Indians. It seemed to me that if the Ordinance was passed and Indians meekly accepted it, this would spell absolute ruin for the Indians in South Africa. I clearly saw that this was a question of life and death to them. Even should memorials and representatives prove fruitless, the community must not sit with folded hands. It was better to die than submit to such a law.

But how were we to die? What should we dare to do so that there would be nothing before us except a choice of victory or death? An impenetrable wall was before me and I could not see my way through.

Here is a brief summary of the measure. Every Indian, man, woman, or child of eight years or upwards, entitled to reside in the Transvaal must register his or her name with the Registrar of Asiatics and take out a certificate of registration. The applicants for registration must surrender their old permits to the Registrar, and state in their application their name, residence, caste, age, etc. The Registrar was to note down important marks of identification upon the applicant's person, and take his finger and thumb impressions. Every Indian who failed thus to apply for registration before a certain day was to forfeit his right of residence in the Transvaal. Failure to apply could be held to be an offence in law for which the defaulter could be fined, sent to prison or even deported, within the discretion of the Court. Parents must apply on behalf of minor children and bring them to the Registrar in order to give their finger impressions. In case of parents failing to discharge this responsibility laid upon them, the minor children on attaining the age of sixteen years must discharge it themselves, and if they defaulted they made themselves liable to the same punishment that could be awarded their parents. The certificate of registration issued to an applicant must be produced before any police officer whenever he might be required to do so. Failure in this respect would be held to be an offence for which the defaulter could be fined or sent to prison. Even a person walking on public thoroughfares could be required to produce his certificate. Police officers could enter private houses in order to inspect certificates. Indians entering the Transvaal from some place outside it must produce their certificates before the inspector on duty. Certificates must be produced on demand in courts which the holder attended on business, and in revenue offices which issued him a trading or bicycle licence.

THE REGISTRATION ORDINANCE

Thus, if an Indian wanted any Government officer to perform any service, the officer could ask to see his certificate of registration before granting his request. Refusal to produce the certificate would be also held to be an offence for which the person refusing could be fined or sent to prison.

I have never known legislation of this nature being directed against any free man in any part of the world. I know that indentured Indians in Natal are subject to a drastic system of passes, but these poor fellows could hardly be classed as free men. However, even the laws to which the indentured labourers were subject were mild in comparison with the Ordinance outlined above, and the penalties imposed were nothing when compared with the penalties laid down in this Ordinance. A trader with assets running into *lakhs* could be deported under this new Ordinance and thus confronted with utter ruin in a moment. There are some drastic laws directed against criminal tribes in India with which this Ordinance might easily be compared in its character and scope.

The giving of finger-prints, required by this Ordinance, was quite a novelty in South Africa. In order to study some literature on the subject, I read a volume on finger-prints by Mr. Henry, a police officer, from which I gathered that full finger-prints are thus required by law only from criminals. I was therefore shocked by this compulsory requirement regarding finger-prints. Again, the registration of women and children under sixteen was proposed for the first time by this Ordinance. This would meet with the strongest objection from the Transvaal Indian community.

The next day a small meeting of the leading Transvaal

Indians was held, to whom I explained the Ordinance word by word. It shocked them intensely, just as it had shocked me. One of them said in a burst of passion: "If anyone came forward to demand a certificate from my wife, I would shoot him on the spot and take the consequences."

Seeing his excitement I asked him to be silent. "This is a very serious crisis," I said, addressing the meeting; "we must judge the whole matter calmly. If the Ordinance is passed and if we acquiesced in its being made law, then it is likely soon to be imitated all over South Africa. It is clearly designed to strike at the very root of our existence in this country as free citizens. This is surely not the last step. It is the first step which is now taken with a view to hounding us out of the country. We are therefore responsible for the safety, not only of the ten or fifteen thousand Indians in the Transvaal, but of the entire Indian community in South Africa. The fate of Indians in Natal and the Cape depends upon our resistance.

"Again, if we fully grasp what this legislation means, we shall find that India's honour is in our keeping. For the Ordinance seeks to humiliate not only ourselves but also India, our Motherland. The humiliation consists of the degradation of innocent men. No one will take it upon himself to say that we have done anything to deserve such an Ordinance directed against us. We are innocent, and an insult offered to a single innocent member of a nation is the same thing as insulting the nation as a whole. It will be wrong, therefore, to be hasty, impatient or angry. That cannot save us from the onslaught. But God will come to our help if only we calmly carry out in time measures of resistance, presenting a united front and bearing the hardships, which such moral resistance is certain to bring in its train."

All the Indian leaders present realized the extreme seriousness of the situation. They resolved at once to hold a public meeting at which a number of strong resolutions should be proposed and passed. The Old Empire Theatre, in Johannesburg, was hired for the purpose, and due notice was given.

CHAPTER VIII

THE SATYAGRAHA OATH

THE MEETING WAS held on September 11, 1906. It was attended by Indian delegates from various places in the Transvaal. But I must confess that even I had not then understood all the implications of the resolutions which I had helped to frame; nor had I gauged all the possible conclusions to which they might lead.

The Old Empire Theatre at Johannesburg was packed from floor to ceiling. In every face I could read the expectation of something strange about to happen. Abdul Gani, Chairman of the Transvaal British Association, presided. He was one of the oldest Indian residents of the Transvaal. The most important among the resolutions passed by the meeting was the famous Fourth Resolution, by which the Indians solemnly determined never to submit to the new Ordinance but to suffer all the penalties, if ever it became law.

I fully explained this resolution to the meeting and received a patient hearing. The business was conducted both in Hindi and Gujarati. There were also Tamil and Telugu speakers, who fully explained the proceedings in their respective languages to those from South India who were present. The meeting was thus followed carefully by all alike. At last the main resolution was duly proposed and seconded and supported by several speakers, one of whom was Sheth Haji Habib. The Sheth was a very old and experienced resident of South Africa and he made an impassioned speech. He was deeply moved and went so far as to say that we must pass this resolution by an oath, having God as our witness, and must never yield a cowardly submission to such a degrading Ordinance. He then went on solemnly to declare, in the name of God, that he would never submit. He advised all present to do the same.

When Sheth Haji Habib came to the solemn declaration on oath, in the name of God, I was at once startled and put on my guard. Only at that critical moment did I realize fully both my own responsibilities and that of the community. For the Transvaal Indians had passed many resolutions before this and had amended them afterwards in the light of further reflection. There were even cases where resolutions that had been passed had never been observed. But no one had introduced the name of God before.

It is true that in the abstract there ought not to be any distinction between a resolution and an oath taken in the name of God. When an intelligent man makes a deliberate resolve, he never swerves from it by a hair's breadth till it is accomplished. With him, his resolution once made carries as much weight as a declaration with God as witness. But the world takes no note of abstract principles. It imagines an ordinary resolution and an oath in the name of God to be poles asunder. A man who makes an ordinary resolution is not ashamed of himself when he deviates from it; but a man who violates an oath is not only ashamed of himself, but is looked upon by society as a sinner. This imaginary distinction has struck such a deep root in the human mind that a person making a statement on oath before a judge is held to have committed perjury if the statement is proved to be false. He receives drastic punishment for such a heinous offence. Possessing, as a lawyer, much experience of the solemnity of such pledges, I was first of all taken aback by Sheth Habib's suggestion of an oath.

In a moment, however, I thought out quickly all the possible consequences, and soon my perplexity gave place to enthusiasm. Although I had never even thought of taking an oath or inviting others to do so, when I went to the meeting, I warmly approved of the Sheth's suggestion. At the same time, it seemed to me that the people who were present ought first to have explained to them carefully the meaning and consequence of an oath. Then after that, if they were prepared to pledge themselves, they should be encouraged to do so; otherwise, it would be understood that they were not yet ready to stand the final test. Therefore I asked the President for permission to explain to the meeting the implications of Sheth Haji Habib's suggestion. The President readily granted leave and I rose to address the meeting.

"I wish to explain," said I, "that there is a vast difference between this resolution and every other which we have passed up to date. This one is so grave that our whole existence in South Africa depends on its faithful observance. The manner of passing the resolution suggested by our friend is a most solemn one and it is entirely new to us as a community. The proposal itself redounds to the credit of Sheth Haji Habib, and it also lays a burden of responsibility upon him. I tender him my congratulations, and deeply appreciate his suggestion. But if you adopt it at this meeting you will share his responsibility. Therefore you yourselves must understand what this responsibility is; and as an adviser and servant of the community, it is my duty fully to explain this to you.

"We all believe in one and the same God, notwithstanding our religious differences. To pledge ourselves, or to take an oath, in the name of God is not a mere trifle. If, after taking such an oath, we violate our pledge we are guilty before God and man. Personally I hold that a man who deliberately and intelligently takes a pledge and then breaks it, forfeits his own manhood. Just as a copper coin treated with mercury not only becomes valueless but also makes its owner liable to punishment for fraud, so a person who lightly pledges his word and then breaks it becomes a man of straw and fits himself for punishment here as well as hereafter. Sheth Haji Habib is now proposing to administer an path of a very serious character. There is no one in this meeting who can be classed as an infant or as wanting in intelligence. You are well advanced in age and have seen the world; many of you are delegates and have discharged important duties, therefore not one of us can hope to excuse himself by saying that he did not know what he was about when he took the oath.

"Pledges and vows are only taken on rare occasions. A man who takes a vow too often is sure to stumble. But if I can imagine a crisis in the history of the Indian community of South Africa, when it would be in the fitness of things to take a pledge, that crisis is surely before us. There is obvious wisdom in taking serious steps with great caution and hesitation. But these things have their limits and the limit is reached. The Government has taken leave of all sense of decency. We shall only be betraying our cowardice if we cannot stake our all at such a time of danger as this.

"Thus the present is the proper time to take an oath. But every one must consider for himself first of all whether he has the will and the ability to keep it. Resolutions of this nature cannot be passed by majority vote. Only those who accept the oath in person can be bound by it. This pledge must not be taken merely with a view to produce an effect on outsiders. Every one must search his own heart, and if the inner voice assures him that he has the requisite strength to carry him through to the end, then only should he pledge himself and then only will his pledge bear fruit.

"If we look to the consequences, we may be assured that if the Indians who take the pledge prove true to their word and if the majority of the community pledge themselves, this new Ordinance will never be passed into law, and even if it is passed it may be repealed. But while, on the one hand, we may hope for the best we must always be prepared for the worst. Imagine that all of us present here, numbering about three thousand, pledge ourselves, and yet the remaining ten thousand Indians in the Transvaal hold back. We may then quite possibly only provoke ridicule in the beginning. But we shall go on till we succeed. Again, it is quite possible that some of those who pledge themselves may weaken at the very first trial. We may have to remain hungry and suffer from extreme heat and cold. Hard labour is likely to be imposed upon us in prison. We may even be flogged by the warders. Or we may not be imprisoned but fined heavily and our property attached and held up to auction for non-payment. Though some of us are wealthy to-day we may be reduced to poverty to-morrow. We may even be deported from South Africa for good.

"Suffering from hunger and similar hardships in jail, some of us may fall ill or even die. Our wisdom therefore lies in pledging ourselves, knowing full well that we shall have to suffer things like these and even worse. If someone asks me when and how the struggle will end, I can assert with confidence that provided the entire community manfully stands the test, the end will be soon. But if many of us fall back, under stress of trial, the struggle will be prolonged. At the same time I can boldly declare that so long as there is even a handful of men true to their pledge, there can only be one end to the struggle, and that is victory.

"Last of all I have to speak about my personal responsibility. If I am warning you of the risks, I am at the same time fully conscious of my own responsibility. It is possible that a majority of those present here may take the pledge in a fit of enthusiasm or indignation but might weaken under the ordeal, and only a handful might be left to face the final test. Even then there is only one course open to me, namely, to die, but not to submit to the law. Even if everyone else were to hold back, leaving me alone, I am confident that I should never violate my pledge. Please do not misunderstand me. I am not suggesting this in a boastful spirit, but I wish earnestly to put you on your guard. I would respectfully suggest that if you have not the will or the ability to stand firm even when you are perfectly isolated, you should not only refuse to take the pledge yourselves but you should here and now declare your opposition to it. Each single man should fully realize his responsibilities and then only pledge himself quite independently of others. He should understand that he himself must be true to his pledge even unto death."

I spoke to this effect and resumed my seat. The meeting heard me, word by word, in perfect silence. Other leaders also spoke. All dwelt upon their responsibility and that of the audience.

Then the President rose. He also made the situation clear, and at last all present, standing with upraised hands, took an oath, with God as witness, not to submit to the Ordinance if it became law.

I can never forget that scene. It is present before my mind's eye as I write. The enthusiasm of those present knew no bounds.

The very next day there was an accident in the theatre owing to which it was wholly destroyed by fire. Friends brought me the news of the fire and congratulated me on the good omen, which signified to them that the Ordinance would meet the same fate as the theatre. But I have never been influenced by such omens and therefore I did not attach any weight to this coincidence, but I have only taken note of it as a demonstration of the courage of those days.

The workers did not let the grass grow under their feet after this great meeting. They went all over the Transvaal. Pledges of passive resistance were taken at every centre. The principal topic of discussion in *Indian Opinion* was the Black Ordinance. Steps were taken at once to meet the Transvaal Government. A deputation waited on Mr. Duncan, the Colonial Secretary, which informed him among other things about the pledges that had been solemnly taken. Haji Habib, who was a member of the deputation, spoke with great emotion to the Minister. "If any officer," he declared, "proceeds to take my wife's finger-prints, I warn you I shall not be able to restrain myself. I shall kill him there and then and die myself."

The Minister stared at the Sheth's face for awhile and said: "The Government are reconsidering whether it is advisable or not to make the Ordinance applicable to women, and I can give you assurance even now that the clauses relating to women will be deleted. The Government has understood your feelings in the matter and desires to respect them. But for the other provisions I am sorry to inform you that the Administration will remain adamant. After due deliberation, General Botha has asked you to agree to this Ordinance. It appears to be essential to the very existence of Europeans in the Transvaal. The Government will certainly consider any suggestion about details which you make, but will not forgo the Ordinance itself. My advice to you, therefore, is that your chief interest should lie in agreeing to the legislation and proposing changes as regards details."

The deputation withdrew, after informing Mr. Duncan that in spite of his advice any acquiescence in the proposed Ordinance was impossible. Sheth Haji Habib thanked him for his implied intention of exempting women from its provisions.

It is difficult to say whether this exemption was the result of the community's firmness or whether the Government had made this concession as an after-thought owing to the practical difficulties involved. It was reported in the Transvaal that the decision to exempt women had been taken independently of the Indian claim. The community, however, were confident that there was some direct connection between their own united action and this exemption. Their fighting spirit rose accordingly.

None of us knew at the time what name to give the movement. I had used at first the term "passive resistance" in describing it; but I had not quite understood the current implications of this English phrase. Some new principle had come into being among us, and I had tried to express it as well as I could in English. Yet as the struggle advanced the phrase "passive resistance" clearly gave rise to confusion. Also it seemed shameful to us to allow this great struggle to be known only by an English title without an Indian equivalent. It could never thus pass as current coin among us; for a great number of Indians in the Transvaal could not speak English. A small prize was therefore offered to the reader who invented the best designation for our struggle. The meaning of what we were doing had been already fully discussed in *Indian Opinion*. Therefore the competitors for the prize had sufficient material to serve as a basis for fashioning an Indian word.

Maganlal Gandhi[1] was one of the competitors and he suggested the word "Sadagraha," meaning "firmness in a good cause." I liked the word, but it did not fully represent the whole idea which I wished to connote. Therefore I corrected the word to "Satyagraha." Satya (Truth) implies Love: and Agraha (Firmness) serves as a synonym for Force. So I began to call the Indian movement "Satyagraha." By this I meant the Force which is born of Truth and Love. After this we gave up the use of the phrase "passive resistance" altogether.

[1] He was Mahatma Gandhi's most trusted lieutenant who died in the year 1927.

THE SATYAGRAHA OATH

As the movement advanced, Englishmen too began to watch it with interest. Although the English newspapers in the Transvaal generally wrote in support of the Europeans and of the Black Ordinance, they willingly published contributions from well-known Indians. They also printed in full Indian representations to Government, or at least made a summary of them. Sometimes they sent their reporters to important meetings, and at other times they kindly made room for the brief reports we sent them. These amenities were of course very useful to us in our struggle. After awhile some leading Europeans came to take a personal interest in the movement.

One of these, Mr. Hosken, was a prominent citizen of Johannesburg. He had always been free from colour prejudice, but his interest in the Indian question deepened after the starting of Satyagraha. The Europeans of Germiston, which is almost a suburb of Johannesburg, had expressed a desire to hear me. A meeting was held; Mr. Hosken was present and explained the movement in his opening address. "The Transvaal Indians," he said, "have only had recourse to passive resistance when all other means of obtaining redress had proved unavailing. They do not enjoy the franchise. They are only a few in number. They are weak and have no military weapons. Therefore they have taken to passive resistance, which is the weapon of the weak."

These observations quite took me by surprise. The speech I had intended to make had to be altered in consequence at a moment's notice. In correcting Mr. Hosken's explanation of "passive resistance" I defined the Indian Movement as "Soul Force." I saw at this meeting that the use of the phrase "passive resistance" was not only inadequate but also in danger of giving rise to terrible misunderstandings.

I do not know when or how the phrase, "passive resistance," came first to be used in English. But lately, among the English people, whenever a small minority did not approve of some obnoxious piece of legislation, instead of rising in rebellion they took the passive resistance step of not submitting to the law and inviting penalties of non-submission upon their heads. For instance, when the British Parliament passed the Education Act some years ago, the Nonconformists offered passive resistance under the leadership of Dr. Clifford. Again, the movement of the English women to obtain the vote was known as "passive resistance." It was in view of these two cases that Mr. Hosken described "passive resistance" as a weapon of the weak or the voteless. Dr. Clifford and his Nonconformists were weak in number, but had the vote. The Suffragettes, on the other hand, had not got any franchise rights, but like the Nonconformists' leaders they were also weak in numbers. Yet their suffrage movement did not eschew the use of physical force. Some of the women fired buildings and even assaulted men. I do not think they ever intended to kill anyone. But they did intend to thrash people when an opportunity occurred, and even thus to make things hot for them.

But brute force had absolutely no place in the Indian movement in any circumstances whatever. No matter how badly they suffered, the Satyagraha never used physical force. Even though they might have used it effectively, they refused to do so.

My point is that in planning the Indian movement

there never was the slightest thought given to the possibility or otherwise of offering armed resistance. Satyagraha is "Soul Force" pure and simple. Whenever and to whatever extent weapons of violence are made use of, to that extent "Soul Force" is rendered impossible.

For these reasons the result of our using the phrase "passive resistance" in South Africa was somewhat unfortunate. For we were mistakenly held to be, like the Suffragettes, a danger to person and property; and even generous friends like Mr. Hosken imagined us to be weak. The power of suggestion is such that a man at last becomes what he believes himself to be. If we continue to believe ourselves and let others believe that on account of our weakness we offer passive resistance, such resistance would never make us strong. At the earliest opportunity we should give up passive resistance as a weapon of the weak.

On the other hand, if we are Satyagrahis and offer Satyagraha, or "Soul Force," believing ourselves to be strong, two clear results follow as a matter of course. By fostering the idea of strength, we grow stronger and stronger ourselves, so that, with the increase in our strength, our Satyagraha becomes more and more effective. Secondly, while there is little scope for love in passive resistance, on the other hand love has its full place in Satyagraha. Not only is hatred excluded, but it is a positive breach of the ruling principle of Satyagraha to have anything to do with violence or hate.

Jesus Christ has been acclaimed as the Prince of passive resisters; but I submit that in His case passive resistance must mean Satyagraha.

There are not many instances in history of passive

resistance in the sense of Satyagraha. A single example of modern times is that of the Doukhobors of Russia cited by Tolstoy. The phrase "passive resistance" was not, I believe, employed to denote the patient suffering of oppression by thousands of devout Christians in the early days of Christianity. I would, therefore, rather class them as Satyagrahis. And if their conduct were ever to be described as passive resistance, then passive resistance in that case would become synonymous with Satyagraha.

In the Transvaal itself we took all necessary measures for resisting the Black Act by moral force alone. We approached the Local Government with petitions and memorials. We held protest meetings. The Legislative Council deleted the clause affecting women, but the rest of the Ordinance was passed practically without any modification. The spirit of our community was then high, and having closed its ranks it was unanimous in opposition to the Ordinance.

No one, therefore, was despondent. We still, however, adhered to our resolution to exhaust all the appropriate constitutional remedies before starting Satyagraha itself in its full form of direct action. The Transvaal was a Crown Colony at that time, so that the Imperial Government was responsible for its legislation. Therefore the royal assent to measures passed by the Transvaal legislature was not a mere formality. Often it might so happen that the King, as advised by his Ministers, might withhold his assent to such measures if they were found to be in conflict with the spirit of the British Constitution. On the other hand, in the case of a Colony enjoying responsible Government, the royal assent to measures

THE SATYAGRAHA OATH

passed by its legislature becomes usually a matter of course.

I submitted to our community that if a deputation were to go to England it was as well that they should first realize more fully their responsibility in the matter, and with this end in view I placed three suggestions before them. First, although we had taken pledges at the great meeting in the Empire Theatre, we should once again obtain individual pledges from leading Indians, so that if any had given way to doubt or weakness they should be immediately found out. One of the reasons advanced by me in support of this suggestion was that if the deputation was backed up by Satyagraha, we should then have no anxiety and could boldly inform the Secretary of State for India and the Secretary of State for the Colonies what the community were resolved to do. Secondly, arrangements for meeting the expenses of the deputation must be made in advance. Thirdly, the maximum number of members of the deputation should be fixed.

The three suggestions were accepted. Signatures were taken. Many signed the pledge, but still I saw even among the Indians who had previously pledged themselves at the meeting that there were some who now hesitated to sign. When once a man has pledged himself he need not hesitate to pledge himself a hundred times. Yet it is not an uncommon thing to find that a man weakens in regard to pledges, when asked to put down a pledge in black and white on paper, which has been given by word of mouth. The necessary funds for the deputation were found without much trouble.

The greatest difficulty, however, was encountered in

selecting the persons who should go to London. It was agreed at once that I should go. But who should go with me? The Committee took much time in arriving at a decision. Many evenings were spent in discussion, and we had a full experience of the bad habits that are generally prevalent in associations. Some proposed to cut the Gordian knot by asking me to go alone, but I flatly refused. There was hardly any Hindu-Muslim problem in South Africa, but it could not be claimed that there was no difference between the two religious sections of our community, and if these differences never assumed an acute form, this was largely because the leaders had unitedly worked together with devotion and frankness. My advice now was that there must be a Musalman delegate going with me, and that the deputation should be limited to two. But the Hindus at once said that as I represented the Indian community as a whole, there should be a representative of Hindu interests. Some even went further and wished for a larger number still. But in the end everyone understood the true position, and only two of us, H. O. Ali and myself, were elected to go as delegates.

H. O. Ali might be regarded as partly a Malay, for his father was an Indian Musalman and his mother was a Malay. His own home language was Dutch. But he had been so thoroughly educated in English that he could speak Dutch and English equally well. He had also cultivated the art of writing to the newspapers. As a member of the Transvaal British Indian Association he had long been taking part in public affairs. He also spoke Hindustani quite freely.

We set to work as soon as we reached England and

printed the memorial which we had already drafted on board the steamer. Lord Elgin was Colonial Secretary, and Mr. Morley was Secretary for India. We met Dadabhai and through him were introduced to the British Committee of the Indian National Congress. The Committee fully approved our policy. Similarly we met Sir Muncherji Bhownaggree, who was a great help to us. He and Dadabhai Naoroji advised us to secure the co-operation of some impartial and well-known Englishman from India who should introduce our deputation to Lord Elgin. Sir W. W. Hunter was no longer alive, and the name of Sir Lepel Griffin was suggested.

We met Sir Lepel Griffin. He had been opposed to the National Congress movement in India; but he was much interested in the Transvaal Indian question and agreed to lead the deputation, not for the sake of courtesy, but for the righteousness of our cause. He read all the papers and became familiar with the problem.

Our deputation waited upon Lord Elgin, who heard everything with careful attention, expressed his sympathy, referred to his own difficulties, and yet promised to do all he could. The same deputation met Mr. Morley, who also declared his own sympathy with us. Sir William Wedderburn was instrumental in calling a meeting of the Committee of the House of Commons for Indian Affairs in the drawing-room of the House and we placed our case before them as well as we could. We met Mr. Redmond, the leader of the Irish Party, and also as many Members of Parliament as possible. The British Committee of the Indian National Congress was very helpful. But according to British customs only men belonging to a certain party and holding certain views would join it, while there were many others who had nothing to do with the Indian National Congress and yet rendered us every possible assistance. We determined to organize a Standing Committee upon which all these could come together and thus be united in watching over our interests. Men of all parties liked the idea.

The burden of carrying on the work of an institution chiefly falls upon the Secretary. The Secretary should not only have full faith in the aims and the objects of the institution he represents, but he should also be able to devote nearly all his time to the achievement of these aims and have great capacity for work. Mr. L. W. Ritch, who belonged to South Africa, was formerly articled to me and was now a student for the Bar in London. He satisfied all the requirements. He was there in England and was also desirous of taking up the work. We therefore ventured to form the South African British Indian Committee.

In England and other Western countries there is one barbarous custom of inaugurating movements at dinners. The British Prime Minister delivers in the Mansion House, on each ninth of November, an important speech in which he adumbrates his programme for the year and publishes his own forecast of the future. Cabinet Ministers, among others, are invited to the dinner by the Lord Mayor of London, and when the dinner is over bottles of wine are uncorked and all present drink to the health of the host and the guest. Speeches are made while this merry business is in progress. The toast of the British Cabinet is proposed and the Prime Minister makes his important speech in reply to it. As in public, so in private, the person with whom some important conversations are to be held is invited to dinner, and the topic of the day is broached either during or after dinner.

Our deputation had to observe this custom not once but quite a number of times, although, of course, we never drank wine. We thus invited our principal supporters to lunch. About a hundred covers were laid. The idea was to tender our thanks to our friends, to bid them good-bye, and at the same time to constitute the Standing Committee. Here, too, speeches were made after the dinner was over and the Standing Committee was organized. We thus obtained greater publicity for our movement in this typically English manner.

CHAPTER IX

IN ENGLAND

AFTER A STAY in England of about six weeks we returned to South Africa. When our steamer reached Madeira, we received a cablegram from Mr. Ritch informing us that Lord Elgin had publicly declared that he was unable, without further consideration, to advise His Majesty the King to sign his name to the Transvaal Asiatic Ordinance.

Our joy at this knew no bounds. The steamer took about a fortnight to reach Cape Town from Madeira, and we had quite a good time during those days building many castles in the air. But the ways of Providence are inscrutable. The castles we then built toppled down.

I must place on record one or two recollections of England that are very dear to me. We had utilized every single minute of our time in that country. The sending out of a large number of circulars could not have been done single-handed, and we were sorely in need of outside help. My experience, ranging over forty years, has taught me that assistance purchased with money can never be compared with purely voluntary service. Fortunately we obtained many volunteers. There were Indian young men in England, engaged in study, who came to visit us, and some of them helped us, day and night, without any hope of reward. None of them refused to do anything, however humble the service, whether it was the writing of addresses, or fixing of postage stamps, or posting and delivering of letters.

IN ENGLAND

But there was an English friend named Symonds who put all the other volunteers into the shade by his self-sacrifice. Whom the gods love die young, and so did this generous young Englishman. When he was in Bombay in 1897 he moved fearlessly among the Indians who had been attacked by the plague and nursed them. It had become a second nature to him never to be daunted by death when ministering to those who were suffering from infectious diseases. He was perfectly free from any racial or colour prejudice. He was independent in temperament, and he believed that truth is always in the minority. It was this belief of his which first drew me to him in Johannesburg, and he often humorously assured me that he would withdraw his support if ever he found me in the majority, since he was of opinion that truth itself is corrupted when it becomes popular. He was private secretary to Sir George Farrar, one of the millionaires of Johannesburg. His knowledge of literature covered a very wide area and he had an unlimited fund of information. As a stenographer he was an expert, and it was fortunate for us that he happened to be in England. I did not know anything about this at the time, but he found us out himself; for our public work had secured for us newspaper advertisement. At once he came to me and expressed his willingness to do anything he could. "I will work," he said, "as a servant if you like, and also if you need a stenographer you will hardly come across anyone more expert than I am. Take me and use me as you will."

We were in need of both kinds of help, and I am not exaggerating things when I say that this noble Englishman toiled for us day and night ceaselessly and without payment. Symonds was all day long at the typewriter, even up till twelve or one o'clock at night. He would carry messages for me and post letters, always with a genial smile. His monthly income was about forty-five pounds, but he spent it all in helping his friends and others. He was about thirty years of age and up to that time he had not married. He wanted to remain unmarried all his life. I pressed him hard to accept some payment, but he flatly refused. "I would be failing," he said, "in my duty if I accepted any remuneration for such service as this."

On the last night, I well remember, he kept awake working till three o'clock in the early morning while we were winding up our business and packing up our things. He parted with us next day, after seeing us off on the steamer, and a sad parting it was.

We were so punctilious in keeping the accounts of the deputation that we preserved even such trifling vouchers as the receipts for money spent for soda water on the steamer. Similarly we kept the receipts for telegrams. I do not remember to have entered a single item under sundries when writing out the detailed accounts. As a rule, sundries did not figure in our accounts at all, and if they did they were intended to cover a few pennies or shillings whose spending we could not recall when writing the accounts at the end of the day.

I have clearly observed in this life that we become responsible agents from the time we reach years of discretion. As long as we are with our parents, we must account to them for money or business they entrust to us. They may be certain of our rectitude and may not ask for accounts, but that does not lessen our responsibility. When we become independent householders, there arises a new responsibility to our own family. We are not the sole proprietors of our acquisitions, our family is co-sharer along with us. We must therefore account for every single farthing for their sake. If such is our responsibility in private life, in public life it is all the greater.

I have observed that voluntary workers are apt to behave as if they were not bound to render a detailed account of the money entrusted to them, because, like Caesar's wife, they are above suspicion. This is sheer nonsense; for the keeping of accounts has nothing whatever to do with trustworthiness or the reverse. It is an independent duty, whose performance is essential to clean living; and if the leading national workers do not ask for accounts, out of a sense of false courtesy or fear, they are equally to blame. If a paid servant is bound to account for work done and money spent by him, the volunteer is doubly bound to do so; for his labour is his own reward.

As soon as we landed at Cape Town, and even more when we reached Johannesburg, we saw that we had sadly overrated the Madeira cablegram. Mr. Ritch, who sent it, was not responsible for this. He cabled only what he had heard about the measure being disallowed. The Transvaal, in the year 1906, was still a Crown Colony. Each colony is represented in England by an Agent, whose duties are to instruct the Secretary of State for the Colonies in all matters affecting Colonial interests. The Transvaal was then represented by Sir Richard Solomon, the noted lawyer of South Africa. Lord Elgin had disallowed the Black Act in consultation with him.

Responsible government was to be conferred on the Transvaal on January 1, 1907. Lord Elgin therefore assured Sir Richard that if an identical measure was passed by the Transvaal Legislature after the grant of responsible government, it would receive the royal assent. But so long as the Transvaal was a Crown Colony, the Imperial Government would be held directly responsible for any class legislation; and as racial discrimination was a departure from the fundamental principles of the British Empire, he could not but advise His Majesty to disallow the measure in question.

If the measure was thus to be disallowed only in name, Sir Richard Solomon had every reason to be satisfied with an arrangement so convenient from his point of view. I have characterized this as crooked policy, but I believe it could be given a still harsher title with perfect justice. The Imperial Government is directly responsible for the legislation of Crown Colonies, and there is no place in its constitution for discrimination on the ground of race or colour. So far, so good. One can also understand that the Imperial Government could not all at once disallow measures passed by the legislatures of Colonies enjoying responsible government. But to hold private conferences with Colonial Agents in advance and promise royal assent to legislation, which is in open violation of the Constitution, is a breach of faith and an injustice.

Lord Elgin by his assurance only encouraged the Transvaal Government all the more in their anti-Asiatic campaign. Yet if such was his intention he should have told this in plain terms to the Indian deputation instead of speaking sympathetically to us. The British Empire cannot really escape responsibility even for the legislation of a Dominion enjoying responsible government. For they are bound to accept the fundamental principles of the British Constitution. No British Dominion, for instance, can revive the institution of legalized slavery. If Lord Elgin disallowed this Black Act of the Transvaal because it was an improper piece of legislation, it was his clear duty privately to have warned Sir Richard Solomon that the Transvaal could not enact such an iniquitous law even after responsible government had been given. If the Transvaal had any intention of doing so, the Imperial Government would be constrained to consider afresh the advisability of granting it the higher responsible status. At least, he should have told Sir Richard that responsible government could be conferred only on the one condition that the rights of the Indians were fully safeguarded.

Instead of following such a straightforward course, Lord Elgin made an outward show of friendliness to the Indians, while at the same time secretly supporting the Transvaal Government and encouraging it to pass the very same law which he had vetoed himself. Unfortunately, this is not the only case of such tortuous diplomacy undertaken in the British Empire. Even an indifferent student of its history will easily recall similar incidents.

In Johannesburg the sole topic of conversation was the deceit practised upon us by Lord Elgin and the Imperial Government. Our disappointment in South Africa was as deep as had been our joy in Madeira. Yet the immediate consequence of this deception was that the Community became even more determined and enthusiastic than before. Everyone said that we must never fear, because our struggle was independent of any help of the Imperial Government. We must look for assistance only to our own selves and to God, in whose name we had pledged ourselves to offer moral resistance. Even crooked policy would in time be straightened out if only we were true to ourselves.

Responsible government was established in the Transvaal. The first measure passed by the new Parliament was the budget; the second was the Asiatic Registration Act. Except for an alteration in the date specified in one of its clauses, which lapse of time made necessary, it was an exact copy of the original Ordinance and it was rushed through all its stages at a single sitting on March 21, 1907. The disallowance of the Ordinance, therefore, was forgotten as if it was a dream. The Indians submitted memorials as usual, but who would listen to them? The Act was proclaimed to take effect from July 1, 1907. Indians were called upon to apply for registration before the end of that month. The delay in enforcing the Act was due, not to any desire to oblige the Indians, but to the exigencies of the case. Some time must elapse before the formal sanction of the Crown to the measure was signified. The forms set forth in schedule had to be prepared. The opening of permit offices at various centres would also have to be arranged. The delay, therefore, was intended solely for the Transvaal Government's own convenience.

When our deputation was on its way to England, I happened to talk about the anti-Asiatic legislation in the Transvaal to an Englishman who had settled in South Africa. When I informed him of the object of our visit to England, he exclaimed, "I see you are going to London in order to get rid of your dog's collar." He thus compared the Transvaal permit to a dog's collar, but I did not quite understand him then, and I cannot exactly say now whether he intended to express his contempt for us by this phrase or whether he merely meant to show his own strong feeling in the matter. In order not to do him an injustice, I would gladly assume the latter.

The Transvaal Government, on the one side, was preparing to fasten the "dog's collar" round our necks, while on the other side the Indians were getting ready to resist it. We were concentrating various measures to strengthen our resolution never to wear that collar. We were writing letters to friends in England, as well as in India, and trying thus to keep in touch with the larger situation from day to day. But the Satyagraha struggle depended very little upon help from outside. After all, it is only internal remedies that are ultimately effective.

One important question before us was what organization we should use for carrying on the struggle. The Transvaal British Indian Association had a large membership and was a powerful body. Satyagraha had not yet seen the light of day when it was established. The Association had resisted in the past, and would have to resist in the future, not one obnoxious law, but quite a host of them. Besides organizing resistance to obnoxious laws, it had many other functions of a political and social nature to perform. But all the members of the Association were not pledged to resist the Black Act through Satyagraha. We should also have to take account of external risks which the Association would run if it was identified with the Satyagraha struggle. The Transvaal Government, for instance, might declare the movement to be seditious and make illegal all institutions supporting it. In such a case, what would be the position of its members who were not Satyagrahis? And what about the funds which were contributed at a time when Satyagraha was not so much as thought of? All these were weighty considerations. Lastly, the Satyagrahis were strongly of opinion that they not only must not entertain any ill will against those who refused to join the struggle, but must maintain their present friendly relations unimpaired and even work side by side with them in all other movements except the Satyagraha struggle.

For all these reasons the community came to the conclusion that the Satyagraha struggle should not be carried on through any of the existing organizations. They might render all help in their power and resist the Black Act in every way open to them. But for the purpose of Satyagraha itself, a new body named the "Passive Resistance Association" was started. It will be seen from this English name that the word Satyagraha had not yet been invented when this new Association came into existence. Time fully justified the wisdom of constituting a fresh body for the work, and the Satyagraha movement might perhaps have suffered serious defeat if any of the existing organizations had been mixed up with it. Numerous members joined the new Association, and the Community provided its funds in a generous manner.

My experience has taught me that no good effort ever stops short for want of funds. This does not mean that

IN ENGLAND

any temporal movement can go on without money, but it does mean that whenever it has good men and true at its helm, it is bound to attract to itself the requisite funds. On the other hand, a movement often takes a downward course from the time when it is afflicted with an excess of money. Whenever, therefore, a public institution is carried on out of its own investments, I dare not call it a sin, but I do say that it is a highly improper procedure. The people should be the bank of all public institutions. No public body should last a day longer than the people wish. An institution conducted with the interest of accumulated capital ceases to be amenable to public opinion. It tends to become autocratic and self-righteous. This is not the place to dwell upon the corruption of many social and religious institutions which depend upon endowments. The phenomenon is so common that he who runs may read.

Lawyers and English-educated persons do not by any means enjoy the monopoly of hair-splitting. Even illiterate Indians in the Transvaal were quite capable of drawing minute distinctions and spinning fine arguments. Some argued that the pledge taken at the Old Empire Theatre, Johannesburg, had been fulfilled because the original Ordinance had been disallowed. Those whose courage had weakened took shelter under this plea. The argument was not quite devoid of force, yet it could not impress those whose resistance was not to the law as a law, but to the vicious underlying principle. All the same, it was found necessary to re-administer the oath of resistance for safety's sake, in order to reinforce the energy of the community and to probe the extent of its weakness. Meetings were therefore held in every place, and the whole situation was explained over again. The oath was administered afresh and in the end the spirit of the community was found to be as high as ever.

Meanwhile the fateful month of July was gradually drawing to a close. On the last day of that month we had resolved to call a mass meeting of Indians at Pretoria, the capital of the Transvaal. Delegates from other places were also invited to attend. The meeting was held in the open air on the grounds of the Pretoria Mosque. After we had started our Satyagraha our meetings were so largely attended that no building was large enough to accommodate them. The entire Indian population in the Transvaal did not exceed thirteen thousand souls, of whom over ten thousand lived in Johannesburg and Pretoria. An attendance at public meetings of two thousand would be considered satisfactory in any part of the world. A movement of mass Satyagraha is impossible on any other conditions.

Where the struggle is wholly dependent upon internal strength, it cannot go on without mass discipline. The active workers, therefore, did not consider that such a large attendance was anything at all surprising. From the very first they had decided to hold public meetings only in the open air. In this way any serious expense was avoided. None had to go back from the meeting place disappointed for want of room. All these meetings were for the most part very quiet. The audiences listened to everything that was said attentively. If those who were far away from the platform could not hear the speaker they would ask him to raise his voice. It need hardly be mentioned that there were no chairs provided. Everyone sat on the ground. There was a very small platform for the use of the Chairman, the speaker, and a couple of friends. A small table and a few chairs or stools were placed upon it.

Yusuf Ismail Mian, the acting-Chairman of the British Indian Association, presided over this inaugural meeting of the Satyagraha in Pretoria.

Since the time for issuing permits under the Black Act was drawing near, the Indians were naturally anxious in spite of all their enthusiasm; but no less anxious were General Botha and General Smuts, notwithstanding the fact that they had all the might of the Transvaal Government at their disposal. No one would like to bend a whole community to his will by sheer physical force. General Botha had therefore sent Mr. Hosken to this meeting to admonish us. The meeting received him cordially.

"You know I am your friend," he said, "and therefore I need scarcely tell you that my feelings in this matter are with you. If at all I had the power, I would gladly make your opponents accede to your demands. But you know as well as I do the hostility of the Transvaal Europeans. I am here at General Botha's request. He has asked me to be the bearer of his message to this meeting. He entertains a feeling of respect for you and understands your sentiments, but he says he is quite helpless in this matter. All the Europeans in the Transvaal unanimously ask for such a law, and he himself is convinced of its necessity. The Indians know full well how powerful the Transvaal Government is. The law itself has been endorsed by the Imperial Government of Great Britain. The Indians have done all they could and have acquitted themselves like men. But now that their opposition has failed, and the law has been passed, the community must prove its loyalty and love of peace by submission. General Smuts will carefully look into any representations you may make suggesting minor changes in the regulations framed in virtue of the Registration Act. My own advice to you is that you should comply with the General's message. I know that the Transvaal Government is firm regarding this law. To resist it will be to dash your heads against a stone wall. I only hope that your community will neither be ruined by fruitless opposition, nor call down needless suffering on your own heads."

I translated this speech to the meeting, word by word, and further put them on their guard on my own behalf. Mr. Hosken retired after his speech amidst cheers.

It was now time for the Indian speakers to address the meeting. One of these was Sheth Ahmad Muhammad Kachhalia, who afterwards became the hero of the whole movement. I knew him only as a client and as an interpreter. He had never before now taken a leading part in public affairs. He had a good working knowledge of English, which he had so far improved by practice that when he took his friends to English lawyers he spoke for them as an interpreter. But this was not his profession; he worked in this respect only as a friend. At first he used to hawk piecegoods for his livelihood and then to trade on a small scale in partnership with his brother. He was a Muhammadan Meman of Surat and enjoyed a high reputation in his religion. His knowledge of Gujarati was limited, but this too had considerably advanced as he was schooled by experience. He had such quick intelligence that he very easily grasped anything that was put to him. He solved legal difficulties with a faculty that often astonished me. He would not hesitate to argue law, even with lawyers, and very often his arguments were worthy of very careful consideration.

I have never come across a man who could surpass Sheth Ahmad Muhammad Kachhalia in courage and steadfastness. He sacrificed everything he had for the community's sake, and was always a man of his word. He was a strict orthodox Musalman, being one of the trustees of the Surati Meman Mosque. But at the same time, he looked upon Hindus and Musalmans with an equal eye. I do not remember that he ever fanatically or improperly sided with Musalmans against Hindus. Perfectly fearless and impartial, he never hesitated to point out their faults to the Hindus, as well as to Musalmans, whenever he found any necessity. His simplicity and humility were worthy of imitation. My close contact with him for years leads me to hold firmly to the opinion that a community can rarely boast of having in their midst a man of the stamp of Sheth Muhammad Kachhalia.

Kachhalia Sheth was one of the speakers at the Pretoria meeting. He made a very short speech. "Every Indian knows," he said, "what the Black Act is and what it implies. I have heard Mr. Hosken attentively and so have you. His speech has only confirmed me in my own resolution. We know how powerful the Transvaal Government is. But it cannot do anything more than enact such an unjust law. It may cast us into prison, confiscate our property, deport us, or hang us. All this we shall bear cheerfully, but we simply cannot put up with this law."

I observed that while saying this, Kachhalia Sheth

was very deeply moved. His face grew red, the veins on his neck and on his forehead were swollen as the blood coursed rapidly through them. His whole body was shaking. Moving the fingers of his right hand to and fro on his neck, he thundered forth: "I swear in the name of Allah that even though I am hanged I will never submit to this law. Let everyone present here take the same oath."

He took his seat. As he moved his fingers on his throat, some of those seated on the platform smiled, and I remember with shame that I joined them. I was doubtful whether Kachhalia Sheth would be able fully to translate his brave words into action. Now every time I think about that scene I am ashamed of that doubt. For Kachhalia Sheth always remained in the forefront, without a moment's flinching, among the many Indians who observed their pledge to the letter in that great struggle.

The whole meeting cheered him as he spoke. Others at that time knew him very much better than I did. They had realized that Kachhalia only said what he meant and meant what he said. There were many other spirited speeches also. But I have singled out Kachhalia Sheth's for special mention because it proved a prophecy of all his subsequent career. Not every one of those enthusiastic speakers that day stood the final test. But Kachhalia Sheth died four years after the struggle was over, in 1918, serving the community to the very last.

Let me close with a reminiscence of this great soul which may not find a place elsewhere. At Tolstoy Farm, there lived with me a number of Satyagraha families. Kachhalia Sheth sent his son Ali, who was twelve years old, to be educated there as an example to the others and in order that the boy might be brought up to a life of simplicity and service. It was due to the example he thus set that other Musalmans likewise sent their boys to the Farm. Ali was a modest, bright, truthful and straightforward boy. God took him unto Himself before his father. If it had been given to this boy to live, I have no doubt that he would have proved himself to be a worthy son of an excellent father.

CHAPTER X

THE FIRST ENCOUNTER

THE FIRST DAY of July in the Transvaal saw the opening of all the permit offices for the issue of registration certificates. The community had decided openly to picket these offices. Volunteers were posted on the roads leading to each of these offices. They were to warn weak-kneed Indians against accepting the certificates. Our sentries were provided with badges and expressly instructed not to be impolite to any Indian taking out a permit. They must ask him his name, but if he refused to give it they must not be violent or rude. To every Indian going into the office to get a permit they were to hand a printed paper detailing what injury to the community any submission to the Black Act would involve. If he could not read, they were to explain what was written on the paper. They must behave to the police with due respect. If the police abused or thrashed them, they must suffer peacefully. Should at any time ill-treatment by the police become insufferable, they were to surrender themselves without resistance. Should any incident of ill-treatment by police occur in Johannesburg, it should be brought to my notice immediately. At other places, the local secretaries were to be informed and further instructions were to be asked for. Each party of pickets had a captain whose orders must be obeyed by the rest.

This was the community's first experience of such duties. All who were above the age of twelve were taken on as pickets, so that there were many young men from twelve to eighteen years of age enrolled. But no one was accepted who was unknown to the local workers. Over and above all these precautions, people were informed by announcements at every public meeting that if anyone who desired to take out a permit was afraid of the pickets, he could ask the workers to detail a volunteer to escort him to the permit office and back. Some did avail themselves of this offer.

The volunteers in every place worked with boundless enthusiasm. They were ever alert and wide awake in the performance of their duties. Generally speaking, there was not much police harshness. When occasionally police violence occurred the volunteers quietly put up with it. They brought to bear upon their work quite an amount of humour, in which the police sometimes joined. On one occasion volunteers were arrested on a charge of obstructing the public traffic. Since non-co-operation did not form part of the struggle in the Transvaal, defence could be made in the Courts.[1] The volunteers were declared innocent and acquitted. This incident further encouraged their high spirits.

Although the Indians who wanted to take out permits were thus saved from any public rudeness and treated with every politeness, I must frankly confess that there also arose a body of men among us, in connection with the movement, who privately threatened those wishing to take out permits. This was a very painful development, and strong measures were adopted by those of us who were in charge to stamp it out as soon as ever it was

---

[1] In the Non-co-operation Movement in India (1920–1923) volunteers arrested were not allowed to defend themselves in the law courts.

discovered. These private threatenings nearly ceased in consequence, though they were not quite eradicated from the struggle. The threats, however, left a bad impression behind them and thus far injured the cause. Those who were privately threatened sought Government protection and got it. Poison was thus instilled into the community, and those who were weak grew weaker still. The poison spread its virulence because the weak are always apt to be revengeful.

Nevertheless, it was not private threatening which prevented men from registering. Two influences—the force of public opinion and the fear of being known as defaulters—acted as powerful deterrents. I do not know a single Indian who considered it right and proper to submit to the Black Act. Those who submitted did so out of sheer inability to suffer hardships or pecuniary losses, and were therefore ashamed of themselves. This sense of shame, as well as the fear of loss of trade following upon the displeasure of big Indian merchants, pressed heavily upon them, and some leading Indians found a way out of the twofold difficulty. They arranged with the Asiatic Department that an officer should meet them in a private house after ten o'clock at night and give them permits. They thought that in this case no one would know anything about their submission to the law for some months at least. They supposed that as they were among the leading men others would follow suit, thus lightening their burden of shame. It did not matter if they were found out later on.

But the volunteers were so vigilant that the community was kept informed of what happened every moment. Even in the permit office itself there would

THE FIRST ENCOUNTER

be some Indian to give information to the Satyagrahis. Others again, though weak themselves, would be unable to tolerate the idea of the Indian leaders thus disgracing themselves. They would inform the Satyagrahis, hoping that they also might be able to face the hardships if only others were quite firm.

In this way we once received information that certain men were going to take out permits in a certain shop on a certain night. We therefore first tried to dissuade these men. The shop was thoroughly picketed. But human weakness cannot be long suppressed. Some leading men took permits late at night in this way, and thus a breach was made. The next day their names were published by the community. But a sense of shame has its limits. Consideration of self-interest drives even shame away and misleads men out of the strait and narrow path. In the end, something like five hundred men took out permits. These were first issued secretly in private houses. But as the sense of shame wore out, some went publicly to the Asiatic Office and obtained certificates of registration.

When the Department found that in spite of all their exertions they could not get more than five hundred Indians willing to register, they decided to arrest one or two leaders. In Germiston there lived many Indians, among whom was Pandit Rama Sundara. This man had a brave look and was endowed with a certain power of fluent speech. He knew a few Sanskrit verses by heart. Hailing from North India, he naturally knew also some stanzas from Tulasi Das's Ramayana, and owing to his designation of Pandit he enjoyed a certain reputation among his people. He delivered a number of spirited speeches in various places. Some malevolent Indians in Germiston suggested to the Asiatic Department that many Indians would take out permits if this man, Rama Sundara, was arrested.

The officer concerned could scarcely resist the temptation thus offered. So Rama Sundara was put under arrest. This being the first case of its kind, the Government as well as the Indians were much agitated over it. Rama Sundara, who before was known only to the people of Germiston, became in a single day famous all over South Africa. Government took special measures which were altogether unnecessary for the preservation of peace. In the Court, Rama Sundara was accorded due respect as no ordinary prisoner. Eager Indians filled the Courtroom. Rama Sundara was sentenced to a month's simple imprisonment. He was kept in a separate cell in the Europeans' ward of Johannesburg jail. People were allowed freely to meet him. He was permitted to receive food from outside, and was entertained every day on delicacies prepared for him by the community. Thus he was provided with everything he wanted.

The day on which he was sentenced was celebrated with great public rejoicing. There was no trace of depression, but on the other hand there was exultation. Hundreds were now ready to go to jail. The officers of the Asiatic Department were disappointed in their hope of a bumper harvest of registrations. They did not get a single registration even from Germiston. Thus the only gainer was the Indian community.

The month was soon over. Rama Sundara was released and was taken in a procession to the place of meeting. Vigorous speeches were made. Rama Sundara was

THE FIRST ENCOUNTER

smothered with garlands of flowers. The volunteers held a feast in his honour, and hundreds of Indians envied his good luck and were sorry that they had not had the same chance of suffering imprisonment in such a pleasant manner.

But Rama Sundara turned out to be a spurious coin after all. There was no escape for him from the month's imprisonment, because his arrest came as a surprise. In jail he had enjoyed luxuries to which he had been a stranger outside. Nevertheless, accustomed as he was to a licentious life and addicted to bad habits, the loneliness and restraint of jail life were too much for him. In spite of all the attention showered upon him by jail authorities, as well as by the community, the confinement in jail appeared irksome to him, and on his release he bade a final good-bye to the Transvaal and to the movement.

There are cunning men in every community and in every movement; and so there were in ours. These knew Rama Sundara through and through. But from the idea that even he might become an instrument for good in the Indian cause, they never let me know his secret history until his bubble had finally burst. I subsequently found that he was an indentured Indian labourer who had deserted the plantation before completing his term of indenture. There was nothing discreditable in his having been an indentured labourer. In the end these labourers in the sugar plantation and mines proved to be a most valuable acquisition to the movement, making their own contribution towards the final victory. But it was certainly wrong of him not to have finished his period of indenture.

The history of Rama Sundara has been thus detailed,

not to expose his faults, but to point out a moral. The leaders of every clean movement are bound to see that they admit only clean fighters into it. But every caution notwithstanding, undesirables cannot altogether be kept out. And yet, if leaders are fearless and true, the entry of undesirable persons into a movement unawares does not ultimately injure the cause. When Rama Sundara was found out, he became a man of straw. The community forgot him, but the movement only gathered fresh strength. The imprisonment which he had suffered for the cause of Satyagraha stood to our credit. The enthusiasm created by his trial remained. Taking advantage of his example, weaklings slipped away out of the movement of their own accord.

No one need point a finger of scorn at Rama Sundara. All men are imperfect, and when imperfection is observed in someone in a larger measure than in others, people are apt to blame him. But that is not fair. Rama Sundara did not become weak intentionally; man can alter his temperament and control it, but he cannot eradicate his inner character. God has not given him so much liberty. Although Rama Sundara fled away, who can tell how he might have repented of his weakness? Or, rather, was not his very flight a powerful proof of his repentance? He could have taken out a permit and steered clear of jail by submission to the Black Act. He would even have become a tool of the Asiatic Department and thus gained popularity with the Transvaal Government. But out of shame for his own weak character he hid his face from the community, and even thus did it a service.

While taking note of the weapons, internal as well as external, employed in the Satyagraha struggle, it is

THE FIRST ENCOUNTER

necessary specially to mention *Indian Opinion*, the weekly journal which continues to be published in South Africa up to this very day. The credit for first starting an Indian-owned printing-press in South Africa is due to a Gujarati gentleman, named Madanjit Vyavaharik. After he had conducted the press for a few years, in the midst of many difficulties, he thought of bringing out a newspaper. So he consulted Mansukhlal Nazar and myself. The newspaper was issued from Durban. Mansukhlal Nazar volunteered to act as unpaid editor. From the very first the paper was conducted at a loss. At last we decided to purchase a farm, to settle all the workers upon it, and print our newspaper from the farm itself. The workers were to constitute themselves into a sort of commonwealth or republic. The farm selected for the purpose is situated on a beautiful hill fourteen miles from Durban. The railway station is two miles distant from the farm and is called Phœnix. Thus the settlement itself is called Phœnix.

Indian Opinion was formerly published in English, Gujarati, Hindi, and Tamil. But the Hindi and Tamil sections were eventually discontinued. The burden they imposed upon us seemed to be excessive, and we could not find Tamil and Hindi writers willing to settle down on the farm. The paper was thus being published in English and Gujarati when the Satyagraha struggle commenced. Among the settlers on the farm were Gujaratis, Hindustanis and Tamils, as well as Englishmen. After the premature death of Mansukhlal Nazar, his place as editor was taken by an English friend, Herbert Kitchin. Then the post of editor was long filled by Henry S. L. Polak, and during our absence the late

Rev. Joseph Doke acted for us. Through the medium of this paper we could disseminate in a thorough manner the news of the week among the community. The English section kept those Indians informed about the movement who did not know Gujarati; and for Englishmen all over the world who have sympathized with the cause *Indian Opinion* has served the purpose of the weekly news-letter.

I believe that a struggle, which chiefly relies upon its own internal strength, cannot be carried on with any completeness without a newspaper. It has also been my experience that we could not have educated the local Indians, or kept Indians and Europeans all over the world in touch with the course of events in South Africa without the aid of *Indian Opinion*. Therefore it proved itself a useful and potent weapon in our struggle.

While the community was transformed as a result of the struggle, *Indian Opinion* was transformed also. In the beginning we used to accept advertisements and execute job-work in the printing-press. Some of our best men had to be spared for this kind of work. Even when we obtained advertisements for publication, there was constant difficulty in deciding which to accept and which to refuse. One might be inclined to refuse an objectionable advertisement, and yet be constrained to keep it because the advertiser was a leading member of the community. He might take it ill if his advertisement was rejected. Some of the best workers had to be set apart for canvassing and realizing outstanding debts from advertisers. They had also to make use of the flattery which advertisers claim as their due.

The view therefore commended itself to me that if

Indian Opinion was conducted, not because it yielded profit but purely with a view to service, then this service should never be imposed upon the community by force, but should be rendered as long as the community wished. And the clearest proof of such a wish would be forthcoming if they became subscribers in sufficiently large numbers to make the paper self-supporting. Finally, it seemed in every way better for all concerned that we should approach the community itself and explain to them the duty of keeping their newspaper going, rather than seek to induce a few traders to place their advertisements with us. The gratifying result would follow that those who were now engrossed in the advertisement department would be able to devote their labours to improving the paper.

The community realized at once their proprietorship of *Indian Opinion*, and their consequent responsibility for maintaining it. The workers were relieved of all anxiety in that respect. Their only care now was to put their best work into the paper so long as the community required it. They were not only not ashamed to ask their fellow-Indians to subscribe, but thought it their duty to do so. A change came over the internal strength and character of the paper, and it became a force to reckon with.

The number of subscribers, which had ranged between twelve and fifteen hundred, increased day by day. The rates of subscription were raised, and yet when the struggle was at its height there were as many as 3,500 subscribers. The number of Indians who could read *Indian Opinion* in South Africa was at the outside twenty thousand in all. Therefore the circulation of over three thousand copies was satisfactory. The community had made the paper their own to such an extent that if copies did not reach Johannesburg at the expected time I was flooded with complaints. *Indian Opinion* generally reached Johannesburg on Sunday morning. I know of many whose first occupation after they had received their paper was to read the Gujarati section through from beginning to end. One of the company would read it, and the rest would surround him and listen. Not all who wanted to read the paper could afford to subscribe to it by themselves. Some of them would therefore club together for that purpose.

Just as we stopped advertisements in the paper so we ceased to take job-work in the press for nearly the same reason. Compositors had now some time to spare, which was utilized in the publication of books. As here also there was no intention of reaping profits, and the books were only printed to help forward the struggle, they commanded good sales. Thus both the paper and the press made their own valuable contribution to the struggle. Satyagraha gradually took root in the community and an upward tendency began to be apparent.

The Transvaal Government failed to reap any advantage from Rama Sundara's arrest. They noticed the spirit of the Indian community rising higher and higher. The officers of the Asiatic Department were diligent readers of *Indian Opinion*. As we kept no secrets, this weekly paper proved an open book to anyone who wanted to gauge the strength and weakness of the community. The workers had realized at the very outset that secrecy had no place with us. The interest of the community demanded that if the disease or weakness was to be

THE FIRST ENCOUNTER

properly eradicated it must be first diagnosed and given due publicity.

When the officers understood the open policy of *Indian Opinion*, the paper became for them a faithful mirror of the current history of the whole Indian community. They at last came to realize that the strength of the movement could not by any means be broken so long as certain leaders were at large. In consequence, we were served with a notice to appear before the magistrate in Christmas week of 1907.

This was an act of courtesy on the part of the officers concerned. They could have had the leaders arrested by warrant if they had chosen to do so. Instead of this they issued notices. Such a procedure, besides being evidence of their courtesy, betrayed their confidence that the Indian leaders were willing and prepared to be arrested. Those who had thus been warned appeared before the Court on the date specified. It was Saturday, December 18, 1907. They were summoned to show why, having failed to apply for registration, as required by law, they should not be ordered to leave the Transvaal within a given period.

One of these was Mr. Leung Quinn, the leader of the Chinese residents of Johannesburg, who numbered three to four hundred and were either traders or farmers. India is noted for its agriculture. But I believe that we in India are not as far advanced in this respect as the Chinese. The modern progress of agriculture in America and other countries defies description, yet I consider it still to be in an experimental stage. China, on the other hand, is an old country like India, and a comparison between India and China would not be uninstructive.

I had carefully observed the agricultural methods of the Chinese near Johannesburg and also had talked with them on the subject. This gave me the strong impression that the Chinese are more intelligent than ourselves. We often allow land to lie fallow, thinking that it is of no more use, while the Chinese would grow good crops upon it, thanks to a minute knowledge of varying soils.

The Black Act applied to the Chinese as well as to the Indians. They therefore joined us in the Satyagraha struggle. Nevertheless, from the first the activities of the two communities were not allowed to be amalgamated. Each worked through its own independent organization. This arrangement produced one beneficial result, that so long as both the communities remained firm, each would be a source of strength to the other. But if one of the two gave way that would leave the morale of the other unaffected, or at least it would steer clear of the danger of total collapse.

Many of the Chinese eventually fell away because their leader played them false. He did not indeed actually submit to the obnoxious law; but one morning someone came and told me that the Chinese leader had fled without handing over charge of the books and money in his possession. It will always be difficult for followers to sustain a conflict in the absence of their leader. Yet for a time this leader did very useful work.

One of the several leading Indians who constituted this first batch of prisoners was Thambi Naidoo. He was a Tamil, born in Mauritius, where his parents had migrated from the Madras Presidency. He was an ordinary trader. While he had received no scholastic education, a wide experience of life had made an excellent schoolmaster for him. He wrote and spoke English fairly well, although his grammar was not free from faults. He spoke Hindustani and had some knowledge of Telugu, though he never learnt the alphabets of these two languages. In addition to this, he had a very good knowledge of the Creole dialect, which is current in Mauritius, and he knew, of course, one of the South African native languages.

A working knowledge of so many languages was by no means a rare accomplishment among the Indians of South Africa. Hundreds of them could claim a general acquaintance with most of these languages. Such men became good linguists almost without effort. Their brains are not fatigued in childhood by education through the medium of a foreign tongue like English. Their memory is sharp. Therefore they acquire these different languages simply by talking to people who speak them and also by observation. This does not involve any considerable strain on their brain-power, but on the contrary the easy mental exercise leads to a natural development of their intellect all round.

Such had been the history of Thambi Naidoo. He had a keen intelligence and could grasp new facts very quickly. His ever-ready wit was astonishing. He had never seen India, yet his love for the homeland knew no bounds. Patriotism ran through his veins, and his courage was pictured in his face. He was very strongly built and possessed tireless energy. He shone equally at meetings, whether he had to take the chair and lead them, or whether he had merely to do hall-porter's work. He would never be ashamed of carrying a load in the public streets. Night and day were the same to him when he set to work. None was more ready than he to sacrifice all he had for the sake of the community. If Thambi Naidoo had not been rash and prone to anger, this brave man could easily have assumed the leadership of the community in the Transvaal, in the absence of Kachhalia. While the Transvaal struggle lasted his good qualities were apparent, but in later years his anger and his rashness have proved to be his worst enemies. However that may be, the name of Thambi Naidoo must ever remain famous in the annals of Satyagraha in South Africa.

The magistrate conducted each case separately and ordered all the accused to leave the Transvaal. The time expired on January 10, 1908. On that day we were called upon to attend the Court for sentence. None of us had any defence to offer. All were to plead guilty to the charge of disobeying the order to leave the Transvaal.

I asked leave to make a short statement, and explained that I thought there should be a distinction between my case and those that were to follow. I had just heard from Pretoria that my compatriots had been sentenced to three months' imprisonment with hard labour, and had been fined a heavy amount for whose non-payment they had served a further period of three months' hard labour. If these men had committed an offence, I had committed a greater offence still and I therefore asked the magistrate to impose upon me the heaviest penalty of all. The magistrate did not accede to my request and sentenced me only to two months' simple imprisonment. I had some slight feeling of awkwardness for a brief moment, which was due to the fact that I was standing as an accused in the very Court where I had often appeared as counsel. But I remembered that the rôle of accused in such a cause was far more honourable than any other. Therefore, when the time came, I did not feel the slightest hesitation in entering the prisoner's box and giving my statement as the accused.

In the Court there were hundreds of Indians as well as some brother members of the Bar in front of me. On the sentence being pronounced, I was at once removed in custody by the police and was then quite alone. The policeman asked me to sit on a bench kept there for prisoners. He shut the door and went away.

At that time, when I was left alone, I fell into deep thought. Home, the law courts where I practised, the public meetings, all passed before me like a dream, and I was now a prisoner. What would happen in these two months? Should I have to serve the full term? If the people courted imprisonment in large numbers, as they had promised, there would be no question of serving the full sentence. But if they failed to fill the prisons, two months would be as tedious as an age. These considerations passed through my mind in less than one-hundredth of the time that it has taken me to put them down on paper.

How vain I had been! I remembered how I had asked the people to consider the prisons as His Majesty's hotels. I had called the suffering consequent upon disobeying the Black Act perfect bliss. I had declared the sacrifice of one's all and even life itself in resisting it as supreme bliss. Where had all this brave experience vanished to-day?

This second train of thought acted upon me like a bracing tonic, and I began to laugh at my own folly.

I wondered what kind of imprisonment would be awarded to the others, and whether they would be kept with me in the same prison. Just then I was disturbed by the police officer, who opened the gates and asked me to go with him. He made me go before him, following me himself. He took me to the prisoners' closed van and asked me to take my seat in it. Thus I was driven to Johannesburg jail.

In jail I was asked to put off my own private clothing. Beforehand, I knew that convicts were stripped naked in jails, and I did not refuse. We had all decided, as Satyagrahis, voluntarily to obey all jail regulations so long as they were not inconsistent with self-respect or religious convictions. The clothes which were given to me to wear were very dirty. I did not at all like to put them on. It was not without pain that I reconciled myself to the idea that I must put up with some dirt.

After the officers had recorded my name and address I was taken to a large cell. There in a short time I was joined by my own compatriots who came in laughing and told me that they had received the same sentence as myself. They explained what had taken place after I had been removed. From them I understood that when my case was over some of the Indians, who were excited, had led out into the streets a procession with black flags in their hands. The police had disturbed the procession and flogged some of its members. We were all happy at the thought that we were to be kept together in the same cell.

The cell door was locked at six o'clock. The door was not composed of bars, but was quite solid, there being high up in the wall a small opening for ventilation,

THE FIRST ENCOUNTER

so that we felt as if we had been locked up in a strong-room.

No wonder the jail authorities did not accord us the good treatment which they had meted out to Rama Sundara. As he had been the first Satyagraha prisoner, the authorities had no idea how he was to be treated. Our batch was fairly large and further arrests were in contemplation. We were therefore kept in the Bantu ward. In South Africa, only two classes of convicts are recognized, namely, the Whites and the Blacks, the Europeans and the Bantus; and the Indians were classed with the latter.

The next morning we found that prisoners without hard labour had the right to wear their own private clothing. If they did not wish to exercise this right, they were given jail clothing assigned to that special class of prisoners. We decided that it was not right to put on our own clothing and that it was appropriate to take the jail uniform. So we informed the authorities accordingly. We were therefore given the clothes assigned to Bantu convicts who were not punished with hard labour. But Bantu prisoners sentenced to simple imprisonment were never very numerous; hence there was a shortage of this class of prisoners' clothing as soon as the other Indians began to arrive. As they did not wish to stand upon ceremony, they readily accepted clothing assigned to hard-labour prisoners. Some of these, however, who came in later preferred to keep their own clothing. I thought this improper, but did not care to insist upon their following the correct procedure in the matter.

From the second or third day the Satyagraha prisoners began to arrive in large numbers. In South Africa, every hawker has to take out a licence. He must show it to the police whenever asked for it. Nearly every day some policeman would ask to see the licences and arrest those who had none to show. The community had resolved to fill up the jail after our arrests, and in this the hawkers took the lead. It was easy for them to be arrested. They must only refuse to show their licences and this was enough to ensure their arrest. In this way the number of Satyagrahis swelled to more than a hundred in one week. As some few were sure to arrive every day, we received the daily budget of news without a newspaper.

When Satyagrahis began to be arrested in large numbers they were sentenced to imprisonment with hard labour, either because the magistrates lost patience or because, as we ourselves conjectured, they had received special instructions from the Government. Even to-day I think that our own conjecture was correct, since apart from the first few cases, in which simple imprisonment was awarded, never afterwards throughout the long-drawn struggle was there any sentence of simple imprisonment. Even Indian ladies were punished with hard labour. If all the magistrates had not received the same orders from higher quarters, and yet by mere coincidence had sentenced all men and women alike to hard labour, then that must be held to be very nearly a miracle.

CHAPTER XI

IMPRISONMENT

THERE WERE ONLY five of us passive resisters in prison at first. On Tuesday, January 14th, Mr. Thambi Naidoo came in along with Mr. Quinn, the president of the Chinese Association. We were delighted to receive them. On the 18th, fourteen others joined us, including Samundar Khan. So the numbers increased day by day. In this chapter, I propose to gather together some of our experiences in prison on different occasions and to explain how we passed our time there.

The question of food is a matter of great moment to many of us, even in ordinary circumstances; but to those in prison it often becomes most important of all. The rule of prison is that a prisoner has to remain content with jail food without procuring any from outside. A soldier also has to submit to his regulation rations; but there is this difference, that a soldier's friend can send food to him from outside and he can take it, while the prisoner is usually prohibited from doing this. Therefore, the prohibition about food is one of the signs of being in prison. Even in general conversation, you will find the jail-officers saying that there should be no question of taste about prison food, and no article should be allowed merely to give relish. In talk with the prison medical officer, I told him that it was necessary for us to have something to eat along with the dry bread that was given to us. He replied that we clearly wanted to eat with relish; but that no palatable thing could be allowed in prison.

According to the regulations, in the first week each Indian got twelve ounces of mealie meal porridge in the morning, without sugar or ghee; at noon, four ounces of rice and one ounce of ghee; in the evening for five days he would get twelve ounces of mealie meal porridge, and for two days twelve ounces of boiled beans and salt. This scale had been modelled on the dietary of the Bantus, the only difference being that they are given crushed maize corn in the evening together with lard or fat, while the Indians get rice. From the second week onward, for two days boiled potatoes and for two days cabbages are given along with maize flour. Those who take meat are given meat with vegetables on Sundays.

The first batch of prisoners resolved to beg for no favours at the hands of the Government. They would take whatever food was served out as long as it was not religiously objectionable. But as a matter of fact, the food I have mentioned was not the proper kind of diet for an Indian at all, though medically it contained sufficient nutrition. Maize is the daily food of the Bantus and therefore the maize diet suits them. Indeed, they thrive on it in jail. But Indians rarely use maize flour in their homes. Only rice suits them. Indians also are not used to eating beans alone, nor could we like vegetables cooked by or for the Bantus. They never clean the vegetables nor season them with any spices. Again, the vegetables cooked for them mostly consist of peelings left over after the vegetables have been prepared for the European convicts. For spices, nothing else except salt is given. Sugar is never dreamt of. Thus the food question was a very difficult one for us all. Still, as we had determined that the passive resisters were neither to solicit nor ask for favours from the jail authorities, we tried to rest content with this unsuitable kind of food.

In reply to his enquiries, we had told the Governor of the prison that the food did not suit us, but we were determined not to ask for any favours from the Government. If Government of its own accord wanted to make a change, it would be welcome; otherwise we would go on taking the regulation diet.

But this determination could not last very long. When others joined us, we thought it would be improper to make them share all this trouble with us. Was it not sufficient that they had shared imprisonment with us? So we began to speak to the Governor on their behalf. We told him that we ourselves were prepared to take any kind of food, but the later batches could not do so. He thought over the matter, and said that he would allow them to cook separately, if they put their complaint down to the ground of religion. But the articles of food would be the same, for it did not rest with him to make any changes.

In the meantime, other Indians had joined us and some of them elected to starve rather than take mealie meal porridge. So I read the jail rules and found out that application in such matters should be made to the Director of Prisons. Therefore I asked the Governor for permission to apply to the Director, and sent a petition accordingly.

As it was an urgent matter I asked for a reply to be sent by wire.

Twenty-one of us had signed the petition and while it was being despatched seventy-six more came in. They also had a dislike for the mealie meal porridge, and so we added a paragraph stating that the new arrivals also objected to the diet. I requested the Governor to send it at once.

He asked his superior's permission by telephone, and allowed at once four ounces of bread in place of the mealie meal porridge. We were all very pleased, and four ounces of bread were given to us both morning and evening. Indeed, in the evening, we got eight ounces, which made up half a loaf. But this was merely a temporary arrangement. A committee was sitting on the question and we heard that they had recommended an allowance of flour, ghee and pulse; but before it could take effect, we had been released, and so nothing more happened.

In the beginning, when there were only eight of us, we did not cook for ourselves; so we used to get badly-cooked rice and vegetables whenever the same were given. Afterwards, we obtained permission to cook for ourselves. On the first day, Mr. Kadva cooked. After that, Mr. Thambi Naidoo and Mr. Jiva both took turns, and during our last days they had to cook for about 150 men. They did their cooking once only, except on vegetable days, which were two in a week. Then they had to cook twice. Mr. Thambi Naidoo took great trouble over his cooking and I used to serve the food.

From the style of the petition it may be understood that it was presented on behalf of all Indian prisoners. We talked with the Governor also on the same lines, and he had promised to look into the jail diet of the Asiatic prisoners. We still hoped that the diet of the Indians would be improved.

IMPRISONMENT

Again, the three Chinese used to get a different diet, and hence annoyance was felt, as there was an appearance of their being considered separate from and inferior to us. For this reason, I applied on their behalf to the Governor and to Mr. Playford, and it was ordered that they should be placed on the same level as Indians.

It is instructive to compare this dietary with that of the Europeans. They get for their breakfast mealie meal porridge and eight ounces of bread; for the midday lunch, bread and soup, or bread and meat, or bread and meat with potatoes or vegetables; and in the evenings bread and mealie meal porridge. Thus they got bread thrice in a day, and so they did not care whether they had the mealie food or not. Again, they got meat and soup in addition. Besides this, they were often given tea or cocoa. This will show that both the Europeans and the Bantus get food suitable to them, and it is the Indians alone who suffer. They had no special dietary of their own. If they were treated like Europeans in food, then the Europeans would have felt ashamed. But no one had the concern to find out what was the food of the Indians. They had thus to be ranked with the Bantus and silently suffer hunger. For this state of things I find fault with our own people, the passive resisters. Some Indians got the requisite food by stealth, others put up with whatever they got, and were either ashamed to make public the story of their distress or had no thought for others. Hence the outside public remained in the dark.

If we were strictly to follow truth and agitate where we get injustice, there would be no room to undergo such inconveniences. If we were to leave self and apply ourselves to the good of others, grievances would get remedied soon. But just as it is necessary to take steps for the redress of such complaints about prison food, so it is necessary to think of certain other things besides. It is but meet that prisoners should undergo certain inconveniences. If there were no suffering, what would be the meaning of being called a prisoner? Those who are the masters of their minds take pleasure even in suffering, and live happily in jails.

There is another evil habit of ours, and that is our tenacity in sticking to our manners and customs in every little particular. We must "do in Rome as the Romans do." When we are living in South Africa we ought to accustom ourselves to what is considered good food in that country. Mealie meal porridge is a good article of diet, as simple and cheap as our wheat. We cannot say that it is insipid. Sometimes it is superior even to wheat. It is my belief that out of respect for the country of our adoption, we should take food which is produced in that country, provided it is not unwholesome. Many Europeans like this mealie food and eat it every morning. It becomes palatable if milk and sugar, or even ghee, be taken with it.

For these reasons and for the fact that we might have to go to jail again in the future, it is advisable for every Indian to accustom himself to these preparations of maize. With this habit formed, when the time comes, even if we take it merely with a little salt, we should not find it hard. All those nations that have advanced have given up certain things where there was nothing substantial to lose. The Salvation Army people attract the people of the land to which they go by adopting their customs and dress, and we should adapt our own ways to South Africa where there is nothing objectionable in doing so.

It would have been a miracle had no one of the 150 prisoners fallen ill. The first to be taken ill was Mr. Samundar Khan. He had been brought into jail ailing and was taken to hospital the next day. Mr. Kadva was a victim of rheumatism, and for some days he remained with us and was treated by the doctor in the prison cell itself, but eventually he had to go to the hospital also. Two others suffered from fainting fits and were taken there. The reason was that it was very hot and the convicts had to remain out in the sun the whole day. We nursed them as best we could. Later on Mr. Nawab Khan also succumbed, and on the day of our release he had to be led out by hand. He had improved a little after the doctor had ordered milk to be given to him. On the whole, however, it may safely be said that the passive resisters fared well.

Our cell had space enough to accommodate only fifty-one prisoners. Later on, when instead of fifty-one there were 150 persons, great difficulty was felt. The Governor had to pitch tents outside, and many had to go there. During our last days, about a hundred were taken outside to sleep and back again in the morning. The area space was too small for this number, and we could pass our time only with difficulty. Added to this there was our evil inborn habit of spitting everywhere, which renders the place dirty and there was danger of disease breaking out. Fortunately our companions were amenable to advice, and assisted us in keeping the compound clean. Scrupulous care was exercised by the inspection officer, and this saved the inmates from disease.

Everyone will admit that the Government was at fault in incarcerating such a large number in so narrow a space. If the room was insufficient, it was incumbent on the Government not to send so many there; and if the struggle had been prolonged it would have been impossible for the Government to commit any more to this prison.

The Government, after wearisome correspondence, had allowed us the use of a table, with pen and ink. We had the free run of the prison library also. I had taken from it the works of Carlyle and the Bible. From the Chinese interpreter, who used to come to the prison, I borrowed the Quran translated into English, the speeches of Huxley, Carlyle's *Life of Burns, Johnson, and Scott*, and Bacon's *Essays*. From my own books I had taken the Bhagavad-Gita, with Manilal Nathubhai's annotations, several Tamil works, an Urdu Book from the Maulvi Sahib, the writings of Tolstoy and Ruskin. Many of these I read for the first time or read over again. I used to study Tamil regularly. In the morning I would read the Gita and at noon mostly the Quran. In the evening I taught the Bible to Mr. Fortoen, who was a Chinese Christian. He wanted to learn English, and I taught it to him through the Bible.

If I had been permitted to work out my full period I might have been able to complete my translation of the books of Carlyle and a book of Ruskin. Since I was fully occupied in the study of these works, I should not have become tired even if my sentence had been longer. Indeed, I should have passed a happy life, believing as I do that whoever has a taste for reading good books is able to bear loneliness in any place with great ease.

IMPRISONMENT

In the West we now see that the State looks after the religion of all its prisoners, and hence we find a special church in the Johannesburg prison for the Whites, who alone are allowed access to it. When I asked for permission for Mr. Fortoen and myself to attend church, the Governor told me that it was only for White Christian prisoners. Every Sunday they went there on parade, and preachers of different denominations gave them lessons of morality and religion.

Several missionaries also came to convert the Bantus, having obtained special permission. There is no church for them; they sit out in the open. Jews also have got their ministers to look after them. It is only the Hindus and the Muhammadans who are left spiritually unprovided for. There are not many Indian prisoners, it is true; but the absence of any such provision for them is hardly creditable to them. The Hindu and Musalman leaders should take counsel together and arrange for the religious instruction of the members of their own community in jail, even if there be only one convict. The preachers, whether Hindus or Maulvis, should be pure-hearted and they should be careful not to offend the convicts by anything they might say to them.

Every prisoner in the jail on getting up in the morning is required to fold his own bedding, and place it in its proper place. He must finish his toilet by six o'clock and be ready to start out at the stroke of the hour. The work begins at seven o'clock. It is of various kinds. The ground to be dug up was very hard. It had to be worked over with spades and hence the work often proved too difficult. Again, it was a very hot time of the year. The place where the convicts were taken was about a mile and a half from the jail. Each one of us started very well indeed. But as no one of us was used to this kind of work, it was not long before we were quite exhausted. Every hour the day advanced the work seemed harder still.

The warder was very strict. He used to cry out every now and then, "Go on, go on." This made the Indians quite nervous. I saw some of them weeping. One of them had a swollen foot. All this caused me a great deal of heart-burning; and yet on every occasion I reminded them of their duty and asked them to perform it as well as possible, with a good heart, and without minding the words of the warder. I also felt myself tired out. My hands were covered with blisters and water was oozing from them. I could hardly work with the spade and felt the weight of it as if it were made of lead. I prayed to God to preserve my honour, to maintain my limbs intact, and to bestow on me sufficient strength to be able to perform my allotted task to the end. I trusted in Him and went on with my work.

The warder would sometimes remonstrate with me when I required an occasional break to get over the fatigue. I told him that it was unnecessary for him to remind me of my duty. I was prepared to go through as much of it as I possibly could, and I was not able to do more.

Just then I saw Mr. Jhinabhai faint. While I was pouring water on his head, the thought came to me that most of the Indians had trusted my word and had submitted themselves to imprisonment on that account. If the advice that I happened to offer them were erroneous, then how great a sin would I be committing in the eyes of God in tendering it to them! They were undergoing all sorts of hardships on account of my advice. With this thought in my mind I heaved a deep sigh. With God as my witness, I reflected on the subject once more, and was immediately reassured that what I had done was right.

I felt that the advice that I tendered to them was the only advice I could give; I had no choice in the matter. In anticipation of future happiness, it was absolutely necessary that we should undergo the hardest trials and sufferings beforehand. There was no reason to be grieved at this. Jhinabhai himself had merely had a fainting fit. But even if it had been death, how could I offer any other advice than what I had already done? It came to my mind that it was much more honourable for anybody to die suffering in that manner than to continue living a life of perpetual enslavement.

On one occasion a warder came to me, and asked me to provide him with two of our men to clean the water-closets. I thought I could do nothing better than clean them myself, and so I offered him my services. In my own case I have no particular dislike to that kind of work. On the contrary, I am of opinion that we ought to get ourselves accustomed to it.

Once I was given a bed in a ward where there were principally Bantu prisoners. Here I passed the whole night in great misery and terror. I did not know then that I was to be taken the next day to another cell which was occupied by Indian prisoners. Fretting that I would be kept incarcerated with such men as those I saw around me, I got very nervous and terror-stricken. And yet I tried my best to reconcile myself to the idea that it was my duty to undergo any suffering that might befall me.

I read from the Bhagavad-Gita that I had with me certain verses suited to the occasion, which I pondered over and I became soon reconciled to the situation.

The chief reason why I got nervous was that in the same room there were a number of wild, murderous-looking, vicious Bantu and Chinese prisoners who had been convicted of violent crime. I did not know their language. One of the Bantus began to ply me with questions. As far as I could gather he seemed to be mocking me indecently. I did not understand what his questions were and I kept quiet. At last he asked me in broken English, "Why have they brought you here?" I gave him a very short reply and again was silent. He was followed by one of the Chinese convicts. He was worse than the other. He approached my bed and looked at me intently as though he had some purpose towards me. I kept on with my silence. He then proceeded towards the bed of the Bantu, which was near. There they began to mock each other indecently. Both of these prisoners were there for crimes of violence. How could I enjoy sleep after seeing these dreadful things?

When at a later period of the Satyagraha struggle I got three months' hard labour, I once again was imprisoned along with my brother Indians and my son in the Volksrust Jail. My experience this time was unique, and what I learnt from it I could not have learnt after years of study. These three months were quite invaluable. I saw many vivid pictures of passive resistance, and I became a more confirmed resister even than before. For all this I had to thank the Government of the Transvaal.

Several officers had betted that I would not get less

IMPRISONMENT

than six months'. My friends, who were old offenders, and my own son had got six months', and so I too wished that the officers might win their bets. Still, I had my own misgivings, and they proved true. When the sentence was given I got only three months', that being the maximum under the law.

After going there, I was glad to meet Dawood Muhammad, Rustomji, Sorabji, Hajura Singh, Pillay, Lal Bahadur Singh and other "resisters." With the exception of about ten of us, all the others were accommodated in tents which were pitched in the jail compound for sleeping. The scene resembled a camp more than a prison. Everyone liked to sleep in the tents if they got a chance.

We were quite comfortable this time about our meals. We used to cook for ourselves as before, and we were able to cook as we liked. We were about seventy-seven passive resisters in all.

Those who were taken out for work had a hard time of it. The road near the Magistrate's Court had to be constructed, so they had to dig up stones and carry them. After the road was finished they were asked to dig up grass from the school-room compound. But they did their work cheerfully. For three days I was also taken out with these gangs for work, but in the meanwhile a telegram was received from Pretoria that I was not to be taken outside for work. I was much disheartened at this because I liked to move out; it improved my health and exercised my body. Generally I take two meals in a day, but in the Volksrust Jail, on account of this physical exercise in the open air, I felt hungry thrice. After I was taken from road-making, I was given the work of a scavenger, but this was no good for hard exercise, and after a time even that work was taken away.

On March 2nd I heard that I was ordered to be sent to Pretoria. The warder asked me to be ready at once, and we had to go to the station in pelting rain, walking on hard roads with my luggage on my head. We left by the evening train in a third-class carriage.

My removal to Pretoria gave rise to various surmises. Some thought that peace was at hand; others thought that, after separating me from my companions, the Transvaal Government intended to oppress me more than otherwise in order to make me surrender. Others thought that in order to stifle discussions in the House of Commons it might be intended to give me greater liberty and convenience.

I did not like to leave Volksrust Prison, since we passed our days and nights pleasantly there, talking to one another. Hajura Singh and Joshi always put us questions that were neither useless nor trivial because they were related to science and philosophy. One did not care to leave such company and such a camp.

But if everything always happened as we wished, we should not be called human beings. So I left the place, quietly saluting Mr. Kaji on the road. The warder and I were put in a single compartment. It was very cold and it rained on the way the whole night. I had my overcoat and I was permitted to use it. Bread and cheese was provided for my meals on the way; but as I had eaten before I left, I gave this to the warder.

We reached Pretoria on March 3rd and found everything altered. The jail was freshly built and the men were new convicts. I was asked to eat, but I had no

MR. GANDHI IN SOUTH AFRICA ABOUT 1900

IMPRISONMENT

inclination to do so. Mealie porridge was placed before me. I tasted a spoonful and then left it untouched. My warder was surprised at this, but I told him that I was not hungry, and he smiled. Then I was handed over to another warder.

"Gandhi," said he to me sharply, "take off your cap."

I did so. Then he asked, "Are you the son of Gandhi?"

"No," I answered. "My son is undergoing six months' imprisonment at Volksrust."

He then confined me to a cell. I began to walk backwards and forwards in it. He watched me from the porthole in the door.

"Gandhi," he shouted at me. "Don't walk about like that. It spoils my floor."

I stopped and stood in a corner quietly. I had nothing to read even, as I had not yet got my books. I was confined at about eight in the morning and at ten I was taken to the doctor. He only asked me if I had any contagious disease and then allowed me to go. At eleven o'clock I was interned in a small room where I passed my whole time.

It seemed to be a cell for one prisoner only. Its dimensions were about ten feet by seven feet. The floor was of black pitch, which the warder tried to keep shining. There was only one small glass window for light and air. This was barred with iron bars. There was electric light kept for the use of the warders to examine the inmates at night, but it was not strong enough to enable one to read. When I went and stood very near to it, I could read only a large-type book. It was put out at eight, but again put on five or six times during the night, to enable the warders to look over the prisoners through the port-holes.

After eleven the Deputy-Governor came and I made three requests to him. The first was for my books; the second was for permission to write a letter to my wife, who was ill; the third was for a small bench to sit on. For the first, he said he would consider; for the second, I might write; for the third, no. Afterwards, I wrote out my letter in Gujarati and gave it to be posted. He endorsed on it that I should write in English. I said my wife did not know English, and my letters were a great source of comfort to her, and that I had nothing special to write in them. Still, I did not get permission, and I declined to write in English. My books were given to me in the evening.

My mid-day meal I had to take standing in my cell with closed doors. At three, I asked leave for a bath. The warder said, "All right, but you had better go there after undressing yourself." I said that if there was no special objection, I would put my clothes on the curtain there and take my bath. "All right, Gandhi," he said, "but do not delay."

Even before I had cleaned my body he shouted out, "Gandhi, have you done?" I said, "I shall be through in a minute." In this prison I could rarely see the face of an Indian.

In the evening I received a blanket and a coir mat to sleep on, but neither pillow nor plank. Even when answering a call of nature, I was being watched by a warder. If he did not happen to know me, he would cry out, "Sammy,[1] come out." But "Sammy" had got the

[1] A corruption of "Swami" often used by Europeans in South Africa because South Indians' names, like Krishnaswami, Appaswami, often end in that word.

bad habit of taking full time on such occasions, so how could I get up at once? Sometimes the warders and also the Bantus would peep in, and at times would sing out, "Get up, Sammy."

The labour given to me next was to polish the floor and the doors. The latter were of varnished iron. What polish could be brought on such a material by rubbing? Nevertheless, I spent three hours on each door rubbing, but found that they were unchanged after all my efforts to brighten them.

I knew that no ghee was given with rice in the evening, and I had thought of remedying the defect. So I spoke to the Chief Warder, but he said that ghee was to be given only on Wednesdays and Sundays, at noon, in place of meat; if a further supply were needed I should see the doctor. Next day I applied to see him and I was taken to him.

I then requested him to order for all Indians ghee in place of fat. The Chief Warder was present and he added that Gandhi's request was not proper. Till then many Indians had used both fat and meat. Those who objected to fat were given dry rice, which they ate without any objection. Passive resisters had also done so, and when they were released they left with added weight.

The doctor asked me what I had to say to that? I replied that I could not quite swallow the story, but, speaking for myself, I should spoil my health if I were compelled to take rice without ghee.

"For you specially," he replied, "I would order bread to be given."

"Thank you," I said; "but I had not applied for myself alone, and I would not be able to take the bread for myself alone until ghee was ordered to be given to all the others." "Very well," said the doctor, "then you should not find fault with me now."

I again petitioned the authorities and came to learn that the food regulations would ultimately be made as in Natal. I criticized that also and gave the reasons why I could not for myself alone accept the ghee. At last, when about a month and a half had passed, I got a reply stating that, wherever there were many Indians prisoners, ghee would invariably be given. Thus it might be said that after a month and a half I broke my fast, and for the last month I was able to take rice, ghee and bread. But I took no breakfast, and at noon, when mealie meal porridge was doled out, I could hardly take ten spoonfuls, as every day it was differently prepared. But I got good nourishment from the bread and rice, and so my health improved. I mention this because when I used to eat once only my health had broken down. I had lost all my strength, and for ten days I was suffering from severe headache. My chest had also shown symptoms of being affected.

Many passive resisters had been told by me that if they left jail with ruined health, they would be considered wanting in the right spirit. We must turn our prisons into palaces. So when I found my own health going wrong I felt apprehensive lest I should have to go to the hospital. It was to be remembered that I had not availed myself of the order for ghee made in my favour, so that there was really a chance of my health getting badly affected: but this did not apply in the case of others, as it was open to each individual prisoner, when he was in jail, to have some special order made in his favour, and thus preserve his health.

IMPRISONMENT

When my warder saw that I was fighting the Government about food, but obeying his own commands unreservedly, he changed his conduct towards me and allowed me to do as I liked. This removed my difficulties. He became so considerate that he scarcely allowed it to be seen that he ordered me to do anything at all. The man who succeeded him was like a Pasha, and he was always anxious to look after my conveniences.

"I love," said he, "those who fight for their community. I myself am such a fighter, and I do not consider you to be a convict." Thus he used to comfort me.

At last the bench, which was refused in the beginning, was sent to me by the Chief Warder himself. In the meantime I had received two religious books from General Smuts. From this I concluded that the hardships I had been obliged to undergo were due, not to his express orders, but to carelessness and indifference. The only object in isolating me appeared to be to prevent me from talking with others. After some trouble, I got permission for the use of a note-book and pencil.

Before I was taken to Pretoria, Mr. Lichtenstein had seen me with special permission. He had come to meet me on office business, but he asked me how my health was. Though at first I was not willing to answer him on that point, he persuaded me to do so. "I will not tell you all," I said to him, "but I will say this much, that they treat me cruelly. General Smuts by this means wants me to surrender; but that will never happen, as I am prepared to undergo whatever befalls me and my mind is at peace."

Mr. Lichenstein communicated this to Mr. Polak, who was not able to keep silent about it in his turn. He spoke to others about me. Mr. David Pollock thereupon wrote to Lord Selborne and an enquiry was held. The Chief Warder thereupon came to enquire from me and I spoke to him the very words I have just mentioned. I also pointed out the defects which I have already described. Thereupon, after ten days he allowed me to have a plank for a bed, a pillow, a night-shirt and a handkerchief. In my memorial to him I had asked him to provide this convenience for all Indians. Really speaking, in this respect the Indians are softer than the whites, and they cannot do without pillows.

The opinion I had come to, in consequence of my treatment in jail in the beginning, was confirmed by what happened now. About four days later I received a summons as a witness in Mr. Pillay's case. So I was taken to Court. I was manacled this time and the warder took no time in putting on the handcuffs. This, I believe, was done without any definite order. The Chief Warder had seen me and from him I obtained leave to carry a book with me. He seemed to be under the impression that I was ashamed of the manacles, and so I had asked permission to carry a book. Hence he asked me to hold the book in my hands in such a way that the handcuffs would be concealed. This made me smile, as I was feeling honoured in thus being manacled. The book that I was carrying was called *The Court of God is in the Mind*. I thought this a happy coincidence, because whatever hardships might trouble me externally, if I were to make God live in my heart, what should I care for them? Thus I was taken on foot, handcuffed, to Court.

In all the troubles given me I calmly acquiesced, with the result that not only was I able to remain calm and

IMPRISONMENT

quiet, but that the warder himself had to remove the handcuffs in the end. If I had opposed him, my strength of mind would have become weakened, and I could not have done the more important things that I had to do. In addition, I should have made the warder my enemy. My food difficulty also was solved at last because I passively resisted and underwent sufferings.

The greatest good I have derived from these sufferings was that by undergoing bodily hardships I could see my mental strength clearly increasing, and it is even now maintained. The experience of those months in prison left me more than ever prepared to undergo all such hardships with ease. I felt that God helps such conscientious objectors, and puts them to the test. He only burdens them with such suffering as they can bear.

Among the many benefits I received, one was the opportunity I got to read good books. At the start I must admit I fell into moods of despondency and anxiety while reading, and was even tired of these hardships, and my mind played antics like a monkey. Such a mental state leads many towards lunacy, but my books saved me. They made up a large measure for the loss of the society of my Indian companions. I always obtained about three hours a day to read.

In this way I was able to go through about thirty books, and to con over others. They comprised English, Hindi, Gujarati, Sanskrit and Tamil works. Out of these, I considered Tolstoy, Emerson and Carlyle worth mentioning. Tolstoy and Emerson related to religion. Tolstoy's books are so simple and easy to study that any man can study and profit by them. Again, he is a man who practises what he preaches. Hence his writings inspire great confidence. I had borrowed a Bible from the jail and studied this also.

Carlyle's *French Revolution* is written in a very effective style. It made me understand that we could hardly learn from the European nations any remedy for the present miseries of India. I am of opinion that the French people have secured no special benefit by their Revolution. This was what Mazzini thought also.

Swami Sankarananda had sent me Gujarati, Hindi and Sanskrit books. These gave me much food for thought. The Upanishads produced in me great peacefulness of mind. One sentence specially has struck me. It means, "Whatever you do, you should do the same for the good of the soul." The words are of great importance and deserve great consideration.

But I derived the greatest satisfaction of all from the writings of Kavi Shri Rajchandra. In my opinion they are such as should attract universal belief and popularity. His life was exemplary and as high as Tolstoy's. I had studied carefully some passages from Sr. Rajchandra's books and also from the Sandhya book.[1] These I learnt by heart and repeated them at night while lying awake. Every morning also for half an hour I used to think over them, and repeat them by heart. This kept my mind in a state of cheerfulness night and day. If disappointment or despair attacked me at times, I would think over what I had read. My heart would instantly become gladdened and thankful to God. Let me say briefly that in this world good books make up for the absence of good companions. Therefore all Indians, who want to live happily in jail, should accustom themselves to reading good books.

[1] Evening prayers.

IMPRISONMENT

What the Tamils achieved in this struggle no other Indian community accomplished. For that reason, if for no other, I thought that to show my sincere gratitude to them, I should seriously read their Tamil books. So I spent my last days in jail in attentively studying their language. The more I studied it the more I felt its wonderful beauties. It is a very sweet language, and from its construction and from all that I have read about it I can see that the Tamils have counted among their own people many highly-gifted and wise authors and men of saintly religious life. If there is to be one nation in India, those who live outside the Madras Presidency must seek to know Tamil.

CHAPTER XII

THE ATTEMPTED SETTLEMENT

ON THIS FIRST occasion of our imprisonment we had only been in jail for a fortnight when fresh arrivals brought news that some negotiations were going on with the Transvaal Government about a compromise. After two or three days Mr. Albert Cartwright, the editor of *The Leader*, a Johannesburg paper, came in to see me.

All the daily papers which were then being conducted in Johannesburg were the property of one or other of the European owners of the gold mines. But except where the interests of these magnates were at stake, the editors were left unfettered in the expression of their own views on all public questions. Only very able and well-known men were selected as editors. For instance, the editor of the *Daily Star* had formerly been private secretary to Lord Milner. He went to England to take Mr. Buckle's place as editor of *The Times*. Mr. Albert Cartwright of *The Leader* was as broad-minded as he was able. He had almost always supported the Indian cause in his columns. He and I had become good friends. After I was sent to jail he had gone to see General Smuts.

General Smuts welcomed his mediation in the struggle. Mr. Cartwright therefore met the Indian leaders who had not yet been imprisoned. "We know nothing," they said to him, "about legal matters, and cannot possibly talk about compromise so long as Gandhi is in jail. We desire a settlement, but if the Government wants it while

THE ATTEMPTED SETTLEMENT

our men are in jail you should see Gandhi. We will ratify any arrangement which he accepts."

Mr. Cartwright thus came to see me and brought with him terms of settlement drafted or approved of by General Smuts. I did not like the vague language of the document, but was prepared myself to put my signature to it with only one alteration. But I informed Mr. Cartwright that I could not sign it without consulting my fellow prisoners, even if I took the consent of Indians outside prison for granted.

The substance of the proposed settlement was that the Indians should register voluntarily, and not under any law; that the details to be entered upon the new certificates of registration should be settled by Government in consultation with the Indian community, and that if the majority of Indians underwent voluntary registration, Government should repeal the Black Act, and take steps with a view to legalizing the voluntary registration. The Draft did not make quite clear the clause which required Government to repeal the Black Act. I therefore suggested a change calculated to place this beyond all doubt from my own standpoint.

Mr. Cartwright did not like even this little addition to the draft he brought with him. "General Smuts," said he, "considered this draft to be final and I have approved of it myself. I can assure you, that if you all undergo the voluntary registration, the Black Act will be repealed."

"Whether or not there is a settlement," I answered, "we shall always be grateful to you for your kindness. I should not like to suggest a single unnecessary alteration in the Draft. I do not object to such language as might uphold the prestige of the Government. But where I myself am doubtful about the meaning I must certainly suggest a change of language. If there is to be a settlement, both the parties must have the right to alter the Draft. General Smuts ought not to confront us with an ultimatum, saying that these terms are final. He has already aimed one pistol in the shape of the Black Act at us. What can he hope to gain by aiming a second?"

Mr. Cartwright had nothing to say against this argument and promised to place my suggestion before General Smuts.

I consulted my fellow prisoners. They too did not like the language, but agreed to the settlement if General Smuts accepted the draft with my amendments. Newcomers to jail brought a message from the Indian leaders outside that I should accept any suitable compromise without waiting for their consent. I got Messrs. Leung, Quinn, and Thambi Naidoo to sign the amended Draft along with myself and handed it to Mr. Cartwright.

On January 30, 1908, Mr. Vernon, the Superintendent of Police, Johannesburg, took me to Pretoria to meet General Smuts, with whom I had a good deal of talk. He told me what had passed between him and Mr. Cartwright. He congratulated me on the Indian community having remained firm even after my imprisonment. "I could never entertain," he said, "a dislike for your people. You know I too am a barrister. I had some Indians as fellow students in my time. But I must do my duty. The Europeans want this law, and you will agree with me that these are for the most part not Boers but Englishmen. I accept the alteration you have suggested in the Draft. I have consulted General Botha also, and I assure you that I will repeal the Asiatic Act as soon as most of you have undergone registration. When the Bill legalizing such voluntary registration is drafted, I will send you a copy for your criticism. I do not wish there to be any recurrence of the trouble, and I wish to respect the feelings of your people."

So saying, General Smuts rose. I asked him, "Where am I to go, and what about the other prisoners?"

The General laughed. "You are free," he said, "this very moment. I am telephoning the prison officials to release the other prisoners to-morrow morning. But I must advise you not to go in for any demonstrations, as in that case Government will find itself in a very awkward position."

"You may rest assured," I replied, "that there will not be a single meeting simply for the sake of a meeting. But I will certainly have to hold meetings in order to explain to the community how the settlement was effected, what is its true nature and scope, and how it has added to our responsibilities."

"You may have as many of such meetings as you please," said General Smuts, laughing. "It is sufficient that you have understood what I desire in this matter."

It was then seven o'clock in the evening. I had not a single farthing in my pocket. General Smuts' secretary gave me the railway fare to Johannesburg. There was no need to stop at Pretoria and announce the settlement to the Indians there. The leaders were all in Johannesburg, which was our headquarters. There was now only one more train to Johannesburg, and I was able to catch it.

I reached Johannesburg at about 9 p.m. and went direct to the Chairman, Sheth Essop Mia. He knew that I had been taken to Pretoria, and therefore was rather expecting me. Nevertheless, it was a pleasant surprise for him and the others to find me unaccompanied by a warder. I suggested that a meeting should be called at once, with such attendance as was possible at a very short notice. The Chairman and other friends agreed with me. As most of the Indians lived in the same quarter, it was not difficult to send round notice of the proposed meeting.

The Chairman's house was near the Mosque, and meetings were usually held in the grounds of the Mosque. There was hence not much to be done by way of arrangement. It was enough to have one light on the platform. The meeting was held that very night at about midnight. In spite of the shortness of the notice and the late hour, the audience numbered nearly a thousand.

Before the meeting was held, I had explained to the leaders present the terms of the settlement. A few opposed the settlement. But all of them understood the situation after they had heard me. They were, however, troubled by one doubt. "What if General Smuts broke faith with us?" they asked. "The Black Act might not then be enforced, but it would always hang over our heads. If in the meanwhile we were to register voluntarily, we should have knowingly played into the hands of our adversary, and surrendered the most powerful weapon in our possession for resisting the Act. The right order for the settlement is that the Act should be repealed first and then we should be called to register voluntarily."

I liked this argument. I felt proud of the keen common sense and high courage of those who advanced it, and saw that such was the stuff which Satyagrahis are made of. "It is an excellent argument," I answered, "and deserves serious consideration. It would obviously be best for all if we were to register voluntarily only after the Act is repealed. But then it would not be in the nature of a compromise. Compromise means that both parties make concessions except where a principle is involved. Our own principle is that we should not submit to the Black Act. To this principle we must adhere at all costs.

"On the other hand, the principle with Government is, that in order to prevent the illegal entry of Indians into the Transvaal, it must get as many as possible to take out non-transferable permits with marks of identification and thus set the suspicion of the Government at rest. They can never give this up. We have admitted this principle of the Government by our conduct up to date, and therefore even if we feel like resisting we may not do so until we find fresh grounds for such a departure. Our struggle aimed, not at the denial of this principle, but at removing the stigma which the Black Act sought to attach to the community. If, therefore, we now utilize the new force which has sprung up in the community for gaining a fresh point, this would ill become us, who claim to be Satyagrahis. So we cannot justly object to the present settlement.

"As for the argument that we must not surrender our weapons before the Act is repealed, it is easily answered. A Satyagrahi bids good-bye for ever to fear. He is therefore never afraid of trusting his opponent. Even if the opponent plays him false twenty times, the Satyagrahi is ready to trust him for the twenty-first time; for an implicit trust in human nature is his creed. To say that in trusting the Government we play into their hands is to betray ignorance of our principles. Suppose we register voluntarily, but the Government fails to repeal the Act. Could we not then resort at once to Satyagraha? We could refuse to show at the proper time the certificates of registration we take out, and then our registration would count for nothing. The Government cannot exercise any control over us without our own active co-operation.

"We are fearless and free, so long as we have the weapon of Satyagraha in our hands. And if anyone thinks that the community will not be as strong afterwards as it is to-day, he is not a real Satyagraha nor has he any true understanding of Satyagraha. For this would imply that the present strength of the community is not real strength, but only a momentary effervescence or intoxication. If that were really true, then we do not deserve to win; and even if we did win, the fruits of victory would slip out of our hands.

"Last of all, suppose the Government first repeals the Act and then we register voluntarily. The Government might still re-enact the same obnoxious law later. What would prevent the Government from pursuing such a course of action except our own strength? If we are doubtful about their strength to-day, then we should be in an equally bad case in such a contingency as I have described. So the community really gains by the compromise. And I am of opinion that when our opponents recognize our modest reasonableness and sense of justice, they will give up their opposition."

I was thus able fully to satisfy the one or two out of the small company collected who struck a discordant note, but I did not even then dream of the storm which was to break out at the midnight meeting. I explained to those present all the terms of the settlement.

"The responsibility of the community," I said, "is largely enhanced by this settlement. We have to register voluntarily in order to show that we do not intend to bring a single Indian into the Transvaal by fraud. If any of us fails to register, he will not be punished at present: but that can only mean that the community does not accept the settlement. It is necessary, indeed, that you should here raise your hands as a mark of your agreeing to the settlement, but that is not enough. As soon as the arrangements for fresh registration are completed, every one of us who raises his hand should take out a certificate of registration at once, and those of you who had volunteered before to explain to the community why they should not register, should now come forward to explain to our compatriots why they should register. It is only when we have thus worthily fulfilled our part that we shall reap the real fruit of victory."

As soon as I finished my speech, a Pathan friend stood up and greeted me with a volley of questions:

"Shall we have to give ten finger-prints under the settlement?"

"Yes and no," I replied; "my own view is that we should give finger impressions without the least hesitation. But those who have any conscientious objection to giving them, or think it contrary to their self-respect, will not be obliged to give them."

"What will you do yourself?" the Pathan friend asked.

"I have decided to give ten finger-prints," I replied. "It would not be right for me to refuse to give them while advising you to do so."

"You were writing a good deal about the ten finger-prints," he said. "It was you who told us that they were required only from criminals. It was you who said that the struggle was about the finger-prints. How do you account for this?"

"Even now," I replied, "I fully adhere to everything I have written about the finger-prints. Even now I say that in India finger-prints are required from criminal tribes. I have said before and say again to-day that it would be a sin in face of the Black Act to give even our signatures, not to speak of our finger-prints. It is true that I have laid great stress on this point about the finger-prints. It was much easier to rouse the community by reference to such a new and startling feature of the Act as the finger-prints than by referring to minor points. But circumstances have now changed, and I say with all force at my command that what would have been a crime yesterday is to-day the hall-mark of a gentleman."

"We have heard," he shouted, "that you have betrayed the community and sold it to General Smuts for £15,000. We shall never give the finger-prints, nor allow others to do so. I swear, with Allah as my witness, that I will kill the man who takes the lead in applying for registration."

"I can understand," I said, "the feelings of my Pathan friends. I am sure no one else believes me capable of betraying the community. The thing is too absurd! I have already said that finger-prints will not be demanded from those who have sworn not to give them. I will render all possible help to any Pathan who wishes to register without giving finger-prints, and I assure him that he will get the certificate without violence being done to his conscience. I must confess, however, that I do object to this threat of death which my friend has held out. I also believe that one may not swear to kill another in the name of the Most High. I therefore take it that it is only in a momentary fit of passion that this friend has taken the oath. However that may be, whether or not he carries out his threat, it is my clear duty to take the lead in giving the finger-prints, and I pray to God that He will graciously permit me to do so."

It is perhaps necessary to explain why those questions were asked. Although no feelings of hatred were entertained against those who had submitted to the Black Act, their action had been condemned in strong terms on the public platform as well as in *Indian Opinion*. Life with them, therefore, was anything but pleasant just then. They never imagined that the community would stand firm and make such a display of strength as to bring the Government to surrender. But when so many Satyagrahis were already in prison and there was talk about a settlement, it was too much for them to endure. There were among them some who even wished that there should be no settlement at all.

Only a few Pathans lived in the Transvaal. Their total number hardly exceeded fifty. Some of them had come over as soldiers during the Boer War and they had settled in the country like many other Indians as well as Europeans who came over as soldiers.

Some of them were my clients, and I was familiar with them. The Pathans are an unsophisticated and credulous race. Brave they are, as a matter of course. To kill and get killed is but an ordinary thing in their eyes. If they are angry with a man, they will thrash him and sometimes even kill him. In these matters they are no respecters of persons. They will behave even to a blood brother in the same way. Even though there were so few of them in the Transvaal, there used to be a free fight every time they quarrelled among themselves, and in such cases I had often acted the part of peacemaker.

A Pathan's anger becomes particularly uncontrollable when he is dealing with anyone whom he takes to be a traitor. When he seeks justice he seeks it only through personal violence. These Pathans had fully participated in the Satyagraha struggle; none of them had submitted to the Black Act. Thus it was an easy thing to mislead them. It was quite possible to create a misunderstanding in their minds about the finger-prints and thus inflame them. This single suggestion, that I must be a traitor, was enough to poison their minds.

Again, there was another party in the Transvaal which was made up of those Indians who had entered the Transvaal by fraud or else were interested in bringing others in secretly, either without a permit or with a false permit. This party knew that any settlement would be detrimental to their interests. As long as the struggle lasted none had to produce his permit and therefore they could carry on their trade without fear and easily avoid going to jail. The longer the struggle lasted, the better for them. Thus this clique also might have instigated opposition among the Pathans.

The Pathan's objections did not make any impression on the meeting. I had asked for a vote on the settlement. The president and others of the leaders were firm. The president made a speech explaining the nature of the settlement and dwelling upon the necessity for endorsing it. He then proceeded to ascertain the sense of the meeting, which unanimously ratified the settlement, with the exception of a couple of Pathans present.

I reached home at about three o'clock in the early morning. Sleep was out of the question, because I had to rise early and go to the jail in order to get the others released. I reached the jail at seven o'clock. The Superintendent had already received the necessary orders on the telephone. He was only waiting for me to arrive. All the Satyagrahi prisoners were released. The Chairman and other Indians were present to welcome them, and from jail all of us proceeded to the place of meeting. That day and a couple of subsequent days were passed in feasting and educating the community on the settlement.

With the lapse of time, if on the one hand the implications of the settlement became clearer, on the other hand misunderstandings began to thicken. I have already discussed the chief causes of misunderstanding. The letter I had written to General Smuts was also open to misrepresentation. The difficulty I experienced in answering various objections was infinitely greater than what I had felt while the struggle actually progressed. In the days of struggle, troubles are difficulties only experienced in our relations with the adversary, and these are easily overcome. But when the fight is over, internal jealousies arise and many take to the easy task of picking holes in what has been accomplished. It is only in the fitness of things, where a democratic basis is aimed at, to provide satisfactory answers for the questions of everyone, great and small. There is a sort of intoxication in fighting the adversary. But misunderstandings between friends are painful. Yet it is only on such occasions that moral courage is put to the real test. Such has been my experience without any exception. Only when passing through such ordeals have I understood the real nature of any struggle.

The Registrar of Asiatics was soon ready to issue registration certificates under the new settlement. The form of the certificates was altogether changed. It had been decided in consultation with the Satyagrahis.

On the morning of February 10, 1908, some of us got ready to take out our registration certificates. The supreme necessity of getting through this business with all possible speed had been fully impressed on the community. It had been agreed that the leaders should be the first to take out the certificates on the very first day of issue.

When I reached my office, which was also the headquarters of the Satyagraha Association, I found Mir Alam and his companions standing outside the premises. Mir Alam was an old client of mine who used to seek my advice in all his affairs. Many Pathans in the Transvaal employed labourers to manufacture straw or coir mattresses, which they sold at a good profit, and Mir Alam did the same. He was over six feet in height and of a large and powerful build. To-day for the first time I saw him standing outside my office instead of inside. Although his eyes met mine, he refrained from saluting me. So I saluted him. Then only he saluted me in return. As usual I asked him, "How do you do?" and my impression is that he answered me politely. But he did not have his usual smile. I noticed his angry eyes and took mental note of the fact. From this, I felt instinctively that something was going to happen. The Chairman,

THE ATTEMPTED SETTLEMENT

Sheth Essop Mia, and other friends arrived, and we set out for the registration office. Mir Alam and his companions followed us.

The Registration Office was at Von Brandis Square. As we were going along Von Brandis Street, outside Arnot and Gibson's premises, not more than three minutes' walk from the Registration Office, Mir Alam accosted me abruptly.

"Where are you going?" he asked.

"I am going," I said, "to take out a registration certificate and I am going to give my ten finger-prints. If you will come with me, I will first get a certificate for you also with an impression only of the two thumbs. Then I will take one out for myself, giving the finger-prints."

I had scarcely finished the last sentence when a heavy cudgel descended on my head from behind. I at once fainted with the words "*Ai Rama!*" ("Oh, God"), and fell prostrate on the ground. After that, I had no notion at all of what followed. But Mir Alam and his companions gave me more blows and also kicks, some of which were warded off by Essop Mia and Thambi Naidoo, with the result that they too became the target for attack in their turn. The noise attracted to the scene some Europeans passing by. Mir Alam and his companions fled, but were caught by the Europeans. The police arrived in the meanwhile and took them into custody. I was picked up unconscious and carried into Mr. J. C. Gibson's office. When I regained consciousness, I saw the Rev. J. Doke bending over me.

"How do you feel?" he asked anxiously, as I lay there.

"All right," I replied, "but there is pain in the teeth and in the ribs. Where is Mir Alam?"

"He has been arrested along with the rest," he replied.

"They must be released," I urged quickly.

"Well and good," said Mr. Doke; "but here you are, lying here, with your lip and face badly lacerated. The police are ready to take you to hospital. But if only you will go with me to my home, Mrs. Doke and I will minister to your needs."

"Oh yes," I replied. "Do please take me to your home. Thank the police; but tell them I will go with you."

So I was taken to the good clergyman's home in Smit Street and a doctor was called in at once. Mr. Chamney, the Registrar of Asiatics, arrived first and I asked him eagerly not to allow anyone to register before me.

"There is no hurry," he said. "The doctor will be here in a minute. Do please rest yourself, Gandhi, and then all will be well. I will give out the certificates, but I will keep a place vacant at the head of the list for you."

"No, no," I urged and entreated. "I am pledged to take out the first certificate, if I am alive to do so and if it is the will of God. The papers must be brought here."

Mr. Chamney, seeing my eagerness, in order to pacify me, went away to bring the papers.

The second thing for me to do at once was to get a telegram sent to the Attorney-General saying that I did not hold Mir Alam and others guilty for the assault committed upon me, and that in any case I did not wish them to be prosecuted but hoped that they would be discharged for my sake.

Dr. Thwaites, who had been summoned to attend me, came in while Mr. Chamney was away. He examined the injuries and stitched up the wounds in the cheek and on the upper lip. He prescribed what was to be applied to the ribs and enjoined silence upon me so long as the stitches remained in my cheek and lip. He also restricted my diet to liquids only. None of the injuries, he said, was serious, and he hoped that I should be able to leave my bed in about a week. But I must be careful not to undertake any physical strain for two months or even more.

Thus any power of speech was forbidden me, but I was still master of my hands. So I addressed a short note to the Indian community through the Chairman, as follows:

"Dear friends, I am well and am now in the brotherly and sisterly hands of Mr. and Mrs. Doke. I hope to take up my duties again shortly.

"Those who have committed the act did not know what they were doing. They thought that I was committing a crime. They had their redress in the only manner they knew. I therefore request that no steps be taken against them.

"Seeing that the assault was committed by a Musalman or Musalmans, the Hindus might feel hurt. But if this happens, they will put themselves in the wrong before the world and their Maker. Rather let the blood spilt to-day cement the two religious communities indissolubly together—such is my heartfelt prayer. May God grant it!

"Assault or no assault, my advice remains the same. The majority of Asiatics ought to give their finger-prints. Those who have conscientious scruples will be exempted by the Government. To ask for more would be to show ourselves acting as children.

"The spirit of Satyagraha rightly understood makes

the people fear no one except God. No cowardly fear therefore should deter the vast majority of sober-minded Indians from doing their duty. The promise to repeal the Act having been given to us, it is the sacred duty of every good Indian to help the Government and the Colony to the uttermost."

Mr. Chamney returned bringing with him the papers, and I gave him my finger-prints, but not without pain. I saw then that there were tears in Mr. Chamney's eyes. I had often occasion to write bitterly against him, but this showed me how a man's heart may be softened by events.

With regard to the assault itself, I found out later that the Europeans of Johannesburg had addressed a strong letter to the Attorney-General, saying that whatever views Gandhi might hold, as regards the punishment of criminals, they could not be given effect to in South Africa. Gandhi himself might not take any steps, but the assault was committed on the high road and was therefore a public offence. Several Englishmen were in a position to tender evidence and the offenders must be prosecuted. Thereupon the Attorney-General re-arrested Mir Alam and one of his companions, who were sentenced to three months' hard labour. But I was not summoned as a witness.

The Rev. J. Doke and his good wife were anxious that I should be at rest. They were therefore pained that I should have had to undergo such mental activity after the assault and they feared that it might react upon my health. By means of making signs and similar devices, they removed all persons from near my bed, and asked me not to write or do anything at all. I made one request in writing, that in order that I might lie down quietly, their daughter Olive, who was then only a little girl, should sing for me my favourite English hymn, *Lead, kindly light*.

Mr. Doke liked this very much and acceded to my request with a smile. He called his daughter Olive and asked her to stand at the door and sing the hymn in a low tone. The whole scene passes before my eyes and I can still almost hear little Olive's voice as she sang that hymn.

I cannot close this incident in my life, which left a very deep impression, without one reminiscence too sacred to be omitted. How shall I describe the service rendered to me by the Doke family?

Mr. Doke was a Baptist minister, then forty-six years old. He had been in New Zealand before he came to South Africa. Some six months before this assault, he came to my office and sent in his card. On seeing the word "Reverend" before his name, I wrongly imagined that he had come, as other clergymen did, to convert me to Christianity or to advise me to give up the struggle, or perhaps to express patronizing sympathy with the movement. Mr. Doke entered. We had not talked many minutes before I saw how sadly I had misjudged him, and mentally apologized to him. I found that he was familiar with all the facts of the struggle that were published in the newspapers.

"Please consider me," he said, "to be your friend in this struggle. I consider it my religious duty to render you such help as I can. If I have learnt any lesson from the life of Jesus it is this—that one should share and lighten the load of those who are weary and heavy laden."

We thus got acquainted with one another, and every time we met marked an advance in our mutual affection and intimacy.

Day and night, one or other member of the family would be waiting on me. The house became a sort of caravanserai so long as I stayed in it. All classes of Indians flocked to the place, from the humble hawker with basket in hand and dirty clothes and dusty boots right up to the Chairman of the Transvaal Indian Association. Mr. Doke would receive them all in his drawing-room with uniform courtesy and gentle consideration, and so long as I stayed with the Dokes, all their time was occupied either with nursing me or else receiving the hundreds of people who looked in to see me. Even at night Mr. Doke would quietly peep twice or thrice into my room. While living under his hospitable roof, I never so much as felt that it was not my home, or that my own dearest and nearest could have looked after me better than the Dokes.

And it must not be supposed that Mr. Doke had not to suffer for according public support to the Indians in their struggle and for harbouring me under his roof. Mr. Doke was in charge of a Baptist Church, and depended for his livelihood upon the congregation of Europeans, not all of whom entertained liberal views and among whom dislike of the Indians was perhaps as general as among other Europeans. But Mr. Doke was unmoved by it. I had discussed this delicate subject with him in the very beginning of our acquaintance.

"My dear friend," he explained to me, "what do you think of the religion of Jesus? I claim to be a humble follower of Him who cheerfully mounted the Cross for the faith that was in Him, and whose love was as wide as the world. I must take a public part in your struggle, if I am at all desirous of representing Christ to the Europeans, who, you are afraid, will give me up as punishment for it. I must not complain if they do thus give me up. My livelihood is indeed derived from them, but you certainly do not think that I am associated with them merely for living's sake, or that they are my cherishers. My cherisher is God; they are but the instruments of His Almighty will. It is one of the unwritten conditions of my connection with them, that none of them may interfere on my account. I am taking my place beside you in this struggle not to oblige the Indians but as a matter of duty. The fact, however, is that I have fully discussed this question with my Deacon. I gently informed him that if he did not approve of my relations with the Indians he might permit me to retire and engage another Minister instead. But he not only asked me not to trouble myself about it but even spoke some words of encouragement. Again, you must not imagine that all Europeans alike entertain hatred against your people. You can have no idea of the silent sympathy of many with your tribulations, and you will agree with me that I must know about it, situated as I am."

About ten days afterwards I had recovered enough strength to move about, and then I took my leave of this godly family. The parting was a great wrench to myself no less than to the Dokes.[1]

[1] For a further account of Mr. Doke see *Mahatma Gandhi's Ideas*, pp. 77-83. I have ventured to repeat sentences already quoted in this volume.

CHAPTER XIII

HELPERS IN THE STRUGGLE

JUST AS I HAD Indians living with me as members of my family, so I had English friends living with me both in Durban and Johannesburg. Not all of those who lived with me liked it. But I persisted in having them. Nor was I wise in every case. I had some bitter experiences, but these included both Indians and Europeans. I do not regret the experiences. In spite of the inconvenience and worry that I have often caused to my friends, I have not altered my conduct and they have borne with me. I hold that believers who have to see the same God in others, whom they see in themselves, must be able to live together with sufficient detachment. The ability to live together can be cultivated, not by fighting shy of unsought opportunities for such contacts, but by hailing them in a spirit of service and at the same time keeping oneself unaffected by them.

I received two Englishmen who had come from Johannesburg. These English friends often caused my wife bitter tears. Unfortunately, she has had many such trials on my account. But this was the first time that I had asked English friends to live with me intimately as members of my own family. I had stayed in English houses during my days in England; but there I had conformed to their ways of living. It was more or less like living in a boarding-house. Here it was different. The English friends became members of my own family. They adopted the Indian style in many matters. Though the arrangements of the house were in the Western fashion, the internal life was for the most part Indian. I do remember having some difficulty in keeping them as members of the family, but I can certainly say that they had no difficulty in making themselves perfectly at home under my roof. In Johannesburg these contacts developed further than in Durban.

Mr. Albert West's intimate association with me dated from some time before the Transvaal struggle. When I opened my office in Johannesburg my wife was not with me. I had received a cable from South Africa and suddenly left India, expecting to return home within a year, and so I was living alone. Mr. West frequented the vegetarian restaurant in Johannesburg, where I regularly had my meals both morning and evening, and we thus became acquainted with each other. He was conducting a printing press in partnership with another European. In 1904, a virulent form of bubonic plague broke out among the Indians in Johannesburg location.[1] I was fully engaged in nursing the patients, and so my visits to the vegetarian restaurant became irregular. Even when I went there to take my food, I used to have my meals served before the other guests in order to avoid any possible danger of infection. Albert West became anxious when he did not find me there, because he had read in the newspapers that I was attending to the plague patients. On the third day, at six o'clock in the morning, I was preparing to go out to the location when he knocked at my door. On opening it, I saw him with his beaming face.

"I am so glad to see you," he exclaimed with relief.

[1] See *Mahatma Gandhi: His Own Story*, p. 155.

"I had been worrying about you. Please tell me if I can do anything for you."

"Will you nurse the patients?" I asked, more in joke than in earnest.

"Why not? I am quite ready," he replied.

Meanwhile I had thought out my plans. "No other answer," said I, "could be expected of you. But there are already many who can help with the nursing. Besides, I propose to put you to still harder work. Mandanjit is here, on plague duty, and there is no one to look after *Indian Opinion*. If you go to Durban and take charge of the press, it will be really a great help. I cannot, of course, offer you any tempting terms. Ten pounds a month and half the profits, if any, is all I can afford."

"That is rather a tough job," he said. "I must have my partner's permission and then there are some dues to be collected. But never mind. Will you wait till the evening for my final answer?"

"Very well," I replied, "let us meet in the park at six o'clock."

So we met in the evening. Mr. West had obtained the permission of his partner. He entrusted me with the recovery of the dues, and left for Durban by the evening train the next day. In a month I had his report that not only was the press not making any profit at all, but it was actually a losing concern. There were large arrears to be collected and the books were badly kept. Even the list of names and addresses of the subscribers was incomplete. There was also mismanagement in other respects. Mr. West did not write all this as a matter of complaint. As he did not care for profit, he assured me that he would not give up what he had undertaken. But he gave me clearly to understand that *Indian Opinion* would not be paying its way for a long time to come.

Mandanjit had come to Johannesburg to canvass subscribers for the paper as well as to confer with me as regards the management of the press. Every month I had to meet a small or large deficit, and I was desirous of having a more definite idea of my possible liabilities. Mandanjit had no idea of the printing press business, and I had been thinking, since the beginning, that it would be well to associate a trained hand with him. The plague broke out in the meantime, and as Mandanjit was just the man for this crisis, I put him to nursing. So I closed with West's unexpected offer and told him that I would like him to go on not merely during the time the epidemic lasted, but for good.

Both the paper and the press had been removed to Phoenix, and West became a member of our community, drawing a monthly allowance of £3, instead of £10 as previously arranged. He was himself fully agreeable to all these changes. I never observed in him the least anxiety about the ways and means of maintaining himself. I recognized in him a deeply religious spirit, although he was not a student of religion. He was a man of perfectly independent temperament. He would say what he thought about all things, and would not hesitate to call a spade a spade. He was quite simple in habits.

When we first met he was unmarried, and I know that he lived a life of spotless purity. Some years later he went to England to see his parents and returned a married man. By my advice he brought with him his wife, his mother-in-law and unmarried sister, who all lived in great simplicity and in every way became fellow members with the Indians at Phoenix. Miss Ada West (or Devi Behn, as we used to call her) has remained unmarried and leads a most pious life. She too rendered to the pioneers at Phoenix services of no mean order. At one time or another she looked after the little children, taught them English, cooked in the common kitchen, swept the houses, kept accounts, and did composing work in the press. Whatever task came to her she never hesitated in doing it. She is not now in Phoenix, but that is because, since my return to India, the press has been unable to meet even her small personal expenditure.

Mr. West's mother-in-law is now nearly ninety years old. She is still a fine hand at sewing, and she used to help the settlement with her skill at tailoring. Everyone in Phoenix called her "Granny" and felt that she was really thus related to him. Mrs. West proved in every way worthy of her husband. When members of the Phoenix settlement were in jail, the Wests along with Maganlal Gandhi took over the whole management of the institution. West would see to the press and the paper, and, in the absence of others and myself, would dispatch to Gokhale the cables which were to be sent from Durban. When West was arrested (though he was soon released), Gokhale at once got nervous and sent over Andrews and Pearson to South Africa.

Then there was Mr. Ritch, about whom I have already written. He had joined my office before the struggle and proceeded to England for the Bar, with a view to filling my place when I was not available. He was the moving spirit of the South African British Indian Committee in London.

The third was Mr. Henry Polak, whose acquaintance

also, like that of Mr. West, I casually made in the restaurant. He left at once the sub-editorship of the *Transvaal Critic* and joined the staff of *Indian Opinion*. Everyone knows how he went to India and to England in connection with the Satyagraha struggle. I called Polak from Phoenix to Johannesburg, where he became my articled clerk and then a full-fledged attorney. Later on he married. People in India are familiar with Mrs. Polak, who was a perfect helpmeet to her husband during the whole struggle. The Polaks did not see eye to eye with us in the later non-co-operation movement in India, but they are still serving India to the very best of their ability.

The next was Mr. Hermann Kallenbach, whom I also came to know before the struggle began. He is a German, and had it not been for the Great War, he would be in India to-day. He is a man of strong feelings, wide sympathies and child-like simplicity. By profession he is an architect, but there is no work, however lowly, which he would consider beneath him. When I broke up my Johannesburg Office I lived with him, but he would have been greatly hurt if I had offered to pay him my share of the household expenses; indeed, he would plead that I was responsible for a considerable saving in his own domestic economy. This was indeed true. But this is not the place to describe my own personal relations with these friends. I am writing about them in their public capacity.

When we thought of accommodating the families of Satyagrahi prisoners in one place, Kallenbach gave us the use of his farm without rent. When Gokhale came to Johannesburg, the Indian community offered him their hospitality at Kallenbach's cottage, which our illustrious guest liked very much. Kallenbach went with me as far as Zanzibar to see Gokhale off. He was arrested along with Polak during the later Satyagraha movement and suffered imprisonment. Finally, when I left South Africa to see Gokhale in England, Kallenbach went with me. But when I returned to India from England, he was not permitted to go with me on account of the war. Like other Germans he was interned in England. When the war was over Kallenbach returned to Johannesburg and recommenced the practice of his profession as an architect. He is working there to-day.

Gokhale had a remarkable power of judging men. The voyage with him from Delagoa Bay to Zanzibar offered us a fine opportunity for quiet talks. He had come in contact with all the Indian and European leaders in South Africa. While minutely analysing for me the principal characters of the Satyagraha drama, he gave the pride of place among them all, Europeans as well as Indians, to Miss Schlesin. "I was astonished," he said, "to see how she sacrificed her all for the Indian cause without expecting any reward whatever. And when you add to this her great ability and energy, these qualities combine to make her a priceless asset to your movement. I need hardly tell you that you must cherish her."

Miss Dick was a Scottish lady working with me as a stenotypist who was a picture of loyalty and purity.[1] Many bitter experiences have been my portion in life; but I have also had the good fortune to claim as my associates a large number of Europeans and Indians of the highest character. Miss Dick left me when she mar-

[1] See *Mahatma Gandhi: His Own Story*, p. 150.

ried, and then Mr. Kallenbach introduced Miss Schlesin to me. "She has been entrusted to me," he said, "by her mother. She is clever and honest, but she is very mischievous and impetuous. Please keep her with you if you can control her."

Miss Schlesin soon made me familiar with the mischievous side of her nature. But in a month's time she had achieved the conquest of my heart by her complete disregard of her own individual comforts and her high standards of work. She was ready to work at all times, whether by day or night. There was nothing difficult or impossible for her.

Mr. Doke was then in charge of *Indian Opinion*. But even he, hoary-headed veteran as he was, would get the articles he wrote for *Indian Opinion* passed by Miss Schlesin. He once told me, "If Miss Schlesin had not been there, I do not know how I could have satisfied even my own self with my work."

Pathans, Patels, ex-indentured men, Indians of all classes and ages surrounded her, sought her advice and followed it.

I feared, and Miss Schlesin hoped, that she might be arrested some day. But although the Transvaal Government were aware of her great ability, her mastery over the "strategy" of the movement, and the hold she had acquired over the Satyagrahis, they adhered to the policy and the chivalry of not arresting her.

Herbert Kitchin was an English electrician with a heart pure as crystal. He worked with us during the Boer War and was for some time editor of *Indian Opinion*. His name will come up more than once in this narrative. His loyalty to the cause made him always ready for sacrifice.

The persons I have thus far mentioned could not be classed among the leading Europeans in the Transvaal who were well known to the general public.

The most influential of such helpers was Mr. Hosken, who held with distinction the post of President of the Association of Chambers of Commerce of South Africa and was a member of the Legislative Council of the Transvaal. He undertook the onerous task of Chairman of the Committee of European sympathizers with the Satyagraha movement. When the movement itself was in full swing, direct communication between Satyagrahis and the local Transvaal Government was obviously out of the question, not because of any objection on principle on the part of the Satyagrahis, but because the Transvaal Government would naturally refuse to deal with those whom they regarded as breakers of the law of the land. This Committee then acted as mediator between the Transvaal Indians and the Government.

I have already mentioned Mr. Albert Cartwright, the editor of *The Leader*. He helped us to the very best of his ability and acted as mediator, as I have described. Then there was the Rev. Charles Phillips, who joined and assisted us even as the Rev. J. J. Doke did. Mr. Phillips had long been a Congregational minister in the Transvaal. His good wife was of one mind with her husband and she too did us much service. The Rev. John Howard also rendered us great assistance, as did Mr. and Mrs. W. M. Vogl. Mr. Gabriel Isaac, a freelance Jewish friend, later cheerfully shared imprisonment with us.

A fourth clergyman who assisted us was the Reverend Dewdney Drew. He had given up his ministry in the Congregational Church in order to take the editorship of the Bloemfontein newspaper called *The Friend*. He constantly supported the Indian cause in his editorials in the teeth of much European opposition. As a speaker on the public platform, he was one of the best in South Africa.

One more spontaneous helper among the editors of the day was Mr. Vere Stent, the editor of the *Pretoria News*. A mass meeting of Europeans was once held in the Town Hall, Pretoria, under the presidency of the Mayor, in order to condemn the Indian movement and to support the Black Act. Mr. Vere Stent alone stood up in opposition to the overwhelming majority of anti-Indian Europeans who were present. He refused to sit down in spite of the President's orders. The Europeans threatened to lay hands on him, yet he stood unmoved and defiant like a lion and the meeting had to disperse at last without passing its resolution.

I have still to tell the story of three ladies, famous in South Africa, who were helpers in the struggle. One was Miss Hobhouse, the daughter of Lord Courtney, who at the time of the Boer War reached the Transvaal against the wishes of Lord Milner and moved single-handed among the Boer women, encouraging them to stand firm when Lord Kitchener set up his "concentration camps." She believed the English policy in respect of the Boer War to be wholly unrighteous, and therefore, like the late Mr. W. T. Stead, she wished and prayed to God for England's defeat. Having thus ministered to the Boers, she was shocked to learn that the same Boers, who had recently resisted injustice, were now led into doing injustice to the Indians through ignorant prejudice. The Boers looked upon her with deepest respect and affection. She was intimate with General Botha, and did her best to commend to the Boers the policy of repealing the Black Act.

The second was Miss Olive Schreiner. The name of Schreiner is one to conjure with in South Africa, so much so that when Miss Schreiner married, her husband adopted her name. This was not due to any false pride, as Miss Schreiner was as simple in habits and humble in spirit as she was learned. I had the privilege of her acquaintance. She knew no difference between the Bantu servants and herself. She was the author of *Dreams* and the *Story of a South African Farm*, yet she never hesitated to cook food, wash the pots or handle the broom. She held that such physical labour stimulated her literary ability and made for a sense of proportion in thought and language. This gifted lady lent to the Indian cause the whole weight of her influence over Europeans of South Africa.

The third was Miss Molteno, an aged member of that eminent family of South Africans, who also did her very best for the Indian cause in South Africa.

What was the result of all this sympathy among the Europeans? The work I have described bears witness to a portion of the result. The very nature of Satyagraha is such that the fruit of the movement is contained in the movement itself. Satyagraha is based on self-help, self-sacrifice and faith in God. One of my objects in enumerating the names of European helpers is to mark the Satyagrahis' gratefulness to them. The history would be justly considered incomplete without such mention. I have not tried to make the list exhaustive, but have tendered the Indians' thanks to all in selecting a few for special mention. Secondly, as a Satyagrahi, I hold to the faith that all activities pursued with a pure heart are bound to bear fruit, whether or not such fruit is visible to us. And last, but not least, I have tried to show that all truthful movements spontaneously attract to themselves every kind of pure and disinterested help. No other effort whatever was made during the struggle to enlist Europeans' sympathy beyond the effort, if effort it can be called, involved in adherence to truth and truth alone. The Europeans were attracted by the inherent power of the movement itself.

I was often on the move between the Transvaal and Natal in connection with my work. From letters of Natal friends I was aware that in Natal, too, the settlement had been grossly misunderstood. And I had received a sheaf of correspondence addressed to *Indian Opinion* in which adverse criticism was passed on the settlement. Although the Satyagraha struggle was still confined to Transvaal Indians, we had to seek the support of the Natal Indians also. The Transvaal struggle was not a mere local affair, and the Indians in the Transvaal struggle were really fighting the battle on behalf of all the Indians in South Africa. Therefore I had to go down to Durban to remove the misunderstanding prevalent there.

A public meeting of the Indians was called in Durban. Some of my friends had warned me beforehand that I would be attacked at this meeting and that I should therefore not attend, or take steps to defend myself. But neither of these two courses was open to me. If a servant when called by his master fails to respond through fear, he forfeits the title of servant. Nor does he deserve the name if he is afraid of his master's punishment. Service of the public for service's sake is like walking on the sword's edge. If a servant is ready enough for praise, he may not flee in the face of blame. I therefore presented myself at the meeting at the appointed time and explained to those assembled how the settlement had been effected, and also answered the questions put by the audience.

The meeting was held at eight o'clock in the evening. The proceedings were nearly over when a Pathan rushed to the platform with a big stick. The lights were put out at the same time. I grasped the situation at once. Sheth Daud Muhammad, the Chairman, stood up on the Chairman's table and tried to quell the disturbance. Some of those on the platform surrounded me to defend my person. The friends who feared an assault had come to the place prepared for what might happen. One of them had a revolver in his pocket and he fired a blank shot. Meanwhile Parsi Rustomji, who had noticed the gathering clouds, went with all possible speed to the police station and informed Superintendent Alexander, who sent a police party. The police made a passage for me through the crowd and took me to Parsi Rustomji's place.

The next day Parsi Rustomji brought all the Pathans of Durban together in the morning, and asked them to place before me all their complaints. I met them and tried to conciliate them, but with little success. They had a preconceived notion that I had betrayed the community, and until this poison was removed, it was useless to reason with them. The canker of suspicion cannot be cured by arguments or explanations.

I left Durban for Phoenix on the same day. The friends who had guarded me on the previous night would not let me go alone. They informed me that they intended to accompany me to Phoenix. "I cannot prevent you," I told them; "if you will insist on coming in spite of me. But Phoenix is a jungle. And what will you do if we, the only dwellers in it, do not give you even food?"

"That will not frighten us," was the reply. "We are well able to look after ourselves. And so long as we are a-soldiering, who is there to prevent us from robbing your pantry?" We thus made a merry party on our way to Phoenix.

The leader of the self-appointed guard was Jack Moodaley, a Natal-born Tamil well known among the Indians as a trained boxer. He and his companions believed that no man in South Africa, whether white or coloured, was a match for him in that branch of sport.

In South Africa, I had for many years been in the habit of sleeping in the open air at all times except when there was rain. I was not prepared to change this habit now, and the self-appointed guard decided to keep watch all night. Though I had tried to laugh these men out of their purpose, I must confess that I was weak enough to feel safer owing to their presence. I wondered if I could have slept with the same ease if the guard had not been there. Probably I should have been startled by some noise or other.

I believe that I have unflinchingly great faith in God. For many years I have accorded intellectual assent to the proposition that death is only a big change in life and nothing more, and should be welcomed as such whenever it arrives. I have deliberately made a supreme effort to cast out from my heart all fear whatever, including the fear of death. Still I remember occasions in my life when I have not rejoiced at the thought of approaching death as one might rejoice at the prospect of meeting a long-lost friend. Thus man often remains weak notwithstanding all his efforts to be strong. Knowledge which stops at the head and does not penetrate into the heart is of but little use in the critical times of living experience. Then again, the strength of the spirit within tends to evaporate when a person gets and accepts support from outside. A Satyagrahi must be always on his guard against such temptations.

While in Phoenix I did just one thing. I wrote a great deal with a view to removing misunderstandings about the compromise, including an imaginary dialogue for *Indian Opinion*, in which I dismissed in ample detail the objections advanced and the criticisms passed against the settlement. I believe that this dialogue produced a good effect. It was found that the Transvaal Indians, whose misunderstandings of the settlement, if persistent, would have led to really disastrous results, did not misinterpret me for long. It was only for the Transvaal Indians to accept or to reject the settlement. They were on their trial as well as myself, their leader and servant.

In the end there were hardly any Indians who did not register themselves voluntarily. There was such a rush of applications for registration that the officers concerned were hard pressed with work and in a very short time the Indians had fulfilled their part of the settlement. Even the Government had to admit this, and I could see that the misunderstandings, though of an acute nature, were quite limited in extent. There was no doubt a great deal of stir when some Pathans violently took the law into their own hands. But such violence, when analysed, often turns out to have no foundation and is only temporary.

Yet it is a power in the world to-day, and we are apt to be unnerved in the face of violence. If, however, we calmly think about it, we shall find that there is no reason for nervousness.

Suppose, for instance, that Mir Alam and his friends, instead of only wounding my body, had actually destroyed it. Suppose also that the community had remained calm and unperturbed and had forgiven the offenders, perceiving that according to their lights they could not have behaved otherwise than they did. Far from injuring the community, such a noble attitude would have greatly benefited them. All misunderstandings would have disappeared, and Mir Alam and party would have had their eyes opened to the error of their ways. As for me, nothing better can happen to a Satyagrahi than meeting death all unsought in the very act of Satyagraha, i.e. pursuing Truth. All these propositions are true only of a struggle like the Satyagraha movement. Here there is no room for hatred. Self-reliance is the order of the day. No one has to look expectantly at another, and there are no leaders and hence no followers. The death of a fighter, however eminent, makes not for slackness but, on the other hand, intensifies the struggle. Such is the pure and essential nature of Satyagraha, not realized in practice, because not every one of us has shed hatred. In actual practice the secret of Satyagraha is not understood by all, and the many are apt unintelligently to follow the few.

Again, the Transvaal struggle was the first attempt at applying the principle of Satyagraha to masses of men. I do not know of any historical example of pure mass Satyagraha. I cannot, however, formulate any definite opinion on that point, as my knowledge of history is limited. But, as a matter of fact, we have nothing to do with historical precedents. Granted the fundamental principles of Satyagraha, it will be seen that the consequences I have described are bound to follow as night follows day. It will not do to dismiss such a valuable force with the remark that it is difficult or impossible of application. Brute force has been ruling the world for thousands of years, and mankind has been reaping its bitter harvest all along, as he who runs may read. There is little hope of anything good coming out of it in the future. Therefore, if light can come out of darkness, then alone can love emerge from hatred.

I had no notion at first that I should have to invest my money in *Indian Opinion*, but I soon discovered that the paper could not go on without my financial help. The Indians and the Europeans both knew that though I was not nominally the editor of *Indian Opinion*, I was virtually responsible for its conduct. It would not have mattered if the journal had never been started, but to stop it after it had once been launched would have been both a loss and a disgrace. So I kept on pouring out money until ultimately I was practically sinking all my savings in it. I remember a time when I had to remit £75 each month.

But after all these years I feel that the journal has served the community well. It was never intended to be a commercial concern. So long as it was under my control, the changes in the journal were indicative of changes in my life. *Indian Opinion* in those days, like *Young India* and *Navajivan* to-day, was a mirror of my own life. Week after week I poured out my soul in its columns, and expounded the principles and practice of Satyagraha as I understood it. During ten years, that is, until 1914, excepting the intervals of my enforced rest in prison, there was hardly an issue of *Indian Opinion* without an article from me. I cannot recall a word of those articles set down without thought or deliberation, or a word of conscious exaggeration, or anything merely to please. Indeed, the journal had become for me a training in self-restraint, and for friends a medium through which to keep in touch with my thoughts. The critic found very little to which he could object. In fact, I know that the tone of *Indian Opinion* compelled the critic to put a curb on his own pen.

Satyagraha would probably have been impossible without *Indian Opinion*. The readers looked forward to it for a trustworthy account of the Satyagraha campaign as also of the real condition of Indians in South Africa. For me it became a means for the study of human nature in all its lights and shades, as I always aimed at establishing an intimate and clean bond between the editor and the readers. I was inundated with letters containing the outpourings of my correspondents' hearts. They were friendly, critical or bitter, according to the temper of the writer. It was a fine education for me to study, digest and answer all this correspondence. It was as though the community thought audibly through this correspondence with me. It made me thoroughly understand the responsibility of a journalist, and the hold I secured in this way over the community made the future campaign workable, dignified and irresistible.

In the very first month of *Indian Opinion* I had realized that the sole aim of journalism should be service. The newspaper press is a great power; but just as an unchained torrent of water submerges whole acres of land and devastates crops, even so an uncontrolled pen serves but to destroy. If the control is from without, it proves more poisonous than want of control. It can be profitable only when exercised from within. If this line of reasoning is correct, how many of the journals in the world would stand the test? But who should be the judge? The useful and the useless must, like good and evil, go on together and man must make his choice.

CHAPTER XIV

A BREACH OF FAITH

THE INDIANS REGISTERED voluntarily, to the satisfaction of the Transvaal Government. It only now remained for the Government to repeal the Black Act, and then the whole Satyagraha struggle for the time being would come to an end. This did not mean the repeal of all anti-Indian legislation in the Transvaal or the redress of all the Transvaal Indian grievances. The further constitutional struggle would have to be taken up later.

But this Satyagraha was directed solely against the one dark and ominous cloud on the horizon in the shape of the Black Act. If accepted by the Indians, this Black Act, when passed, would have utterly humiliated them and prepared the way for their final extinction, first in the Transvaal and then throughout the whole of South Africa. Thus the repeal of the Black Act was a matter of life and death to us all. But now instead of repealing it, as we had fully expected, General Smuts suddenly took a fresh step forward.

He maintained the Black Act on the statute-book in spite of his promise to me. He then introduced into the Transvaal Legislature a measure validating the voluntary Indian registration already effected and the certificates already issued subsequent to the date mentioned in the Black Act. In this way he took the holders of voluntary registration certificates out of its operation and made further provision for the registration of Asiatics. Thus there came into force two concurrent pieces of legislation with one and the same object in view. Freshly arriving Indians, as well as also later applicants for registration, were still subject to the Black Act. Only those who had already voluntarily registered were made exempt.

I was simply astonished when I read the new Bill. I did not know how I should be able to face the community. Here was excellent material for the Pathan friend who had severely criticized me at the midnight meeting in Johannesburg.

But far from shaking my faith in Satyagraha, this blow made it all the stronger. I called a meeting of our Satyagraha committee and explained the new situation to them in detail.

"There you are," said someone tauntingly to me. "Did we not expressly warn you of this? Why did you take no notice? We have told you again and again that you are too credulous. You believe everything that is said to you. It would not matter much if you were so hopelessly gullible in your private affairs, but you must surely realize that the community has to suffer for your credulity in public matters. It is very difficult now to rouse the same spirit of passive resistance and going to jail which our people had exhibited before. You know the stuff we Indians are made of. We are men whose momentary enthusiasm must be taken at the flood. If you neglect the tide, you are done for."

There was no bitterness in these taunting words. Such things had been addressed to me before on other occasions. "Well," I said with a smile, "what you call my credulity is part and parcel of myself. It is not credulity but trust. It is the duty of everyone of us to trust our fellow men. But even granting that it is a defect in me, you must take me as you find me with all my defects. I cannot concede that the enthusiasm of this community is a mere temporary effervescence. You must remember that you, as well as I, are members of the community. I should consider it an insult if you characterized my enthusiasm as effervescent.

"In a great struggle like ours there is always a tide and an ebb. However clear may be your understanding with the adversary, what is there to prevent him from breaking faith?

"There are many among us who pass promissory notes to others. What can be clearer and more free from doubt than a man's putting his signature to a document? Yet suits must be filed against them; they will oppose the suits and offer all kinds of defence. At last there are decrees and writs of attachment which take a long time to execute. Who can guarantee against the repetition of such flagrant behaviour? I would therefore advise you patiently to deal with the problem before us. We have to consider what we can do in case the struggle has to be resumed. Personally, I am inclined to think that if only we are true to ourselves, others will not be found wanting, and even if they are inclined to weakness, they will be strengthened by our example."

About this time Mr. Kachhalia began to show his mettle and come to the front. On every point he would announce his considered opinion in the fewest words possible and then stick to it through thick and thin. I do not remember a single occasion on which he betrayed weakness or doubt about the final result. A time came when Yusuf Mia was not ready to continue at the helm in troubled waters. We all with one accord acclaimed Kachhalia as our captain, and from that time forward to the end he held unflinchingly to his responsible post. He fearlessly put up with hardships which would have daunted almost any other man.

As the struggle advanced, there came a stage when going to jail was a perfectly easy task for some and a means of getting a well-earned rest, whereas it was infinitely more difficult to remain outside, minutely to look into things, to make various arrangements and to deal with all sorts and conditions of men.

At a later time in the struggle, the European creditors of Kachhalia caught him as in a noose. Many Indians are entirely dependent on European firms, which sell them lakhs of rupees worth of goods on credit on mere personal security. That Europeans should repose such trust in Indian traders is an excellent proof of the general honesty of Indian trade. Kachhalia likewise owed large sums of money to many European firms, which asked him at once to meet their dues. The firms gave Kachhalia to understand that they would not press him for immediate payment if he left the Satyagraha movement. But if he remained in it, they were afraid of losing their money, as he might be arrested any time by the Government, and therefore demanded immediate satisfaction in cash.

Kachhalia bravely replied that his participation in the struggle was his own personal affair, which had nothing to do with his trade. His religion, the honour of the community and his own self-respect were bound up in the struggle. He thanked his creditors for the support they had extended to him. Their money was perfectly safe with him, and as long as he was alive he would repay them in full at any cost. But if anything happened to him, his stock as well as the book debts owing to him were at their disposal. He therefore wished his creditors to continue to trust him as before.

This was a perfectly fair argument, and Kachhalia's firmness was an additional reason for his creditors continuing their trust in him, but on this occasion it failed to impress them. We can rouse from his slumbers a man who is really asleep, but not him who only makes pretence of sleep all the while he is awake. So it was with these European traders, whose sole object was to bring undue pressure to bear upon Kachhalia. Otherwise their money was perfectly safe.

A meeting of the creditors was held in my office on January 22, 1909. I told them clearly that the pressure to which they were subjecting Kachhalia was purely political and unworthy of merchants. They were incensed at my remark. I showed them Kachhalia's balance sheet and proved they could have their twenty shillings in the pound. Again, if the creditors wanted to sell the business to someone else, Kachhalia Sheth was ready to hand over the goods and the book debts to the purchaser. If this did not suit them, the creditors could take over the stocks in Kachhalia's shop at cost price. If any part of their dues still remained unsatisfied they were free to take over the book debts due to him sufficient to cover the deficit.

If they had agreed to this arrangement the European merchants would have had nothing to lose. I had on many occasions effected such arrangements with the creditors of some of my clients who were hard pressed. But the merchants at this juncture did not seek justice. They were out to bend Kachhalia. Kachhalia's firmness would not bend. Bankruptcy proceedings were instituted against him, and he was declared insolvent, though his estate showed a large access of assets over liabilities.

Far from being a blot on his escutcheon, this insolvency was perfectly honourable to him. It enhanced his prestige among the community, and all congratulated him on his firmness and courage. But such heroism is rarely met with. The man in the street cannot understand how insolvency can cease to be a disgrace and become an honour, but Kachhalia realized it at once.

Many traders had submitted to the Black Act merely from fear of insolvency. Kachhalia could have warded off insolvency if he had wished, not by leaving the struggle—that was out of the question—but by borrowing from his many Indian friends who would have gladly helped him out of this crisis. But it would not be becoming to him to save his trade by such means. The danger of being any day imprisoned he shared in common with all the Satyagrahis. It would therefore be hardly proper for him to borrow from a fellow Satyagrahi to pay the European creditors.

Again, we thought that if Kachhalia allowed himself to be declared an insolvent, his insolvency would serve as a shield for others; for if not in all, at least in an overwhelmingly large majority of cases of insolvency, the creditors stand to lose something. They are quite pleased if they realize ten shillings in the pound. They consider fifteen shillings almost as good as full payment.

A BREACH OF FAITH

For big traders in South Africa generally reap a profit not of 6 but of 25 per cent. As full payment is hardly ever realized from a bankrupt's estate, creditors are not anxious to reduce their debtors to a state of insolvency. As soon, therefore, as Kachhalia was declared insolvent, there was every likelihood that the European traders would cease to threaten other Satyagrahi traders who were their debtors. And that was exactly what happened. The Europeans wanted to compel Kachhalia either to give up the struggle or else to pay them in cash. They failed to achieve either object, and the actual result was the very reverse of what they had expected. They were dumbfounded by the first case of a respectable Indian trader welcoming insolvency, and were quiet ever afterwards.

In a year's time the creditors realized twenty shillings in the pound from Kachhalia's stock-in-trade. This was the first case in South Africa, to my knowledge, in which creditors have been paid in full from an insolvent debtor's estate. Thus even while the struggle was in progress, Kachhalia commanded great respect among the European merchants, who showed their readiness to advance to him any amount of goods in spite of his leading the movement.

But Kachhalia was every day gaining strength and an intelligent appreciation of the struggle. No one could now tell how long the struggle would last. We had therefore resolved after the insolvency proceedings that the Sheth should not take any large commitments in trade during the continuance of the movement, but confine his operations within such moderate limits as would suffice to provide him with his daily bread. He therefore did not avail himself of the European merchants' offers.

Kachhalia became Chairman some time after the resumption of the struggle (September 10, 1908), and his insolvency came about five months later.

But to return to the Committee meeting. When it was over, I wrote a letter to General Smuts, saying that his new Bill constituted a breach of the compromise, and drawing his attention to the following passage in his Richmond speech delivered within a week of the settlement. "The Indians' second contention was that they would never register until the law had been repealed. . . . He had told them that the law would not be repealed so long as there was an Asiatic in the country who had not registered. . . . Until every Indian in the country had registered the law would not be repealed." I did not receive any satisfactory reply to my letters.

I met Albert Cartwright, who had been our mediator. He was shocked. "Really," he exclaimed, "I cannot understand General Smuts at all. I perfectly remember that he promised to repeal the Asiatic Act. I will do my best, but you know nothing can move General Smuts when he has once taken up a stand. Newspaper articles are as nothing to him. So I am afraid that I may not be able to help you." I also met Mr. Hosken, who wrote to General Smuts, but could elicit only a very unsatisfactory reply.

While, on the one hand, we were trying to induce General Smuts to fulfil his part of the settlement, we were, on the other hand, enthusiastically engaged in "educating" the community. We found the people

A BREACH OF FAITH

everywhere ready to resume the struggle and go to jail. Meetings were held in every place, where we explained the correspondence which was being carried on with the Government. The weekly diary in *Indian Opinion* kept the Indians fully abreast of current events, and they were warned of the impending failure of voluntary registration. They were asked to hold themselves in readiness to burn the certificates if the Black Act were not repealed after all. Thus we would let the Government note that the community was fearless and firm and ready to go to prison. Certificates were collected from every place with a view to making a bonfire of them.

The Government Bill was about to pass through the Legislature, on which a petition was presented on behalf of the Indians, but in vain. At last an "ultimatum" was sent to the Government by the Satyagrahis. The word "ultimatum" was not used by us, but by General Smuts, who thus had styled the letter we had addressed to him signifying the determination of the community. "The people," said the General, "who have offered such a threat to the Government have no idea of its power. I am sorry that some agitators are trying to inflame poor Indians who will be ruined if they succumb to their blandishments."

As the newspaper reporters wrote on this occasion, many members of the Transvaal Assembly became angry at this "ultimatum." The House unanimously and enthusiastically passed the Bill introduced by General Smuts.

The so-called ultimatum may be thus summarised: "The point of the agreement between the Indians and General Smuts clearly was that if the Indians registered voluntarily, he on his part would bring forward in the

Legislature a Bill to validate such registration and to repeal the Asiatic Act. It is well known that the Indians have registered voluntarily to the satisfaction of the Government, and therefore the Asiatic Act must be repealed. The community has sent many communications to General Smuts and taken all possible legal steps to obtain redress, but thus far to no purpose. We regret to state that if the Asiatic Act is not repealed in terms of the settlement, and the Government's decision to that effect is not communicated to the Indians before a specified date, the certificates collected by the Indians will be burnt, and they will humbly but firmly take the consequences."

One reason why this letter was held to be an ultimatum was that it prescribed a time limit for reply. Another reason was that the Europeans looked upon the Indians as a barbarous people unfit to be reasoned with as civilized human beings. If the Europeans had considered the Indians to be their equals, they would have found this letter perfectly courteous, and would have given it most serious consideration. But the fact that the Europeans thought Indians to be barbarians was a sufficient reason for the Indians to write such a letter. The Indians must either confess to their being barbarians and must consent to be suppressed as such, or else they must take active steps in repudiation of the charge of barbarism. This letter was the first of such steps. If there had not been behind the letter an iron determination to act up to it, it might have been held to be an impertinence, and the Indians would have proved themselves to be a thoughtless and foolish people.

The charge of barbarism was really repudiated in

A BREACH OF FAITH

1906, when the Satyagraha pledge was taken. And it should be remembered that the Satyagraha pledge came in almost by accident, and the subsequent imprisonment followed as an inevitable corollary. The community then gained largely in stature, but unconsciously.

But when this letter was written there was a deliberate intention of claiming full knowledge and high prestige. Now, as well as before, the object aimed at was the repeal of the Black Act. But there was a change in the style of language used and in the methods of work selected, and in other things besides. When a slave salutes his master, and a friend salutes a friend, the manner of salute may be the same in either case, but there is a world of difference between the two, which enables the detached observer to recognize the slave and the friend at once.

There was much discussion among ourselves when the ultimatum was forwarded. Would not the demand for reply within a stated period be considered impudent? Might it not be that it would stiffen the Government and lead them to reject our terms which otherwise they might have accepted? Would it not be sufficient indirectly to announce the community's decision to the Government?

After giving due weight to all these considerations we unanimously came to the conclusion that we must do what we thought right and proper. We must run the risk of being charged with discourtesy as well as the risk of Government refusing in anger what otherwise they might have granted. If we do not admit our inferiority as human beings in any sense whatever, and if we believe that we possess the capacity for unlimited suffering for any length of time, we must adopt a straightforward course without hesitation.

There was therefore some novelty and distinction about the step now taken, which had its reverberations in the Legislature and in European circles outside. Some congratulated the Indians on their courage and others got very angry, and asked for condign punishment to be awarded to the Indians for their insolence. Either section acknowledged the novelty of the Indians' fresh move.

This letter created a greater stir than even the commencement of Satyagraha, which was a novelty when it started. The reason is obvious. When Satyagraha was started no one knew what the Indians were capable of, and therefore neither such letter nor the language in which it was couched would have been fitting for that initial stage. But the community had already had its baptism of fire. Everyone had observed that the Indians had the capacity to suffer the hardships incidental to an attempt to get their wrongs righted, and therefore the language of the "ultimatum" appeared in the light of a natural growth and not at all inappropriate.

The ultimatum was to expire on the same day that the new Asiatic Bill was to be carried through the Legislature. A meeting had been called, some two hours after the expiry of the time limit, in order to perform the public ceremony of burning the certificates. The Satyagraha Committee thought that the meeting would not be fruitless even if quite unexpectedly a favourable reply was received from the Government. For in that case the meeting could be utilized for announcing the Government's decision to the community.

The Committee, however, believed that the Government would not reply to the ultimatum at all. We had reached the place of meeting early, and arranged for the Government's reply, if any, to be brought promptly to the meeting, which was held at four o'clock in the grounds of the Haminia Mosque at Johannesburg (August 16, 1908). Every inch of space available was taken up by Indians of all classes. It seemed as though the entire Indian community had come forward to condemn the Government action. A cauldron, of the largest size available in the market, had been requisitioned and set up on a platform for the purpose of burning the certificates.

As the business of the meeting was about to commence, a volunteer arrived on a cycle with a telegram from the Government. The telegram stated that the Government regretted the determination of the Indian community and announced their inability to change their line of action. The telegram was read to the audience, who received it with cheers, as if they were glad that the auspicious opportunity of burning the certificates had not after all slipped through their hands.

It is difficult to pronounce any opinion about such feelings of gladness without the knowledge of the motive which prompted those who greeted the Government reply with applause. This, however, can be said, that these cheers were a happy token of the enthusiasm of the meeting. The Indians had now some consciousness of their own strength.

The meeting began. The Chairman put those present on their guard and explained the whole situation to them. Afterwards, I clearly detailed the various stages of the protracted negotiations.

"If there is any Indian," I said to them, "who has handed his certificate to be burnt, but now wants it to be returned, let him step forward and receive it. Merely the burning of the certificates is no crime, nor will it enable those who court imprisonment to win it. By burning the certificates we only desire to declare our solemn resolution never to submit to the Black Act, and divest ourselves of the power of even showing the certificates. But it is open to any one to-morrow to take out another, and if there are any persons here who contemplate such a cowardly act, or doubt their own ability to stand the ordeal, there is still time for them to have their certificates returned to them."

"No one," I continued, "need be ashamed of getting his certificate back just now. In doing so he will be exhibiting a certain kind of courage. But it would be not only shameful, but also detrimental to the interests of the community to get a copy of the certificate afterwards. Again let us take note that it is going to be a protracted struggle. We know that some of us have fallen out of the marching army, and the burden of those who remain has been made heavier to that extent. I would advise you to ponder over all these considerations and only then take the plunge you propose to-day."

Even during my speech there were voices saying: "We don't want the certificates back! Burn them! Burn them!"

At the end of my speech I suggested that if anyone wished to oppose the resolution, he should come forward; but no one stood up. Mir Alam too was present at this meeting. He announced that he had done wrong in assaulting me as he did, and to the great joy of the audience handed in his original certificate to be burnt. (He had not taken out a voluntary certificate.) I took hold of his hand, pressed it with joy, and assured him that I had never harboured in my mind any resentment against him.

The Committee had already received upwards of two thousand certificates to be burnt. These were all thrown into the cauldron, saturated with paraffin, and set ablaze by Mr. Essop Mia. The whole gathering rose to its feet and made the place resound with continuous cheers during the burning process. Some of those who had still withheld their certificates brought them to the platform, and these too were consigned to the flames. One of these friends, when asked why he handed his certificate only at the last moment, said that he did so because it would create more impression on the onlookers. Another frankly admitted his want of courage and a feeling that the certificates might not be burnt after all. But he could not possibly withhold his certificate after he had witnessed the bonfire itself. Such frankness was a matter of frequent experience during the struggle.

The reporters of English newspapers present were profoundly impressed with the whole scene and sent a graphic description of our meeting to the press in South Africa. A vivid account was also sent to the London *Daily Mail* by its Johannesburg correspondent. He compared the act of the Indians in burning their certificates to the Boston Tea Party which started the American Revolution. I do not think that this comparison did more than justice to the Indians, seeing that if the whole might of Great Britain was ranged against the hundreds of thousands of able Europeans in America, here in South

Africa a helpless body of thirteen thousand Indians had challenged the powerful Government of the Transvaal.

Our only weapon was our faith in God. To the devout spirit, this faith is all-sufficient and all-powerful. As God is the strength of the weak, it is well that they are despised by the world. For thus God's strength is made manifest.

CHAPTER XV

THE STRUGGLE RENEWED

DURING THE SAME year in which the Black Act was passed through the Legislature, another Bill called the Transvaal Immigrants' Restriction Bill (Act No. 15 of 1907) was passed, which was ostensibly of general application, but was chiefly aimed at Indians. This Act followed the main lines of similar legislation in Natal, but it treated as prohibited immigrants even those who could pass education tests and yet were ineligible for registration under the Asiatic Act. It was thus indirectly made the instrument for preventing a single Indian newcomer entering into the Transvaal.

It was absolutely essential for the Indians to resist this fresh inroad on their rights and liberties, but the question was whether it should be made another plank in the Satyagraha struggle or not. The community was not in any way bound as to the oxact time and subject on which they should offer Satyagraha. In deciding such questions they must only refrain from transgressing the limits prescribed by wisdom and also by a right judgment of their own capacity. Satyagraha offered on every occasion, seasonable or unseasonable, would degenerate into violence and untruth. If anyone unwisely takes to Satyagraha, and afterwards sustains a defeat, he not only disgraces himself but also brings the matchless weapon of Satyagraha itself into disrepute by his folly.

The Satyagraha Committee saw that the Indians' resistance was being offered only against the Black Act, and that if the Black Act was once repealed, the Immigration Restriction Act would lose its sting. Yet if the Indians did not take steps regarding the Immigration Act from an idea that a separate movement against it was unnecessary, their silence might be misconstrued as implying their consent to the total prohibition of all Indian immigrants into the Transvaal. The Immigration Act, therefore, must also be opposed, and the only question remained whether this should be included in the present Satyagraha struggle or not. The community's view was that they should include any fresh attack on their rights made while the struggle was still in progress.

Correspondence was therefore carried on with the Transvaal Government on the subject. We could not induce General Smuts to agree to a change in the law, but it provided him with a fresh handle for condemning the community and myself. General Smuts knew that many more Europeans, besides those who were publicly helping us, were privately in sympathy with our movement, and he naturally wished that their sympathy should be alienated. He therefore charged me with raising a fresh point. He explained and also wrote to our supporters that they did not know me as well as he did. If he yielded an inch, I would ask for an ell, and therefore he was not repealing the Asiatic Act.

When Satyagraha started, there was no question about fresh immigrants. Now, when he was legislating to prevent the fresh entry of any more Indians, in the interests of the Transvaal, there too I had threatened Satyagraha. He could not any more put up with this "cunning." I might do my worst, and every Indian might be ruined, but he would not repeal the Asiatic Act, nor would the

Transvaal Government give up the policy they had adopted regarding the Indians. In this just attitude they were entitled to the support of all Europeans.

A little reflection will show how totally unjust and immoral this argument was. When there was nothing like the Immigrants' Restriction Act at all in existence, how were the Indians or myself to oppose it? General Smuts talked glibly about his experience of what he called my "cunning," and yet he could not bring forward a single case in support of his statement. And I do not remember to have ever resorted to cunning during all the years that I lived in South Africa. I may now go even further, and say without the least hesitation that I have never had recourse to cunning in all my life. I believe that cunning is not only morally wrong, but also politically inexpedient, and have therefore always discountenanced its use even from the practical standpoint. It is hardly necessary for me to defend myself.

It is evident from all this how difficult was the obstruction we encountered during the Satyagraha struggle and how imminent was the danger to the movement if even by a hair's breadth we swerved from the strait and narrow path. The rope-dancer, balancing himself upon a rope suspended at a height of twenty feet, must concentrate his attention upon the rope, and the least little error in so doing means death for him, no matter on which side he falls. My eight years' experience of Satyagraha in South Africa has taught me that a Satyagrahi has to be, if possible, even more single-minded than the rope-dancer. The friends before whom General Smuts levelled this charge at me knew me well, and therefore it had an effect upon them exactly the opposite of what General

Smuts had desired. They not only did not give me up or the movement, but grew more zealous in supporting me, and the Indians saw later on that they would have come in for no end of trouble if their Satyagraha had not extended to the Immigration Act as well.

My experience has taught me that a law of progression applies to every righteous struggle. But in the case of Satyagraha the law amounts to an axiom. As the Ganges advances, other streams flow into it, and hence at the mouth it grows so wide that neither bank is to be seen and a person sailing upon the surface of the river cannot make out where the river ends and the sea begins. So also, as a Satyagraha struggle flows onwards, many other elements help to swell its current. There is a constant growth in the result to which it leads. This is really inevitable, and is bound up with its first principles. For in Satyagraha the minimum is also the maximum, and as it is the irreducible minimum, there is no question of retreat. The only movement possible is an advance. In other struggles, even when they are righteous, the demand is first pitched a little higher so as to admit of future reduction. Hence the law of progression does not apply to all of them without exception.

But I must explain how the law of progression comes into play when the minimum is also the maximum, as in Satyagraha. The Ganges does not leave its course in search of tributaries. Even so the Satyagrahi does not leave his path, which is as sharp as the sword's edge. But as the tributaries spontaneously join the Ganges, while it advances, so it is with the river that is called Satyagraha.

Seeing that the Immigration Act was included in the Satyagraha struggle, some Indians, ignorant of the principles of Satyagraha, insisted upon the whole mass of the anti-Indian legislation in the Transvaal being similarly treated. Others, again, suggested a mobilization of Indians all over South Africa and the offering of Satyagraha against all the anti-Indian legislation in Natal, Cape Colony, and the Orange Free State while the Transvaal struggle was on. Both the suggestions involved a breach of principle. I said distinctly that it would be dishonest to take up a position which was not in view when Satyagraha started. No matter how strong we were, the present struggle must close when the demands for which we were agitating were accepted.

I am confident that if we had not adhered to this principle, then, instead of winning, we should not only have lost all along the line, but also have forfeited the sympathy which had been enlisted in our favour. On the other hand, if the adversary himself creates new difficulties for us while the struggle is in progress, these become automatically included in the struggle itself. A Satyagrahi, without being false to his faith, cannot disregard new difficulties which confront him while he is pursuing his course. The adversary is not bound by any limit of maximum or minimum. He can try if he wishes to frighten the Satyagrahi by raising novel issues. But the latter has renounced all fear; he confronts by Satyagraha the later difficulty as well as the former, and trusts that it will help him to hold his own against all odds. Therefore when the struggle is prolonged by the adversary, it is the adversary who stands to lose from his own standpoint, and it is the Satyagrahi who stands to gain. We shall come across other illustrations of the working of this law in the later stages of this struggle.

Since Satyagraha was now made to embrace the Immigration Act as well, Satyagrahis had to test the right of educated Indians to enter the Transvaal. The Committee decided that the test should not be made through any ordinary Indian. The idea was that some Indian, who did not come under the definition of a prohibited immigrant in the new Act, should enter the Transvaal and go to jail. We had thus to show that Satyagraha is a force containing within itself seeds of progressive self-restraint. There was a section in the Act to the effect that any person who was not conversant with a European language should be treated as a prohibited immigrant. The Committee therefore proposed that some Indian who knew English but who had not been to the Transvaal before should enter the country. Several young Indians volunteered for the purpose, out of whom Sorabji Shapurji Adajania was selected.

Sorabji was a Parsi. There were not perhaps more than a hundred Parsis in South Africa. I held in South Africa the same views about the Parsis that I have expressed in India. There are not more than a hundred thousand Parsis in the world. It speaks volumes for their high character that such a small community has so long preserved its prestige, clung to its religion, and proved itself second to none in the world in point of charity. Sorabji turned out to be pure gold. I was slightly acquainted with him when he joined the struggle. His letters as regards participation in Satyagraha left a good impression on me. Just as I am a lover of the great qualities of the Parsis, so I am not unaware of some of their defects as a community. I was therefore doubtful whether Sorabji would be able to stand quite firm in critical times. But it was a rule with me not to attach any weight to my own doubts where the person concerned himself asserts the contrary. I therefore recommended to the Committee that they should take Sorabji at his word, and eventually he proved himself to be a first-class Satyagrahi. Not only was he one of the Satyagrahis who suffered the longest terms of imprisonment, but he also made such a deep study of the struggle that his views commanded respectful hearing from all. His advice always betokened firmness, wisdom, charity and deliberation. He was slow to form an opinion as well as to change it.

After the struggle was over, Doctor Mehta offered a scholarship in order to enable some good Satyagrahi to proceed to England for the Bar. I was charged with the selection. There were two or three deserving candidates, but all the friends felt that Sorabji could not be approached in maturity of judgment and ripeness of wisdom, and he was selected accordingly. The idea was, that on his return to South Africa he should take my place and serve the community. Sorabji went to England carrying the blessings of everyone with him, and was duly called to the Bar. He had already come in contact with Gokhale in South Africa, and his relations with him became closer in England. Sorabji won Gokhale's heart. He asked him to join the Servants of India Society when he returned to India. Sorabji became extremely popular among the students. He would share the sorrows of all, and he was not tarnished by the luxury and the artificiality of English life. When he went to England he was over thirty years old and he had only a working knowledge of English. But the difficulties vanished at the touch of the man's perseverance. Sorabji lived the pure life of a student and passed his examinations. The Bar examinations in my time were easy. Barristers nowadays have to study very much harder. But Sorabji did not know what it was to be defeated.

When the ambulance corps was established in England[1] he was one of the pioneers, as also one of those who remained in it till the last. This corps had to offer Satyagraha, in which many members fell back; but Sorabji was at the head of those who would not give in. Let me state in passing that this Satyagraha of the ambulance corps was also crowned with victory.

After being called to the Bar in England, Sorabji returned to Johannesburg, where he began to practise law as well as to serve the community. Every letter I received from South Africa was full of praise of Sorabji: "He is as simple in habits as ever, and free from the slightest trace of vanity. He mixes with all, rich and poor alike."

But God seems to be as cruel as He is merciful. Sorabji caught acute phthisis and died in a few months, leaving the Indians whose love he had freshly won to mourn his loss. Thus within a very short period God bereft the community of two outstanding personalities, Kachhalia and Sorabji. If I were asked to choose between the two, I should be at a loss to decide. In fact, each was supreme in his own field. Sorabji was as good an Indian as he was a good Parsi, even as Kachhalia was as good an Indian as he was a good Musalman.

---

[1] At the beginning of the European War Mahatma Gandhi offered to form an Indian Ambulance Corps as he had done in South Africa. The offer was accepted.

Thus Sorabji entered the Transvaal after having previously informed the Government of his intention to test his right to remain in the country under the Immigrants' Restriction Act. The Transvaal Administration was not at all prepared for this and could not at once decide what to do with Sorabji, when he publicly crossed the border and deliberately entered the Transvaal. The Immigrants' Restriction Officer knew him personally. Sorabji told him that he was deliberately entering the country for a test case, and asked him either to examine him in English or to arrest him, just as he pleased. The officer replied that there was no question of examination in English with him as he was aware of his knowledge of that language. Furthermore, he had no orders to arrest him. Therefore he gave orders that Sorabji might enter the country. The Transvaal Government, if they wished, might arrest him. Thus, contrary to our expectations, Sorabji reached Johannesburg and we welcomed him into our midst. No one had expected that the Government would permit him to proceed even an inch beyond the frontier station at Volksrust.

Very often it so happens that when we take steps deliberately and fearlessly as Satyagrahis, the Administration at first is not ready to oppose us. The reason for this lies in the very nature of the Government itself. An official does not ordinarily make his department so much his own as to arrange his ideas on every subject beforehand and make preparations accordingly. Again, the officer has not one but many things to attend to, and his mind is divided between them. Thirdly, the official suffers from the intoxication of power, is thus apt to be careless and believes that it is child's play for the authorities to deal with any movement whatever. On the other hand, the public worker knows his ideal as well as the means of achieving his end. Therefore, if he has definite plans, he is perfectly ready on the spot to carry them out, and his work is the only subject of his thoughts night and day. If, therefore, he takes the right steps with decision, he is always in advance of the Government. Many movements fail, not because Governments refrain from exercising extraordinary powers, but because the leaders are lacking in firmness and decision.

In short, whether through negligence or the set design of the Government, Sorabji reached as far as Johannesburg. The local officer had neither any idea of his duty in a case like this nor any instructions from his superiors. Sorabji's arrival increased our enthusiasm, and some young men thought that the Government were defeated and would soon come to terms. They saw their mistake, however, very soon. They even realized that a settlement could hardly be purchased except by the self-devotion and sacrifice of many young men.

Sorabji informed the Police Superintendent, Johannesburg, about his arrival and let him know that he believed himself entitled to remain in the Transvaal, according to the terms of the new Immigration Act, as he had an ordinary knowledge of English and in this respect he was ready to submit to an examination by the officer if he so desired. No reply to this letter was received, or rather the reply came after some days in the form of a summons.

Sorabji's case came before the Court on July 9, 1908. The Court-house was packed full of Indian spectators. Before the case began we held an Indian meeting in the grounds of the Court, and Sorabji made a brave and fearless speech, in which he announced his readiness to go to jail as often as necessary for victory and to undergo all dangers and risks. In the meanwhile, I had got fairly familiar with Sorabji and assured myself that he would do credit to the community. The Magistrate took up the case in due course. I defended Sorabji, and at once asked for his discharge on the grounds of the summons being defective. The Public Prosecutor also put forward an argument; but the Court upheld my contention and discharged Sorabji. But immediately afterwards he received a warning to appear before the Court the next day.

On July 10th the Magistrate ordered Sorabji to leave the Transvaal within seven days. After the Court's order was served upon him, Sorabji informed Superintendent J. A. G. Vernon that it was not his desire to leave the Transvaal. He was accordingly brought to the Court once more, on the 20th, charged with failing to obey the Magistrate's order, and sentenced to a month's imprisonment, with hard labour.

The Government, however, did not arrest the local Indians, as they saw that the more arrests were made the higher the spirit of the Indians rose. Again, Indians were sometimes discharged, thanks to legal technicalities in the cases, which were instituted against them, and this also served to redouble the ardour of the community.

The Transvaal Government had now carried through the Legislature all the laws they wanted. Many Indians had indeed burnt their certificates, but they had proved their right to remain in the country by their registration. The Administration therefore saw no sense in prosecuting them simply in order to send them to jail, and thought that the Satyagrahi workers would cool down if they found no outlet for their energies, in view of the masterly inactivity of the Government. But they were reckoning without their host. The Indians took fresh steps to test the Government's patience, which was soon exhausted. When they saw through the Administration's game of tiring them out by Fabian tactics they felt bound to take further steps. A Satyagrahi is never tired so long as he has the capacity to suffer. The Indians were therefore in a position to upset all the calculations of the Government.

There were several Indians in Natal who possessed ancient rights of domicile in the Transvaal. They had no need to enter the Transvaal for trade, but the community held that they had the right of entry. They also had some knowledge of English. Again, there was no breach of the principles of Satyagraha in educated Indians like Sorabji entering the Transvaal. We therefore decided that two classes of Indians should enter the Transvaal: (1) those who had previously been domiciled in the country, (2) those who had received an English education.

Of these, Sheth Daud Mahommed and Parsi Rustomji were big traders, and Surendrarai Medh, Pragji Khandubhai Desai, Ratansi Mulji Sodha, Harilal Gandhi and others were educated men. Daud Sheth came in spite of his wife being dangerously ill.

Sheth Daud Mahommed was president of the Natal Indian Congress and one of the oldest Indians who had come out to South Africa as traders. I have only seen a few Indians in South Africa who equalled him in tact.

THE STRUGGLE RENEWED

He had excellent powers of understanding. He had not much literary education, but spoke both English and Dutch. He was skilful in his business intercourse with European traders. His liberality was widely known. About fifty guests would dine with him every day. He was one of the chief contributors to Indian monetary collections. His son was a precious jewel who far surpassed his father in character. The boy's heart was as pure as crystal. Daud Sheth never came in the way of his son's aspirations. Indeed, it would be no exaggeration to say that the father almost worshipped his son. His one wish was that none of his own defects should appear in the boy, so he had sent him to England for education. But Daud Sheth lost this treasure of a son in his early youth. Phthisis claimed Husain for its victim. This was a sore wound which had never healed. Along with Husain died all the high hopes which the Indians had cherished about him. He was a most truthful lad, and Hindu and Musalman were to him as the left eye and the right eye. Even Daud Sheth is now no more with us. Death lays his hand on us all.

I have already introduced Parsi Rustomji. These chapters are not being written to immortalize any names, but only to explain the secret of Satyagraha, and to show how it succeeded, where obstacles beset its path, and how these obstacles were removed. Even where I have mentioned names I have done so in order to point out how men who might be considered illiterate distinguished themselves in South Africa, how Hindus, Musalmans, Parsis and Christians worked harmoniously together; how traders, "educated" men and labourers fulfilled their duty. When a man of high merit has been mentioned, praise has been bestowed, not upon him, but upon the character.

When Daud Sheth thus arrived on the frontier with his "army" of Satyagrahis, the Government of the Transvaal was ready to meet him. The Government would become an object of ridicule if they allowed such a large troop to enter the Transvaal. They were therefore bound to arrest them. So they were arrested. On August 18, 1908, they were brought before the Magistrate, who ordered them to leave the Transvaal within seven days. They, of course, disobeyed the order, were re-arrested at Pretoria on the 28th and deported without trial. They re-entered the Transvaal on the 31st and finally on September 8th were sentenced at Volksrust to a fine of fifty pounds or three months' imprisonment with hard labour. Needless to say, they cheerfully elected to go to jail. This was what they had all along desired.

The Transvaal Indians were now in high spirits. If they could not compel the release of their Natal compatriots, they must certainly share their imprisonment. They therefore cast about for some means which would bring them within the prison walls. There were several ways in which they could have their heart's desire. If a domiciled Indian did not show his registration certificate, he would not be given a trading certificate and it would be an offence on his part if he traded without a licence. Again, an Indian must show the certificate if he wanted to enter the Transvaal from Natal. He would be arrested if he had none to show. The certificates had already been burnt and the line was therefore clear. The Indians employed both these methods. Some began to hawk without a licence, while others were arrested for not showing certificates upon entering the Transvaal.

The movement was now in full swing. Every Indian was on his trial. Other Natal Indians followed Sheth Daud Mahommed's example. There were many arrests also in Johannesburg. Things came to such a pass that everyone who wished could get himself arrested without any difficulty. Jails began to be filled. "Invaders" from Natal used to get three months'. The Transvaal hawkers got anything from four days' to three months'.

Among those who thus courted arrest was our "Imam Sahib."[1] Imam Abdul Kadar Bawazir was arrested for hawking without a licence and sentenced on July 21, 1908, to imprisonment for four days with hard labour. The Imam Sahib's health was so delicate that people laughed when they heard that he was courting arrest. Some people came to me and asked me not to allow the Imam Sahib to go to prison for fear he might bring discredit on the community. I disregarded this warning. It was none of my business to judge the strength or weakness of the Imam Sahib. He never walked barefoot; he was fond of the good things of the earth, had a Malay wife, and kept a well-furnished house. He went about in a horse-carriage.

All this was well known, but who could read the depths of his mind? After he was released the Imam Sahib went to jail again, lived there as an ideal prisoner, and took his meals after a spell of hard labour. At home he would have new dishes and delicacies every day; in jail he took mealie meal porridge and thanked God for it. Not only was he not defeated, but he became simple

[1] The Imam leads prayers in the Mosque.

in habits. As a prisoner he broke stones, worked as a sweeper and stood in a line with the other prisoners. At Phoenix he fetched water and even set types in the press. Everyone at the Phoenix Ashram was bound to acquire the art of type-setting, and the Imam Sahib set types to the best of his ability. But there were many such who experienced self-purification in jail.

Joseph Royappen, barrister-at-law, a graduate of Cambridge University, had been born in Natal of parents who were indentured labourers; but he had fully adopted the European style of living. He would not go barefoot even in his own house—unlike the Imam Sahib, who must wash his feet before prayers and must also pray barefooted. Joseph Royappen left his law books, took up a basket of vegetables and was arrested as an unlicensed hawker. He, too, suffered imprisonment. "But should I travel third class?" asked Royappen. "If you travel first or second class," I replied, "how can I ask of the rest to travel third? Who in jail is going to recognize the barrister in you?" That was enough to satisfy Royappen. Many lads sixteen years old went to jail. One, Mohanlal Manji Ghelani, was only fourteen.

The jail authorities left no stone unturned to harass the Indians, who were given scavengers' work; but they did it with a smile on their face. They were asked to break stones, and they broke stones with the name of Allah or Rama on their lips. They were made to dig tanks and set to perform pickaxe work in hard rocky ground. Their hands soon became hardened with the work. Some of them even fainted under the unbearable strain, but they did not know what it was to be beaten.

It must not be supposed that there were no internal

THE STRUGGLE RENEWED

jealousies or quarrels in jail. Food constitutes the perpetual apple of discord, but we successfully avoided bickerings even over food.

I also was arrested again. At one time as many as seventy-five Indians were prisoners in Volksrust jail. We cooked our own food. I became the cook, since only I could adjudicate on the conflicting claims to the rations supplied. Thanks to their love of me, my companions took without a murmur the half-cooked porridge I prepared without sugar.

Government thought if they separated me from the other prisoners it might chasten me as well as the others. They therefore took me to Pretoria jail, where I was confined in a solitary cell reserved for dangerous prisoners. I was taken out only twice a day for exercise. Unlike Volksrust jail, in Pretoria no ghee was provided for the Indian prisoners.

Yet, in spite of all hardships, the Indians would not take defeat. The Transvaal Government was in a state of utter perplexity. How many Indians could be sent to jail after all? Also, it meant additional expenditure. The Government began to consider carefully other means of dealing with the situation.

CHAPTER XVI

GENERAL BOTHA'S OFFER

THE OBNOXIOUS ACTS provided for three kinds of punishment—fine, imprisonment, and deportation. The Courts were empowered to award all these punishments simultaneously, and Magistrates were given jurisdiction to impose the maximum penalties. At first, deportation meant taking the "culprits" across the border into Natal, the Orange Free State, or Portuguese East Africa, beyond the Transvaal frontier, and leaving them there. The Indians who crossed over from Natal were deported beyond Volksrust station and there left to their own devices. Deportation of this kind was a farce, pure and simple. It involved only a little inconvenience, and instead of disheartening the Indians encouraged them still further.

The local Government therefore had to find out a fresh means of putting us to trouble. The jails were already overcrowded.

The officials thought that the Indians would be so thoroughly demoralized as to surrender at discretion if they were deported to India. There was some ground for this belief. Therefore, a large batch of Indians were deported without any appeal direct to India. These deportees suffered great hardships. They had nothing to eat except what the Government chose to provide for them on the steamer, and all of them were sent as deck passengers. Again, some of them had their property and business in South Africa. Many had their families in the Transvaal, while others were also in debt. Not many people would be ready to lose their all for the sake of Satyagraha and be turned into bankrupts.

Notwithstanding, many Indians remained perfectly firm. Many more, however, weakened and ceased to court arrest, although they did not give way to the extent of getting duplicates of the burnt certificates. Only a few were intimidated into registering afresh.

At the same time, there was a considerable number of stalwarts who were so brave that some of them, I truly believe, would have mounted the scaffold with a smile on their faces and gone to their death. If they cared little for life, they cared still less for property.

But many of those who were deported to India were poor, simple folk who had joined the Satyagraha movement in a spirit of faith. That these should be oppressed so heavily was almost too much for us to endure. Yet it was difficult for us to see our way to assist them. Our funds were meagre, and then there was the real danger of losing the fight altogether if we proceeded to give temporary help. Not a single person hitherto had been permitted to join the movement from pecuniary motives; for otherwise our cause might have been hindered by men joining it on the strength of selfish hopes. We felt, however, that it was incumbent upon us to help the deportees with our active sympathy.

I have seen from experience that money cannot go as far as fellow-feeling truly expressed. If a man, who is eager to obtain riches, receives money from another but no real sympathy, he will give him up in the long run. On the other hand, one who has been conquered by love is ready to encounter all kinds of difficulties along with him who has given him this love.

We therefore resolved to do for the deportees everything that kindness could possibly do. We comforted them with the promise that proper arrangements would be made for them in India. Many of them were ex-indentured labourers and had no relatives in India. Some were even born in South Africa. To all of them India was almost like a strange land on account of long absence. It would be sheer cruelty to these helpless people if upon being landed in India they were merely left to shift for themselves. We therefore promised them that suitable arrangements would be made for them in India as soon as ever they disembarked.

But this was not enough. The deportees could not be comforted unless some leader went with them to be their companion and guide. This was the first batch of deportees, and their steamer was to start in a few hours. There was not much time for making a selection. I quickly thought of P. K. Naidoo, one of my co-workers.

"Will you escort these poor brothers to India?" I asked him.

"Why not?" he replied.

"But the steamer is starting just now."

"Very well," said he; "I am ready."

"What about your clothes and food?"

"This suit I have on will suffice," he answered, "and I will get food on board the steamer all right."

Such promptness was a most agreeable surprise for me. The conversation took place at Parsi Rustomji's house. I procured some clothes and blankets for him at once and sent him on board.

GENERAL BOTHA'S OFFER

"Take care," said I to him on leaving. "Look after these brothers on the way. Consider their comforts first, and then your own. I am cabling to G. A. Natesan at Madras, and you must follow his instructions."

"I will try," said Naidoo, "to prove myself a true Satyagrahi."

He left for the pier. Victory must be certain, I thought to myself, with such valiant fighters. P. K. Naidoo was born in South Africa and had never been to India before. I gave him a letter of introduction to Mr. Natesan and also sent a cablegram.

In those days G. A. Natesan stood almost alone in India as a student of the hardships of Indians abroad. He was their helper, and a systematic well-informed exponent of their case. I used to have regular correspondence with him. When the deportees reached Madras, Natesan rendered them full assistance. He found his task easier owing to the presence of an able man like P. K. Naidoo among the deportees. He made local collections, and did not allow them to feel for a moment that they had been deported to a strange country.

These deportations by the Transvaal Government were as illegal as they were cruel. People are generally unaware that Government often deliberately violates its own laws. In face of an emergency there is no time to pass fresh legislation. Governments, therefore, often break laws and do what they please. Afterwards they either enact new laws or else make the people forget their breach of the old laws.

The Indians started a powerful agitation against this lawlessness of the local Government, which was adversely commented upon in India also. Thus the Government every day found it more and more difficult to deport Indians. We took all possible legal steps and successfully appealed against the deportations, with the result that Government had to stop the practice.

But this policy was not without its effect upon the Satyagrahi "army" itself. Not all could overcome the fear of being deported to India. Many more fell away, and only the real fighters remained.

This was not the only step taken by the Government to break the spirit of the Indians. Officials often did their utmost to harass the Satyagrahi prisoners, who were put to all manner of tasks, including the breaking of stones. But that was not all. At first all prisoners were kept together. Now the Government adopted the policy of separating them in every jail. Winter in the Transvaal is very severe; the cold is so bitter that one's hands are almost frozen while working in the morning. Winter, therefore, was a hard time for the prisoners, some of whom were kept in a road camp where no one could even go to see them. One of these prisoners was a young Satyagrahi, eighteen years old, named Swami Nagappan, who observed the jail rules and did the task set him. Early each morning he was taken to work on the roads, where he contracted double pneumonia. He died of this after he was released (July 7, 1909). Nagappan's companions say that he thought only of the struggle till he breathed his last. He never repented going to jail and embraced death for his country's sake as he would embrace a friend.

Nagappan was "illiterate" according to our standards. He had learnt English, but was by no means an educated man. Still, if we consider his fortitude, his patience, his patriotism, his firmness unto death, there is nothing left which we might desire him to possess. The Satyagraha movement went on successfully, even though it was not joined by many highly educated men. But where would it have been without soldiers like Nagappan?

Just as Nagappan died of ill-treatment in jail, so also the hardships of deportation proved to be the death of Narayanswami (October 16, 1909). Nevertheless, the Indian community stood unmoved; only weaklings slipped away. But even the weaklings had done their best. Let us not despise them. Those who march forward are generally apt to look down upon those who fall back and to consider themselves very brave fellows, whereas often the facts are just the reverse. If a man who can afford to contribute a hundred rupees subscribed only fifty, and if he who can afford to pay only five rupees contributes that amount in full, then he who gives the five must be held to be more generous than he who gives ten times that amount. Yet very often he who contributes fifty rupees is needlessly elated at the false notion of his own superiority over the contributor of five rupees. In the same way, if a man who falls back through weakness has done his utmost, he is really superior to another who leaves him behind, but has not put his whole soul into the march. Therefore even those who slipped away when they found things too hard for them rendered useful service to the community.

A time now came when greater calls were made on our patience and courage. The stalwarts who held to their posts were equal to the service required. Day by day the trial grew still more severe for the Indians.

The Government became violent in proportion to the strength put forth by the community.

There are always special prisons where dangerous prisoners, or prisoners whom the Government wants to bend, are kept. One of these was the Diepkloof Convict Prison, where there was a harsh jailer and the labour exacted from the prisoners was also hard. Yet Indians under his charge successfully performed their allotted task. But though they were prepared to work, they would not put up with the insults offered them by the jailer; and therefore they went on hunger strike. They solemnly declared that they would take no food until either the jailer was removed from the prison or they themselves were transferred to another prison.

This was a perfectly legitimate strike. The strikers were quite honest and were not likely to take food secretly. There was not as much room in the Transvaal for such public agitation as a case of this kind would evoke in India. Again the jail regulations in the Transvaal were particularly drastic. Outsiders did not seek interviews with prisoners even on occasions of this nature. A Satyagrahi, when he once found himself in jail, had generally to shift for himself. The struggle was on behalf of the poor and was conducted as a poor man's movement. Thus the vow, which these strikers took, was fraught with great risk. Yet they remained firm and succeeded in getting themselves transferred to another prison after a seven days' fast. As hunger strikers were a rarity in those days, these Satyagrahis are entitled to special credit as pioneers. This happened at a later period of the struggle in November, 1910.

Thus the Satyagrahis continued to be imprisoned and

deported. There was sometimes a lull and then a storm, but both parties had somewhat weakened. The Government saw that they could not hope to subdue the Satyagrahi stalwarts by sending them to jail. The policy of deportations had only put the Administration into a false position. Some cases also which had been taken to the Courts against Indians were lost. The Indians on their part were not in a position to put up a really strong fight. There was not a sufficient number of Satyagrahis for that purpose. Some Indians were war-weary, while others had become entirely defeatists and therefore looked upon the staunch Satyagrahis as so many fools. The "fools," however, knew themselves to be wise, and had faith in God. They were confident that "Great is Truth and it shall prevail."

Meanwhile, there was a continuous movement going forward in South African politics. The Boers and the British were anxious to secure a higher status by effecting a union of the four different Colonies in the sub-continent. General Hertzog stood for a total breach of the British connection, while others preferred to keep up a nominal association with the British Empire. Englishmen would never agree to total secession, and any higher status in view could only be attained through the British Parliament. The Boers and the British in South Africa therefore decided that a deputation should visit England on their behalf and present their case before the British Cabinet and Crown.

The Indians observed that if a union of the four Colonies took place, their last state would be worse than their first. All the South African Colonies were desirous of suppressing the Indians, and it was clear, in view of their anti-Indian tendency, that it would go very hard with the community when they came closer together. In order that not a single avenue might remain unexplored, the Indians resolved to send once again a deputation to England, although there was every likelihood of their small voice being drowned amid the loud roar of British and Boer lions.

On this occasion Sheth Haji Habib, a Meman gentleman from Porbandar,[1] was appointed as my colleague on the deputation. The Sheth had carried on a long-established trade in the Transvaal and was a man of very wide experience. He had not received any English education, yet he easily understood English, Dutch, and Zulu. His sympathies were with the Satyagrahis, but he could not be described as a full Satyagrahi himself. Mr. Merriman, the famous veteran statesman of South Africa, was our fellow passenger on board the R.M.S. *Kenilworth Castle*, which took us to England. We left Cape Town on June 23, 1909. Mr. Merriman was going to London with a view to the unification of the four colonies into one South African Dominion. General Smuts and others were already in England. A separate deputation of the Indians in Natal also visited England about this time in connection with their special grievances.

Lord Crewe was Secretary of State for the Colonies, and Lord Morley Secretary of State for India. There were many discussions, and we interviewed a large number of people. There was hardly a journalist or member of either House within reach of an introduction

---

[1] Porbandar is Mahatma Gandhi's own birthplace. It is a small port on the western border of Kathiawar, in Western India.

whom we did not meet. Lord Ampthill rendered us invaluable service. He used to meet Mr. Merriman, General Botha and others, and at last he brought a message to us from the General himself.

"General Botha," said he, "appreciates your feelings in the matter and is willing to grant all your minor demands. But he is not ready to repeal the Asiatic Act or to amend the Immigrants' Restriction Act. He also refuses to remove the colour bar which has already been set up as the law of the land.[1] To maintain this racial bar is a matter of principle with the General; and even if he felt like doing away with it, the South African Europeans would never listen to him. General Smuts is of the same mind as General Botha, and this is their final decision and final offer. If you ask for more you will only be inviting trouble for yourselves as well as for your people. Therefore, whatever you do, do it after giving due consideration to this attitude of the Boer leaders. General Botha has asked me to tell you this and give you an idea of your responsibilities."

After this message had been delivered to us, there followed a personal interview with Lord Ampthill.

"You see," said he, "how General Botha concedes all your minor practical demands, and in this work-a-day world we must necessarily give and take. We cannot have everything our own way. I would therefore strongly advise you to close with this offer. If you wish to fight for principle's sake, you may do so later on. You and the Sheth had better think it over and let me have your reply at your convenience."

[1] It was the law of the Boer Republics in both the Transvaal and Orange Free State.

Upon hearing this I looked to Sheth Haji Habib, inviting him to speak first. "Tell him from me," said he, "that I accept General Botha's offer on behalf of the conciliation party. If he makes these concessions, we shall be satisfied for the present and then later on struggle for the principle itself. I do not like to see the community going on suffering any more. The party I represent constitutes the majority and it holds the major portion of the community's wealth."

I translated the Sheth's sentences on behalf of the conciliation party word by word. Then I spoke in turn on behalf of the Satyagrahis. "We are both highly obliged to you," I said warmly, "for the trouble you have taken on our behalf. My colleague is right when he says that he represents a numerically and financially stronger section. The Indians for whom I speak are comparatively poor and inferior in numbers, but they are resolute unto death. They are fighting not only for practical relief, but for the principle as well. If they must give up either of the two, they will refuse to accept the former and fight for the principle. We have a clear idea of General Botha's might, but we attach still greater weight to our pledge. Therefore we are ready to face the worst. We shall be patient in the confidence that if we stick to our solemn resolution, God, in whose name we have made our vow, will see to its fulfilment."

Then I added some further sentences in order to make my position quite clear. "I can grasp your position fully," I said. "You have done much for us and we are very thankful. We shall not take it amiss if you now withhold your support from a handful of Satyagrahis. Nor shall we forget the debt of gratitude under which you have laid us. But we trust that you on your side will excuse us for our inability to accept your advice. You may certainly tell General Botha how the Sheth and myself have received his offer, and inform him that the Satyagrahis, though in the minority, will observe their pledge and hope in the end to soften his heart by their self-suffering, and to induce him to repeal the Asiatic Act."

"You must not suppose," Lord Ampthill replied, "that I will give you up. I, too, must play the gentleman's part. Englishmen are not willing at once to relinquish any task they have undertaken. Yours is a righteous and honourable struggle, and you are fighting with clean weapons. How can I possibly give you up? At the same time you can realize my own delicate position. The suffering, if any, must be borne by you alone, and therefore it is my duty to advise you to accept any settlement possible in the circumstances. But if you, who have to suffer, are prepared to undergo any amount of suffering for principle's sake, I must not only refrain from pressing you further but even congratulate you. I shall therefore continue to act as President of your Committee and help you to the best of my ability. But you must remember that I am but a junior member of the House of Lords and do not command much influence. However, you may rest assured that what little influence I possess will be continually exerted on your behalf."

We were both pleased to hear these words of encouragement.

One delightful feature of this interview has perhaps not escaped the reader. As I have already observed, Sheth Haji Habib and myself held divergent views, and yet there were such friendship and mutual confidence between us that the Sheth did not hesitate to communicate his difference of opinion through me. He relied upon me to present his case fully to Lord Ampthill.

During my stay in England I had occasion to talk with many Indian anarchists. My booklet, *Indian Home Rule*,[1] written during the return voyage to South Africa on board the R.M.S. *Kildonan Castle* (November, 1909), and published soon afterwards in *Indian Opinion*, had its origin from the necessity of having to meet their arguments as well as to solve the difficulties of Indians in South Africa who held similar views. I had also discussed the main points of the book with Lord Ampthill in order that he might not feel for one moment that I had misused his name and his help for my work in South Africa by suppressing my own views.

This discussion with Lord Ampthill has always remained imprinted on my memory. He found time to meet me in spite of illness in his family. Although he did not agree with my views, as expressed in *Hind Swaraj*, he accorded his support to our struggle till the last, and my relations with him were always cordial.

Our deputation, which now returned from England, did not bring good news with it. But I did not mind what conclusions the community would draw from our conversations with Lord Ampthill. I knew who would stand by us till the end. My ideas about Satyagraha had now matured, and I had realized its universality as well as its excellence. I was therefore perfectly at ease. *Hind Swaraj* was written in order to demonstrate the sublimity of Satyagraha. That book is a true measure

---

[1] Called *Hind Swaraj*. This was published in Hindi and English.

of my faith in its efficacy. I was perfectly indifferent to the numerical strength of the fighters on our side.

But I was not free from anxiety on the score of finance. It was indeed hard to prosecute a long and protracted struggle without funds. I did not realize then as clearly as I do now that a struggle can be carried on without funds, that money very often spoils a righteous fight, and that God never gives a Satyagrahi or Mumukshu[1] anything beyond his strict needs. But I had faith in God, who did not even then desert me, but raised me from the slough of despondency. Though I had to tell the Indians on our landing in South Africa that our mission had failed, yet God relieved me at the same moment from financial difficulty. Just as I set my foot in Cape Town I received a cable from England that Ratanji Jamshedji Tata of Bombay had given Rs. 25,000 to our funds.

But the largest possible gift of money could not by itself help forward the Satyagraha struggle; for a fight on behalf of Truth consists chiefly in self-purification and self-reliance. Such a moral warfare is impossible without capital in the shape of character. Just as a splendid palace deserted by its inmates looks like a ruin, so does a man without character. The Satyagrahis now saw that no one could tell how long the struggle would last. They could not impose a time limit on their responsibilities. Whether the campaign lasted one year or many, it was all the same to them.

But what about their families in the meantime? No one would engage as an employee a man who was constantly going to jail. When he was released, how was

[1] A Pilgrim of eternity.

he to maintain himself as well as those dependent upon him? Even a Satyagrahi may be excused if he feels troubled at heart from want of his daily bread. There cannot be many in this world who would fight the good fight in spite of being compelled to condemn their nearest and dearest to the same starvation which they suffered in their own person.

Till now the families of all jail-going Satyagrahis were maintained by a system of monthly allowances in cash according to their need. It would not do to grant an equal sum to all. A Satyagrahi who had a family of five persons dependent upon him could not be placed on the same level with another who was unmarried and without any family responsibilities. Nor was it possible to recruit only unmarried people for our "army." The one principle generally observed was, that each family was asked to name the minimum amount, adequate for its own needs, and was paid accordingly on trust.

There was considerable room here for fraud, and we might be certain that some rogue would not fail to take full advantage of it. Others were honest, but were accustomed to live in a particular style and naturally expected such help as would enable them to keep it up. I saw that at this rate the movement could not be conducted for any length of time. There was always the risk of injustice being done to the deserving and undue advantage being taken by the unscrupulous. There was only one solution for this difficulty, which was that all the families should be kept together in one place and should become members of a sort of co-operative commonwealth.

Clearly it would not be at all easy to live a simple,

inexpensive life amid the varied distractions of Johannesburg. Again, in the city, there could not be found a place where so many families could prosecute some useful industry in their own homes. It was therefore clear that the place selected should be neither too far from nor too near to the mining capital. There was of course Phoenix, where *Indian Opinion* was being printed, and where there was also some farming already being carried on. Phoenix was also convenient in many ways. But it was more than three hundred miles away from Johannesburg and only to be reached by a train journey of thirty hours. It would therefore be difficult and expensive to take the families such a distance and bring them back again. Besides, the Indian families in the Transvaal would not be ready to leave their homes and go to such a far-off place; and even if they were ready, it seemed impossible to send them, as well as the Satyagrahi prisoners on their release, such a long distance.

Mr. Kallenbach had bought a farm of about 1,100 acres. On May 30, 1910, he gave the use of it to Satyagrahis free of any rent or charge. Upon this farm there were nearly one thousand fruit-trees and a small house at the foot of a hill with accommodation for half a dozen people. Water was supplied from two wells and also from a spring. The nearest railway station, Lawley, was about a mile from the farm and Johannesburg was twenty-one miles away. We decided to build houses upon this farm and to invite the families of Satyagrahis to settle there. Oranges, apricots, and plums grew in such abundance that during the fruit season the Satyagrahis could have their fill of fruit and yet have a surplus besides. The spring was about five hundred yards distant from our quarters, and the water had to be fetched on carrying-poles, which afforded excellent daily exercise.

Here we insisted that we should not have any servants, either for the household work or as far as might be even for the farming and building operations. Everything, therefore, from cooking to scavenging, was done by our own hands. As regards the arrangements for families, we resolved from the first that the men and women should be housed separately. The houses therefore were built in two separate blocks, each at some distance from the other. For the time it was considered sufficient to provide room for ten women and sixty men. Then, again, we had to erect a house for Mr. Kallenbach, and by its side a schoolhouse, as well as a workshop for carpentry and shoemaking.

We wanted to be self-reliant, as far as possible, even in erecting our buildings. The architect, of course, was Mr. Kallenbach himself, and he got hold of a European mason. A Gujarati carpenter, Narayandas Damania, volunteered his services free of charge, and brought other carpenters to work at reduced rates. As regards unskilled labour, the settlers all toiled with their own hands. Some of them, who had supple limbs, literally worked wonders. A fine Satyagrahi named Vihari did half of the carpenters' work. The lion-like Thambi Naidoo was in charge of sanitation and marketing, for which he had to go in to Johannesburg.

One of the settlers was Pragji Desai, who had never hitherto been accustomed to discomfort all his life. But at Tolstoy Farm he had often to put up with bitter cold at night and early morning, with sometimes the sun burning hot in the daytime and also sharp drenching rains. In the very beginning, we lived in tents for about two months while the buildings were under construction. The structures were all of corrugated iron and therefore they did not take long to erect. The timber also could be had ready-made in all sizes required. The only thing we had to do was to cut it to measure. There were not many doors or windows to be prepared. Hence quite a number of simple buildings were erected within a very short space of time. But all this labour was a heavy tax on Pragji's physical health at first. The work was certainly harder on the farm than in jail. One day he actually fainted owing to great fatigue and heat. But he was not the man to give in. He fully trained up his body there, and in the end he stood abreast of us all as a good worker.

Then there was Joseph Royappen, a barrister, free from all a barrister's pride. He could not undertake very heavy work at first. It was difficult, for instance, for him to fetch down loads all the way from the railway train and to haul them on to our cart to the settlement, but he did his best. The weak became strong on Tolstoy Farm, and labour proved to be a tonic to all of us without exception.

CHAPTER XVII

"HIND SWARAJ"

THE POET TULSIDAS[1] has said: "Of religion, pity (or love) is the root, as egotism is of the body. Therefore, we should not abandon pity so long as we are alive." This appears to me to be a scientific truth. I believe in it as much as I believe in two and two being four. The force of love is the same as the force of the soul or of truth. We have evidence of its working at every step. The universe would disappear without the existence of that force of love.

If we ask for historical evidence, it is necessary to know what history means. If history means the doings of kings and emperors, there can be no evidence of soul-force or passive resistance in such history. We cannot expect to get silver ore out of a tin mine. History, as we know it, is a record of the wars of the world; and so there is a proverb among Englishmen that a nation which has no history—that is, no wars—is a happy nation. How kings acted, how they became enemies of one another, and how they murdered one another—all this is found accurately recorded in history; and, if this were everything that had happened in the world, it would have been ended long ago.

If the story of the universe had commenced with wars, not a man would have been found alive to-day. Those people who have been warred against have disap-

---

[1] Tulsidas was the writer of the *Ramayana* in Hindi. This chapter is taken from Mr. Gandhi's book called *Hind Swaraj*.

peared, as, for instance, the natives of Australia, of whom hardly a man was left alive by the intruders. Mark, please, that these natives did not use soul-force in self-defence, and it does not require much foresight to know that the Australians are likely to share the same fate as their victims. "Those that take the sword shall perish with the sword." With us, the proverb is that professional swimmers will find a watery grave.

The fact that there are so many men still alive in the world shows that the world is based not on the force of arms, but on the force of truth or love. Therefore the greatest and most unimpeachable evidence of the success of this force is to be found in the fact that, in spite of all these wars, the world still lives on.

Thousands, indeed hundreds of thousands, depend for their existence on a very active working of this force. Little quarrels of millions of families in their daily lives disappear before the exercise of this force. Hundreds of nations live in peace on this account. History does not, and cannot, take note of this fact. History is really a record of every interruption of the even working of the force of love or of the soul.

Two brothers quarrel; one of them repents and re-awakens the love that was lying dormant in him; the two again begin to live in peace; nobody takes note of this. But if the two brothers, through the intervention of solicitors or some other reason, take up arms or go to law—which is another form of the exhibition of brute force—their doings would be immediately noticed in the press, they would be the talk of their neighbours, and would probably go down to history. And what is true of families and communities is true of nations. There is no reason to believe that there is one law for families and another for nations. History, then, is a record of an interruption of the course of nature. Soul-force, being natural, is not noted in history.

When I refuse to do a thing that is repugnant to my conscience I use soul-force. For instance, suppose the Government of the day has passed a law which is applicable to me. I do not like it. If, by using violence, I force the Government to repeal the law, I am employing what may be termed body-force. If I do not obey the law, and accept the penalty for its breach, I use soul-force. It involves sacrifice of self.

Everybody admits that sacrifice of self is infinitely superior to the sacrifice of others. Moreover, if this kind of force is used in a cause that is unjust, only the person using it suffers. He does not make others suffer for his mistakes. Men have before now done many things which were subsequently found to have been wrong. No man can claim to be absolutely in the right, or that a particular thing is wrong, because he thinks so, but it is wrong for him so long as that is his deliberate judgment. It is therefore meet that he should not do that which he knows to be wrong, and should suffer the consequence, whatever it may be. This is the key to the use of soul-force.

When we do not like certain laws, we do not break the heads of law-givers, but we suffer and do not submit to them. That we should obey other laws whether good or bad is a new-fangled notion. There was no such thing in former days. The people disregarded those laws they did not like, and suffered the penalties for their breach. It is contrary to our manhood if we obey laws repugnant to our conscience. Such teaching is opposed to religion, and means slavery. If the Government were to ask us to go about without any clothing, should we do so? If I were a passive resister, I would say to them that I would have nothing to do with their law. But we have so forgotten ourselves and become so compliant that we do not mind any law, however degrading.

A man who has realized his manhood, who fears only God, will fear no one else. Man-made laws are not necessarily binding on him. Even the Government do not expect any such thing from us. They do not say: "You must do such and such a thing," but they say: "If you do not do it, we will punish you." We are sunk so low that we fancy that it is our duty and our religion to do what the law lays down. If man will only realize that it is unmanly to obey laws that are unjust, no man's tyranny will enslave him. This is the key to self-rule or home-rule.

It is a superstition and an ungodly thing to believe that an act of a majority binds a minority. Many examples can be given in which acts of majorities will be found to have been wrong, and those of minorities to have been right. All reforms owe their origin to the initiation of minorities in opposition to majorities. If among a band of robbers a knowledge of robbing is obligatory, is a man of religion to accept the obligation? So long as the superstition that men should obey unjust laws exists, so long will their slavery exist. And a passive resister alone can remove such a superstition.

To use brute-force, to use gunpowder, is contrary to passive resistance, for it means that we want our opponent to do by force that which we desire but he does not. And, if such a use of force is justifiable, surely he is entitled to do likewise by us. And so we should never come to an agreement. We may simply fancy, like the blind horse moving in a circle round a mill, that we are making progress. Those who believe that they are not bound to obey laws which are repugnant to their conscience have only the remedy of passive resistance open to them. Any other must lead to disaster.

Thus passive resistance, that is, soul-force, is matchless. It is superior to the force of arms. It cannot be considered merely a weapon of the weak. Physical-force men are strangers to the courage that is requisite in a passive resister. Do we believe that a coward can ever disobey a law that he dislikes? But a passive resister will say he will not obey a law that is against his conscience, even though he may be blown to pieces at the mouth of a cannon.

Wherein is courage required—in blowing others to pieces from behind a cannon or with a smiling face to approach a cannon and to be blown to pieces? Who is the true warrior—he who keeps death always as a bosom-friend or he who controls the death of others? Believe me that a man devoid of courage and manhood can never be a passive resister.

This, however, I will admit: that even a man weak in body is capable of offering this resistance. One man can offer it just as well as millions. Both men and women can indulge in it. It does not require the training of an army; it needs no ju-jitsu. Control over the mind is alone necessary, and, when that is attained, man is free like the king of the forest, and his very glance withers the enemy.

Passive resistance is an all-sided sword; it can be used anyhow; it blesses him who uses it and him against whom it is used. Without drawing a drop of blood, it produces far-reaching results. It never rusts, and cannot be stolen.

Kings will always use their kingly weapons. To use force is bred in them. They want to command. But those who have to obey commands do not want guns; and these are in a majority throughout the world. They have to learn either body-force or soul-force. Where they learn the former, both the rulers and the ruled become like so many mad men. But where they learn soul-force, the commands of the rulers do not go beyond the point of their swords; for true men disregard unjust commands. Peasants have never been subdued by the sword, and never will be. They do not know the use of the sword, and they are not frightened by the use of it by others. That nation is great which rests its head upon death as its pillow. Those who defy death are free from all fear. For those who are labouring under the delusive charms of brute force, this picture is not overdrawn. The fact is that, in India, the nation at large has generally used passive resistance in all departments of life. We cease to co-operate with our rulers when they displease us. This is passive resistance.

I remember an instance when, in a small principality, the villagers were offended by some command issued by the prince. The former immediately began vacating the village. The prince became nervous, apologized to his subjects and withdrew his command. Many such instances can be found in India. Real home-rule is possible only where passive resistance is the guiding force of the people. Any other rule is foreign rule.

It is difficult to become a passive resister unless the body is trained. As a rule, the mind, residing in a body that has become softened by pampering, is also soft, and where there is no strength of mind, there can be no strength of soul. We shall have to improve our physique in India by getting rid of infant marriages and luxurious living.

I have known a lad of fourteen years become a passive resister; I have known also sick people doing likewise; and I have also known physically strong and otherwise happy people being unable to take up passive resistance. After a great deal of experience, it seems to me that those who want to become passive resisters for the service of the country have to observe perfect chastity, adopt poverty, follow truth, and cultivate fearlessness.

Chastity is one of the greatest disciplines without which the mind cannot attain requisite firmness. A man who is unchaste loses stamina, becomes emasculated and cowardly. He whose mind is given over to animal passions is not capable of any great effort. This can be proved by innumerable instances. What, then, is a married person to do? is the question that arises naturally; and yet it need not arise. When a husband and wife gratify the passions, it is no less an animal indulgence on that account. Such an indulgence, except for perpetuating the race, is strictly prohibited. But a passive resister has to avoid even that very limited indulgence, because he can have no desire for progeny. A married man, therefore, can observe perfect chastity.

Several questions arise: How is one to carry one's wife with one? What are her rights, and such other questions? Yet those who wish to take part in a great work are bound to solve these puzzles.

Just as there is necessity for chastity, so is there for

poverty. Pecuniary ambition and passive resistance cannot well go together. Those who have money are not expected to throw it away, but they are expected to be indifferent about it. They must be prepared to lose every penny rather than give up passive resistance.

Passive resistance has been described as truth-force. Truth, therefore, has necessarily to be followed, and that at any cost. In this connection, academic questions such as whether a man may not lie in order to save a life, etc., arise, but these questions occur only to those who wish to justify lying. Those who want to follow truth every time are not placed in such a quandary, and, if they are, they are still saved from a false position.

Passive resistance cannot proceed a step without fearlessness. Those alone can follow the path to the end who are free from fear, whether as to their possessions, their false honour, their relatives, the government, bodily injuries, death.

These observances are not to be abandoned in the belief that they are difficult. Nature has implanted in the human breast ability to cope with any difficulty or suffering that may come to man unprovoked. These qualities are worth having.

A physical-force man has to have many other useless qualities which a passive resister never needs. And we shall find that whatever extra effort a swordsman needs is due to lack of fearlessness. If he is an embodiment of the latter, the sword will drop from his hand that very moment. He does not need its support. One who is free from hatred requires no sword. A man with a stick suddenly came face to face with a lion, and instinctively raised his weapon in self-defence. The man saw that he had only prated about fearlessness when there was none in him. That moment he dropped the stick, and found himself free from all fear.

Finally, let each of us do his duty. If I do my duty, that is, serve myself, I shall be able to serve others. I will take the liberty of repeating:

1. Real home-rule is self-rule or self-control.
2. The way to it is passive resistance; that is, soul-force or love-force.

CHAPTER XVIII

TOLSTOY FARM

EVERYONE HAD to go now and then into Johannesburg on some errand or other. Our children used to like to make the journey just for the fun of the thing. Kallenbach and I also had to go there on business. We made a strict rule that no one could travel by rail except on direct public business connected with our little commonwealth. Then, too, if we went on public business we had to travel third class. Anyone who wanted to go on a pleasure trip must go on foot, and carry homemade provisions with him. None must spend anything on his food in the city. Had it not been for these drastic rules, the money saved by living in the country would have been wasted on railway fares and city picnics in Johannesburg. But by this discipline we were able to avoid all waste of public funds.

The provisions carried by us on our journey were of the simplest possible character. They consisted of home-baked bread made out of coarse wheat flour, from which the bran had not been extracted, ground-nut butter prepared at home, and home-preserved marmalade. We had purchased an iron hand-mill for grinding the ground-nuts. This butter was four times cheaper than ordinary butter. We had plenty of oranges on the Farm itself. We scarcely used cow's milk at all, and generally managed with condensed milk.

But to return to the different trips to town. If anyone wished to go to Johannesburg for pleasure, he had to go there on foot and return on the same day. It was twenty-one miles to Johannesburg and the same distance back. We saved hundreds of rupees by this rule of going on foot, and those who went walking were much benefited by it. Some acquired anew the habit of walking. The usual practice was for the intending traveller to rise at two o'clock in the morning long before daylight and start at once. He would then reach Johannesburg after six hours' continuous walking. The record for the minimum time taken on this journey was four hours eighteen minutes.

This common discipline did not operate upon the settlers as a hardship at all. Indeed, it was accepted cheerfully. It would have been impossible to have had a single settler if compulsion had been employed. Everyone thoroughly enjoyed the work on the Farm and the pleasant errands to the city.

It was difficult to prevent the youngsters from playing pranks while engaged in work. No more work was given them than they could willingly and cheerfully render, and I never found the work done unsatisfactory either in quantity or quality.

In spite of the large number of settlers living in one place, refuse and night-soil were not to be found anywhere on the Farm. All rubbish was buried in trenches dug for the purpose. No waste water was permitted to be thrown on the roads. This was collected in buckets and used to water the trees. Scraps of food and vegetable refuse were also utilized as manure. A square pit, one foot and a half deep, was dug out to receive the night-soil, which was afterwards fully covered with the excavated earth and therefore did not give out any smell. There were no flies, and no one would imagine that night-soil had been buried there. We were thus not only spared a nuisance, but what might have been a possible annoyance was converted into valuable manure for the Farm. If night-soil were properly utilized in India we could get manure worth lakhs of rupees and also secure immunity from a number of diseases. But by our bad habits we spoil our sacred river banks and furnish breeding grounds for flies. Owing to our criminal negligence these settle down upon uncovered night-soil and then settle upon us. Thus they defile our bodies after we have bathed. Such acts of gross neglect are a sin against God as well as man. They betray a sad want of public spirit and consideration for others.

The work before us at Tolstoy Farm was to keep the place a busy hive of industry, and thus to save expense. In the end our main aim was to make the families self-supporting. If we achieved this goal, we could then carry on our struggle with the Transvaal Government for an indefinite period.

The use of shoes in a hot climate is harmful, because all the perspiration is absorbed by the feet which thus grow tender. No socks are really needed in the Transvaal just as none are needed in India. But we thought that the feet must be protected against thorns and sharp stones. We therefore determined to learn to make our own leather sandals.

At Marianhill, near Pinetown in Natal, there is a Monastery of German Catholic monks, called Trappists, where useful industries of this nature are carried on. Kallenbach went there and acquired the art of making good leather sandals. Afterwards he returned and taught this art to me, and I in my turn taught the art to others. Thus several young men learnt this work of making sandals, and we commenced selling them to our friends. I need scarcely add that many of my pupils easily surpassed me in the art.

Another handicraft introduced was that of carpentry. Having founded a sort of village at Tolstoy Farm we needed all manner of things large and small, from benches to boxes, and we made all these ourselves. Those unselfish carpenters, already referred to, helped us for several months. Mr. Kallenbach was the head of the carpentry department. As such he gave us, every moment, clear evidence of his mastery and exactitude.

A school was quite indispensable for the youngsters and the children. This was the most difficult of all our tasks, and we never achieved complete success till the very last. The burden of the teaching work was largely borne by Mr. Kallenbach and myself. The school could be held only in the afternoon, when both of us were thoroughly exhausted by our morning's work, and so were our pupils. The teachers therefore would often be dozing as well as the boys. We used to sprinkle water on our eyes, and by playing with the children try to make them attentive and also pull up ourselves, but sometimes in vain. The body peremptorily demanded rest and would not take any denial.

But this was only one of the least of our teaching problems. For the classes were conducted somehow in spite of these dozings. But what were we to teach pupils who spoke three languages, Gujarati, Tamil or Telugu? How were we to teach them and what books were we to use? I was anxious to make the vernaculars the medium

A BAND OF SATYAGRAHIS WITH MR. GANDHI IN THE CENTRE

of instruction. I knew a little Tamil but no Telugu. What could one teacher do in these circumstances? I tried to use some of the young men as teachers, but the experiment was not quite a success. Pragji's services were requisitioned.[1] Some of the youngsters were mischievous and lazy and always on bad terms with their books. A teacher could not expect to make much headway with such refractory pupils. Again we could not be regular in our teaching. Business sometimes took Hermann Kallenbach as well as me to Johannesburg. We had to drop our teaching in order to go there, and this hurt our work.

Religious teaching presented another tough problem. I would like the Musalmans to read the Quran, and the Parsis to study the Avesta. There was one Khoja child whose father had laid upon me the responsibility of teaching his child the special doctrine of the sect.[2] Little by little I collected books bearing on Islam and Zoroastrianism. Also I wrote out the fundamental doctrines of Hinduism according to my own light. If this document were now in my possession, I should have inserted it here at this point as a landmark in my spiritual progress. But I have thrown it away or burnt it, as I have many such things in my life. Such papers as I felt it unnecessary to preserve, I destroyed. To have preserved them would have been burdensome and expensive to me. It would have involved my keeping cabinets and boxes, and this would have been an eyesore to one who has taken the vow of poverty.

---

[1] He is now in South Africa at Phoenix, editing *Indian Opinion* along with Mahatma Gandhi's son, Manilal.
[2] The Khojas are a special sect of Islam.

The children were saved from the infection of religious intolerance. They learnt to view one another's religions with a large-minded charity. They also learnt to live together as blood-brothers. And from what little I know about the later activities of some of the children of Tolstoy Farm, I am certain that the education which they received there has not been in vain. Even if imperfect, it was a thoughtful and religious experiment, and among the happiest reminiscences of Tolstoy Farm, this imperfect teaching experiment is no less pleasant than the rest.

Hardly ever has any school-teacher had to take the kind of heterogeneous class that fell to my lot. It contained pupils of all ages and of both sexes. There were boys and girls of about seven years of age. Young men were there aged twenty. There were also young girls of twelve or thirteen. Some of the boys were wild and mischievous.

What, then, was I to teach this ill-assorted group? What language should I use in talking to them in their classes? Tamil and Telugu children knew their own mother-tongue and sometimes a little Dutch and English. I could speak to these children in English. So I divided the class in two sections, the Gujarati section to be talked to in Gujarati and the rest in English. For the principal part of the teaching, I arranged either to read or tell to them interesting stories. Also I proposed to bring them into close mutual contact and to lead them to cultivate together a spirit of friendship and service. Then there was to be imparted in addition some general knowledge of history and geography and in some cases of arithmetic. Writing was also taught, and so were the religious hymns which formed part of our prayers.

The boys and girls met freely. My experiment of co-education on Tolstoy Farm was the most fearless of its type. To-day I dare not either allow, or train children to enjoy, the liberty which I had fearlessly granted to the Tolstoy Farm class. My mind then used to be more innocent than it is now, and my experiment was due partly to my ignorance. Since then I have had bitter experiences, and have sometimes burnt my fingers badly. Persons whom I took to be thoroughly innocent have turned out corrupt. I have observed the roots of evil deep down in my own nature; and timidity has claimed me for its own. Nevertheless, in spite of repeated failure, I do not repent having made this school experiment. My conscience bears witness that it did not do them any harm. But as a child who has burnt himself with hot milk blows even into cold whey, so my present attitude with regard to children's education is one of extra caution.

A man cannot borrow faith or courage from others. The doubter is marked out for destruction, as the Gita puts it. My faith and courage were at their highest point in Tolstoy Farm. I have been constantly praying to God to permit me to re-attain that height, but the prayer has not yet been fulfilled. For the number of such suppliants before the Great White Throne is legion. The only consolation is that God has as many ears as there are suppliants. Therefore I repose full faith in Him and know that my prayer will at last be accepted when I have fitted myself for His grace.

Here, then, was my experiment in co-education. I sent the boys reputed to be mischievous and the innocent young girls to bathe in the same spot at the same time. I had fully explained the duty of self-restraint to the children, who were all familiar with my Satyagraha principles. I knew, and so did the children, that I loved them with a mother's love. The spring of water where they bathed together was at some distance from the kitchen. Was it folly to let the children meet there for their bath and yet expect them to be innocent? My eye always followed the girls as a mother's eye would follow a daughter. The time was fixed when all the boys and girls went together for a bath. There was an element of safety in the fact that they went in a body for this mixed bathing. Solitude was always avoided. Generally I also would be at the spring at the same time.

All of us slept in an open veranda. The boys and the girls would spread themselves around me. There was hardly the distance of three feet between any two beds. Some care was exercised in arranging the beds; but any amount of care would have been futile in the case of a wicked mind. I can see that God alone safeguarded the honour of these boys and girls. I made the experiment from the belief that boys and girls could thus live together without harm, and the parents with their boundless faith in me allowed me full liberty to make it.

One day, one of the young lads made fun of two girls, and the girls themselves or some child brought me the information. The news made me tremble. I made enquiries and found the report to be true. So I remonstrated with the young lads, but that was not enough. I wished the two girls to have some sign on their persons to warn every young man that no evil eye might be cast upon them, and as a lesson to every girl that no one dare to assail their purity. The passionate Ravana could not so much as touch Sita with evil intent while Rama was thousands of miles away.[1] What mark should the girls bear so as to give them a sense of security and at the same time sterilize the sinner's eye? This question kept me awake all night. In the morning, I gently suggested to the girls that they might let me cut off their fine long hair. On the Farm we all shaved ourselves and cut each other's hair. We therefore kept scissors and clipping machines. At first the girls would not listen to me. I had already explained the situation to the elderly women of our settlement. They could not bear to think of my suggestion, but yet understood my motive; and they had finally accorded their support to me. The two girls were both of them noble in character. One of them is now dead. She was very bright and intelligent. The other is living and she has to-day children of her own. They came round to my point of view after all, and at once the very hand that is narrating this incident set to cut off their hair. Afterwards I analysed and explained my procedure before my class, with excellent results. The girls in question did not lose in any case. Indeed, they gained more than can be described. I hope the youths still remember this incident and keep their eye from sin.

Experiments such as I have placed on record here are not, of course, meant for imitation. Any teacher who imitates them would be incurring grave risks. I have only at this point taken note of them to show how far a man can go in certain circumstances and to stress the purity of heart required for the Satyagraha struggle. This very

[1] Ravana was the Demon King of Lanka who carried off Sita, the chaste wife of Rama.

purity was a guarantee of victory. Before launching on such experiments the teacher has to be both father and mother to his pupils and to be prepared for all eventualities whatsoever. Only the hardest penance can fit him to conduct them.

This act of mine was not without effect on the entire life of these settlers on the Farm. As we had intended to cut down expenses to the barest minimum, we changed our mode of dress also. In the city the Indian men, including the Satyagrahis, had been accustomed to wear full European dress. Such elaborate clothing was not needed on the Farm. We had all become labourers and therefore we now put on labourer's dress in the European style, that is to say, only the ordinary labourer's trousers and shirt. These were imitated from the prisoners' uniform. We used cheap trousers and shirts which could be obtained ready-made. They were of coarse blue cloth. Most of the Indian ladies were good hands at sewing and took charge of the tailoring department.

For our food we usually had rice, dal, vegetables and wholemeal bread with porridge occasionally added. All this was served in a single dish which was like the bowl supplied to prisoners in jail. We had made spoons out of wood for ourselves. There were three meals each day. We had bread and home-made wheaten "coffee" at six o'clock in the morning; rice, dal, and vegetables at eleven; wheat porridge and milk, or bread and "coffee," at half-past five in the evening. After the evening meal we sang Bhajans,[1] and sometimes had readings from the Ramayana[2] or the books of Islam. The Bhajans were in English, Hindi and Gujarati. Sometimes we had one hymn from

[1] Hymns.   [2] The sacred epic composed by Tulsidas.

each of the three languages, and sometimes only one. Everyone retired to rest at nine o'clock.

Many observed the Ekadashi Fast on the Farm.[1] We were joined by P. K. Kotwal, who had had much experience of fasting, and some of us had followed him in keeping the Chaturmas[2] form of fasting. The Ramazan Fast of Islam also arrived in the meanwhile.[3] There were Musalman young men among us, and we felt that we must encourage them to keep their special Fast. We arranged for them to have meals in the evening after sunset as well as in the early morning. Porridge was prepared for them in the evening. There was no meat, of course, nor did anyone ask for it. In order to keep the Musalman friends company the rest of us had only one meal just before sunset; so the only difference was that the others had just finished their supper at the time when the Musalman boys were commencing theirs. These boys were so courteous that they did not put anyone to extra trouble, although they were observing fasts; and the fact that the non-Musalman children supported them in fasting left a good impression on all. I do not remember that there ever was a quarrel between the Hindus and the Musalman boys on the score of religion. On the other hand, I know that although staunch in their beliefs, they all treated one another with respect and assisted one another in their respective religious observances.

---

[1] A Hindu fast strictly kept on the eleventh day of the moon for the whole day and night, accompanied by prayer.
[2] Another Hindu fasting period of a sacrificial character which continues over four months.
[3] The great Muhammadan fasting month during which no food or water is taken before sunset.

Although we were living far away from all the amenities of city life, we did not keep even the commonest appliances or medicines against any possible attacks of illness. I had in those days as much faith in the nature cure of diseases as I had in the innocence of children. I felt that there should not be disease if we lived a simple life. But if there was any disease, I was confident in being able to deal with it. My booklet on health is a note-book of my experiments and of my living faith in those days. I was proud enough to believe that illness for me was out of the question. I held that all kinds of disease could be cured by nature treatment, such as earth bandages, water hip-baths, fasting, and changes of diet. There was not a single case of illness on the Farm during those years for whose remedy we went back to the use of drugs or called in a doctor.

But I have lost courage, and in view of my own two serious illnesses in the years 1914 and 1918, I felt at last that I had forfeited the right to make such experiments in future.

On the Farm there was an ebb and flow of Satyagrahis. Some of them would be expecting to go to prison while others had just been released from it. Once it so happened that there arrived at the Farm two Satyagrahis who had been remitted by the magistrate without bail on personal recognizance. They had to attend the Court on the very next day in order to receive the sentence. It happened they were so engrossed in conversation that the time was up for the last train back to Johannesburg. So it was a doubtful question whether they would succeed in taking that train and reaching Johannesburg in time. They were both young men and good athletes. They ran for all they were worth along with some of us who wanted to see them off.

While still on the way I heard the whistle of the train as it steamed into the station. When there was a second whistle, indicating the departure, we had just reached the precincts of the station. The young men increased their speed every moment, and I lagged behind. The train had started. Fortunately, the station-master saw them running and stopped the train, thus enabling them to catch it after all. I tendered my thanks to the station-master when I reached the station.

Two points emerge out of this incident. First of all, it shows the eagerness of the Satyagrahis in seeking jail and in fulfilling their promises. Secondly, it reveals the happy relations cultivated between the Satyagrahis and the local officials. If the two young men had missed the train, they could hardly have attended the Court on the next day. No surety had been required of them, nor had they been asked to deposit any money with the Court. The Satyagrahis had acquired such prestige that magistrates did not think it necessary to ask them for bail, because they knew that they were courting imprisonment. The young Satyagrahis were therefore deeply anxious at the prospect of missing the train and ran as swiftly as the wind.

At the commencement of the struggle Satyagrahis were somewhat harassed by officials. The jail authorities in certain places were unduly severe. But as the movement advanced, we found the bitterness of the officials softened and not seldom it became even changed to sweetness. Where there was long-continued intercourse with them, they even began to assist us, like the station-master I have referred to. The Satyagrahis never bribed these officials in any shape or form, in order to secure any amenities from them. But where kindnesses were offered through courtesy, they were freely accepted. In this way, the Satyagrahis had been in the habit of enjoying kindly facilities in many places. If a station-master is ill-disposed he can harass the passengers in a variety of ways, keeping himself all the while within the four corners of the railway rules and regulations. No complaint can be preferred against such harassment. On the other hand, if the official is well-disposed, he can grant many facilities without violating the rules. All such kindness, which would be freely granted, we had been able to secure from the station-master at Lawley Station because of our courtesy, patience and capacity for self-suffering.

For about the last thirty years I have been fond of making experiments in dietetics from the religious, economic and hygienic standpoints. This predilection for food reform still persists. People around me would naturally be influenced by my different experiments. Side by side with dietetics I have made experiments in treating diseases with natural curative agents such as earth and water, without recourse to drugs. When I practised as a barrister, cordial relations were established with my clients so that we looked upon one another almost as members of one family. The clients therefore made me a partner of all their joys and sorrows. Some of them sought my advice after having become familiar with my experiments in nature cures.

Stray patients of this class would sometimes arrive at Tolstoy Farm. One of these was Lutavan, an aged client, who had first come out from North India as an indentured labourer. He was over seventy years old and suffered from chronic asthma and bronchitis. He had given long trials to Vaidyas'[1] powders and doctors' mixtures. In those days I had boundless faith in the efficacy of my methods of curing diseases, and therefore I agreed not indeed to treat him, but to try one of my experiments upon him if he consented to live on the Farm and observe all my conditions. One of these was that he should give up tobacco, to which he was strongly addicted. I made him fast for twenty-four hours. At noon, every day, I commenced giving him a Kuhne bath in the sun, as the weather then was not extra warm. For food he had a little rice, some olive oil, honey, and, along with honey, porridge. Sometimes I gave him oranges, and at other times grapes and wheaten coffee. Salt and all condiments were forbidden. Lutavan slept in the same building with me but in an inner apartment. For sleeping purposes everyone at Tolstoy Farm was given two blankets, one for spreading and the other for covering. We all had wooden pillows.

A week passed. There was an accession of energy in Lutavan's body. His asthma gave less trouble, but I noticed that he had more fits of coughing at night than by day. Therefore I had my suspicion that he was smoking secretly, and I asked him if this was true. Lutavan said he did not. A couple of days passed and since still there was no improvement, I determined to watch him. Everyone slept on the floor, and the place was full of snakes. Mr. Kallenbach had therefore given me an elec-

---

[1] Doctors in India who use the Ayurvedic system, the ancient method of Hindu India. The Muslim system is called Yunani (literally, Greek).

tric torch and kept one for himself. I always slept with this torch by my side. One night I resolved to lie in bed awake. My bed was spread on the verandah just near the door, and Lutavan slept inside but also near the door. Lutavan coughed at midnight, lighted a cigarette and began to smoke. I slowly went up to his bed and switched on the torch. Lutavan at once understood that he was found out and became nervous. He ceased smoking, stood up and touched my feet. "I have done," he confessed, "a very wrong and deceitful thing. Henceforth I will never smoke again. Alas, I have deceived you. Please forgive me."

So saying he almost began to sob. I consoled him and said that it was in his interest not to smoke. His cough ought to have been cured. I told him that when I found he was still suffering I suspected that he was smoking secretly and had watched him. Lutavan gave up smoking. His asthma and cough grew less severe after two or three days, and in a month he was perfectly cured. He was now full of vigour and took his leave of us.

The station-master's son, a child of two years, had an attack of typhoid. This good man had come to know about my curative methods, and therefore sought my advice. On the first day I gave the child no food at all, and from the second day onwards I gave the half of a banana well mashed with a spoonful of olive oil and a few drops of sweet orange juice. At night I applied a cold mud poultice to the child's abdomen, and in this case also my treatment was successful. It is possible that the doctor's diagnosis was wrong and it was not a case of typhoid at all.

I made many such experiments on the Farm, and I do

TOLSTOY FARM

not remember to have failed in even a single case. But to-day I would not venture to employ the same treatment. I would now shudder to have to give banana and olive oil to a patient suffering from typhoid. In the autumn of the year 1918 I had an attack of dysentery myself and I failed to cure it. Even to this day I cannot be certain whether it is due to my own want of self-confidence, or to the difference in climate, that the same treatment which was effective in South Africa is not equally successful in India. But this I know, that the home treatment of diseases and the simplicity of the life on Tolstoy Farm were responsible for saving a very large sum of public money. The settlers learned to look upon one another as members of the same family. The Satyagrahis secured a place of refuge. Little scope was left for dishonesty or hypocrisy. Thus the wheat became easily separated from the tares.

My dietetic regulations were made from a hygienic standpoint, but I conducted a most important experiment upon myself which was purely spiritual in its nature. I had long pondered deeply and read widely over the question whether, as vegetarians, we had any right to take milk. Then one day, when I was living on the Farm, some book or newspaper fell into my hands wherein I read about the inhuman treatment accorded to cows in Calcutta in order to extract the last drop of milk from them. Once when I was discussing with Mr. Kallenbach the necessity for taking milk, in the course of the discussion I told him about this horrible practice in Calcutta, pointing out several other spiritual advantages which seemed to flow from the rejection of milk in our diet. Mr. Kallenbach, with his usual spirit of a knight-errant, was ready at once to launch upon an experiment of doing without milk, as he highly approved of my observations.

The same day both he and I gave up milk, and in the end we came to restrict ourselves to a diet of fresh and dried fruit, having eschewed all cooked food as well. I cannot here go into the later history of this experiment or tell how it ended,[1] but I may say this, that during the five years in which I lived a purely vegetarian and fruitarian life I never felt weak, nor did I suffer from any diseases. Again, during the same period I possessed such a perfect capacity for bodily labour that one day I walked fifty-five miles. At this time forty miles was an ordinary day's journey for me. I am firmly of opinion that this experiment yielded excellent spiritual results. It has always been a matter of regret to me that I was compelled somewhat to modify my fruitarian diet. If I were free from my political pre-occupations, even at this advanced age of my life and at the risk of bodily health, I would revert to the fruit diet to-day in order further to explore its spiritual possibilities. The lack of spiritual insight in doctors and Vaidyas has also been an obstacle in my path.

Such experiments as these could only have their place in a struggle whose very essence was self-purification and spiritual development. Tolstoy Farm proved to be a centre of spiritual purification and penance for the final campaign. I have serious doubts as to whether the struggle could have been prosecuted for eight years,

---

[1] The account of how Mahatma Gandhi returned to a diet of milk—taking goat's milk instead of cow's milk—will be found in *Mahatma Gandhi: His Own Story*, p. 295.

whether we could have secured such large funds, whether the thousands of men and also the women, who participated in its last phase, would ever have borne their full share of suffering, if there had been no Tolstoy Farm. It was there the struggle was won.

Tolstoy Farm was never placed in the limelight. Yet a deserving institution attracts public sympathy to itself. Indians knew that the Tolstoy Farmers were doing what they themselves were not prepared to do and what they themselves looked upon in the light of a hardship. This public confidence was a great asset to the movement when it was organized afresh on a larger scale.

CHAPTER XIX

MR. GOKHALE'S VISIT

THUS THE SATYAGRAHIS went on pursuing the even tenor of their way on Tolstoy Farm, preparing themselves day by day for whatever the future had in store for them. They did not know, nor did they care, when the struggle would end. They were only under one pledge. They must refuse submission to the Black Act and suffer whatever hardships were involved in such disobedience. For a fighter the fight itself is victory; he takes a delight in that alone. And as it rests with him to prosecute the fight, he believes that victory or defeat, pleasure or pain, depends upon himself alone. For him, indeed, there is no such word as pain or defeat. The famous verse of the Gita is found to be true which says that pleasure and pain, victory and defeat, to him are both alike.

Stray Satyagrahis now and then went to jail. But in the intervals when no occasion offered for going to prison, anyone who casually observed the external activities of the Farm could hardly believe that true Satyagrahis were living there, or that they were preparing for another hard struggle. Whenever a sceptic happened to visit the Farm, then if he was a friend he would pity us, and if a critic he would censure us. "These fellows," he would remark, "have grown quite lazy and are therefore eating the bread of idleness in this secluded spot. They are obviously sick of going to jail and are enjoying themselves here in this fruit garden instead, away from all the din and roar of city life."

MR. GOKHALE'S VISIT

How could it be explained to this critic that a Satyagrahi cannot go to jail by violating the moral law; that his very peacefulness and self-restraint constitute his preparation for "war"; that the Satyagrahi, bestowing no thought on human help, relies upon God as his sole refuge?

In the end there happened, or God brought to pass, events which none of us had expected. Help also arrived which was equally unforeseen. The ordeal came unawares, and at last there was achieved a tangible victory which he who runs may also read.

I had been requesting Gokhale and other leaders to go out to South Africa in order to study the condition of the Indian settlers on the spot. But I doubted whether any of them could really come over. Mr. Ritch had also been trying in London to get some Indian leader to visit us. But who would dare to go when the struggle was at such a very low ebb? Gokhale was in England during the year 1911. He was a close student of our struggle in South Africa. He had initiated debates in the Viceroy's Legislative Council and had moved a resolution on February 25, 1910, in favour of the complete prohibition of further recruitment of indentured labour for Natal. This resolution was carried and was the first blow struck against the whole evil system of Indian indentured labour. I had been in communication with him all along. He conferred with the Secretary of State for India in London and informed him of his intention to proceed forthwith to South Africa and acquaint himself with the facts of the Indian position at first hand. The Minister approved of Gokhale's mission. Gokhale wrote to me to arrange a programme for a six weeks' tour, indicating the latest date when he would be obliged to leave South Africa.

No Indian leader had been to South Africa before, or for that matter to any other place outside India to which Indians had emigrated, with a view to examine their condition. We therefore realized the immense importance of this visit of a great leader like Gokhale and determined to accord him a reception which even princes might envy, conducting him to the principal cities of South Africa. Satyagrahis and other Indians alike cheerfully set about making grand preparations of welcome. Europeans were also invited to join and did generally join in the reception. We also resolved that public meetings should be held in different town halls wherever possible, and the mayor of the place should generally occupy the chair, if he consented to do so. We undertook to decorate the principal stations on the railway line and succeeded with some difficulty in securing the necessary permission in most cases. Such permission is not usually granted. But our grand preparation impressed the authorities, who evinced as much sympathy in the matter as they could. For instance, in Johannesburg alone the decoration at Park Station took us about a fortnight, including, as they did, a large ornamental arch of welcome designed by Hermann Kallenbach.

Even in England itself, Gokhale had a foretaste of what South Africa was like. The Secretary of State for India had informed the Union Government of his high rank and his position in the British Commonwealth. But who would think of booking his passage or reserving a good cabin for him? Gokhale's health was so delicate that he would be obliged to have a comfortable cabin where he would be able to enjoy some privacy. The authorities of the Steamship Company roundly stated that there was no such cabin.

I do not quite remember whether it was Gokhale or some friend of his who informed the India Office about this. But a letter was addressed from the India Office to the Directors of the Company and the best cabin was placed at Gokhale's disposal in the same steamer where none had been available before. Thus good came of this initial evil. The captain of the steamer received instructions to accord good treatment to Gokhale, and consequently he had a very happy and peaceful voyage to South Africa. He was just as full of fun and humour as he was serious and earnest. He participated in all the various games and amusements on the steamer, and thus became very popular among his fellow-passengers. The Union Government offered Gokhale their hospitality beforehand during his stay at Pretoria and placed at his disposal the State railway saloon. He conferred with me on the point and then accepted their offer.[1]

Gokhale landed at Cape Town on October 22, 1912. His health was very much more delicate than I had ever anticipated. He had to restrict himself to a particular diet, and he could not endure any fatigue. The programme which I had framed beforehand was therefore much too heavy for him, and I had to cut it down ruthlessly. He himself was prepared to go through with the whole programme, as it originally stood, if no modifications could be made. Needless to say, I deeply repented

---

[1] Indians in South Africa, along with all non-Europeans, are obliged to travel in a special compartment marked "reserved" and are not allowed to sit in the restaurant car owing to the colour bar. These difficulties would be overcome by using the State saloon.

of my folly in drawing up such an onerous itinerary without consulting him. Some changes were made, but much had to be left as it was.

I had not grasped the necessity for securing absolute privacy for him, and afterwards I had the greatest difficulty in securing it. Still, I must in all humility state, in the interests of truth, that since I was proficient in waiting upon the sick and the elderly, as soon as I had realized my folly, all the arrangements were drastically revised so as to give Gokhale privacy and peace. I acted as his secretary throughout the tour. The volunteers, one of whom was Kallenbach, were wideawake, and I do not think that he underwent any discomfort or hardships for want of help.

It was clear that we should have a great meeting in Cape Town. Senator W. P. Schreiner, the head of that illustrious family, was asked to take the chair for the occasion. There was a big meeting attended by a large number of Indians and Europeans. Mr. Schreiner welcomed Mr. Gokhale in well-chosen words and expressed his sympathy with the Indians of South Africa. Gokhale made a speech, concise, full of sound judgment, firm but courteous. This immensely pleased the Indians and fascinated the Europeans. In fact, he won the hearts of the different people of South Africa from the first day that he set foot on South African soil.

From Cape Town, Gokhale was to go to Johannesburg by a railway journey of two days. The Transvaal was the field of battle. As we went from Cape Town the first large border station in the Transvaal was Klerksdorp. Gokhale had to stop there and also to attend meetings at the intermediate stations of Potchefstroom and Krugersdorp as well as at Klerksdorp itself. He therefore went on from Klerksdorp by a special train. The mayors of all these places presided at the meetings and at none of the stations did the train halt longer than one or two hours.

The train reached Johannesburg punctually to the minute. There was a platform specially erected for the occasion covered with rich carpets. Along with other Europeans, Mr. Ellis, the Mayor of Johannesburg, was present, and placed his car at Gokhale's disposal during his stay in the Golden City. An address was presented in the station itself. The Johannesburg address was engraved on a solid heart-shaped plate of gold from the Rand mounted on Rhodesian teak. The plate represented a map of India and Ceylon and was flanked on either side by two gold tablets, one bearing an illustration of the Taj Mahal and the other a characteristic Indian picture. Indian scenes were beautifully carved on the woodwork as well.

Introductions, reading the address, the reply, and receiving other addresses, did not take more than twenty minutes. The address was short enough to be read in five minutes. The volunteers maintained such excellent order that there were no more persons on the platform than it had been expected easily to accommodate. There was no noise or confusion. A huge crowd waited outside, yet no one was at all hampered either in coming or going.

Gokhale received hospitality in a beautiful cottage belonging to Hermann Kallenbach perched on a hill-top five miles from Johannesburg. He liked the place immensely because the scenery was magnificent, the atmosphere was soothing and the house, though simple, was full of art. A special office was hired in the city for Gokhale to receive all visitors. There were three rooms and a private chamber, with also a waiting-room for visitors. He was taken to make personal calls on some distinguished men in the city. A special meeting of leading Europeans was organized so as to give him a thorough understanding of their standpoint.

Besides this, a banquet was held in Gokhale's honour to which were invited four hundred persons, including about 150 Europeans. Indians were admitted by tickets, costing a guinea each—an arrangement which enabled us to meet the expenses of the banquet. The whole of the cooking was attended to by volunteers.

It is difficult to give an adequate idea of this banquet. Hindus and Musalmans in South Africa do not observe the usual restrictions as to interdining. The vegetarians among them do not take meat. Some of the Indians were Christians, with whom I was as intimate as with the rest. These Christians are mostly the descendants of indentured labourers and many of them make their living by serving in hotels as waiters. It was with the assistance of these latter that culinary arrangements could be made on such a large scale without difficulty. We had altogether about fifteen items on the banquet menu. It was quite a novel and wonderful experience for the Europeans of South Africa to sit at dinner with so many Indians at the same table and then to have purely vegetarian fare and to do entirely without wines or liquors. For many of them, the three features were completely new, while two features were a novel experience for all.

To this gathering Gokhale addressed his longest and most important speech in South Africa. In preparing this speech he subjected us who were leaders to a very full examination. He declared that it had been his lifelong practice not to disregard the standpoint of local men, but always to try to meet it as far as he possibly could. Therefore he asked me to inform him about everything I could tell him from my own point of view. I was to put this on paper and undertake not to be offended even if he did not utilize a single word or idea from my draft, which should be neither too short nor too long, and yet should not omit a single point of any consequence.

I may say at once that Gokhale did not make use of my language at all. Indeed, I should never expect such a master of English as Gokhale was to take up my phraseology. I cannot even say that Gokhale adopted my ideas. But as he acknowledged the importance of my views, I took it for granted that he must have in some way incorporated them into his utterances. Indeed, Gokhale's train of thought was such that one could never tell whether or not any room had been left to one's own ideas. I listened to every speech made by Gokhale, but I do not remember a single occasion when I could have wished that he had expressed a certain idea differently or had omitted a certain qualifying adjective. The clearness, firmness and urbanity of his utterances was the result of his indefatigable labour and his unswerving devotion to truth.

In Johannesburg we were also to hold a mass meeting of Indians only. I have always insisted on speaking either in my mother tongue, Gujarati, or else in Hindustani, at Indian meetings. Thanks to this insistence I have been able to establish close relations with the Indians in South Africa. I was therefore anxious that Gokhale also should speak in Hindustani. I was well aware of his views on the subject. Broken Hindi[1] would not do for him, and therefore he would speak either in Marathi or in English. It seemed artificial to him to speak in Marathi in South Africa, because there were only a small number who spoke that language. His speech would therefore have to be translated into Hindustani for the benefit of his audience.

Fortunately for me, I had one argument which Gokhale would accept as conclusive in favour of making a Marathi speech. There were some Konkani Musalmans as well as a few Maharashtra Hindus[2] in Johannesburg, all of whom were eager to hear Gokhale speak in Marathi. They specially asked me to request Gokhale to speak in their mother tongue. I told Gokhale that these friends would be highly delighted if he spoke in Marathi, and I would translate his Marathi into Hindustani.

Gokhale burst into laughter. "I have quite fathomed," he said, "your knowledge of Hindustani, an accomplishment upon which you cannot exactly be congratulated. But how do you propose to translate Marathi into Hindustani? May I know, my friend, where you acquired such profound knowledge of Marathi?"

"What is true of my Hindustani," I replied, "is equally true of my Marathi. I cannot speak a single word of Marathi, but I am confident that I can gather the purport of your Marathi speech on a subject with which I am familiar. In any case you will see that I do not misinterpret you to the people. There are others well versed

[1] Hindi is the language of North India, with Sanskrit roots, spoken chiefly by Hindus where they predominate. Urdu is the language framed on Hindi, with a Persian and Arabic vocabulary. Hindustani is a name given to a language blend between Hindi and Urdu.
[2] Konkani people live along the coast to the south of Bombay. Maharashtra is the old name for the Maratha country.

in Marathi, who could act as your interpreter, but you will not perhaps approve of such an arrangement. So please bear with me and please do speak in Marathi. I, too, am desirous of hearing your Marathi speech in common with our Konkani friends."

"You will always have your own way," said Gokhale, laughing. "And also there is no help for me, as I am here at your mercy!"

Gokhale thus laughingly fell in with my suggestion; and from this point onwards right up to Zanzibar he always spoke in Marathi at similar meetings and I served as translator by special appointment. I do not know if I was able to bring Gokhale round to the view, that rather than speak in perfect idiomatic English it was more desirable to speak in Marathi in South Africa. After he had made some speeches I could see that he also was gratified with the result of the experiment. In this way, on many occasions, in cases not involving a question of principle, he showed that there was real merit in pleasing his followers.

After Johannesburg, Gokhale visited Natal. Last of all he returned to the Transvaal and proceeded to Pretoria, where he was put up by the Union Government at the Transvaal Hotel. Here he was to meet the Ministers of the Government, including General Botha and General Smuts. It was my usual practice to inform Gokhale of all engagements, fixed for the day, early in the morning or on the previous evening if he so desired. The coming interview with the Union Ministers was a most important affair.

We came to the conclusion that I should not go with Gokhale, nor indeed even offer to go. My presence would raise a sort of barrier between Gokhale and the Ministers, who would be handicapped in speaking out freely concerning what they considered to be the mistakes of the local Indians, including my own. Then again they could not with an easy mind make any statement of future policy. Since for all these reasons Gokhale must go alone, it added largely to his own burden of responsibility. What was to be done if he quite inadvertently committed some mistake of fact which had not been first brought to his notice, but was put to him by the Ministers? Or suppose he was called upon to accept some arrangement on behalf of the Indians in the absence of any one of their responsible leaders? What was he to say?

Gokhale solved this difficulty at once. He asked me to prepare a summary historical statement of the condition of the Indians up to the present time, and also to put down in writing how far they were prepared to go. And Gokhale said that he would at once admit his ignorance if anything outside this "brief" cropped up at the interview.

It now remained for me to prepare the statement and for him to read it over. It was hardly possible, however, for me to narrate the vicissitudes of the Indians' history in all the four Colonies, ranging over a period of eighteen years, without writing ten or twelve pages at the least, and there was hardly any time left for Gokhale to look it over. There would be many questions he would like to put to me after reading the paper. But Gokhale had an infinite capacity for taking pains as he had also an exceptionally sharp memory. He kept himself and others awake the whole night, posted himself fully on every point, and went over the whole ground again in order to make sure that he had rightly understood everything. He was at last satisfied. As for me, I never had any fears.

Gokhale's interview with the Ministers lasted for about two hours. When he returned he was full of hope. "You must return to India," he said to me, "in a year. Everything has been settled. The Black Act will be repealed. The racial bar will be removed from the immigrant law. The £3 tax will be abolished."

He did not convince me. "I doubt it very much," I replied. "You do not know the Ministers as I do. Being an optimist myself I love your optimism, but having suffered frequent disappointments, I cannot be as hopeful in the matter as you are. But I have no fears either. It is enough for me that you have obtained this undertaking from the Ministers. It is my duty to fight the matter out only where it is necessary and to demonstrate that ours is a righteous struggle. The promise given to you will serve as a proof of the justice of our demands and will redouble our fighting spirit if it comes to fighting after all. But I do not think that I shall have the opportunity of returning to India in a year or before many more Indians have gone to jail."

"What I have told you," said Gokhale, "is bound to come to pass. General Botha has promised me that the Black Act would be repealed and the £3 tax abolished. You must return to India within twelve months, and I will not have any of your lame excuses."

During this visit to Natal, Gokhale came in contact with many Europeans in Durban, Maritzburg and other places. At Durban public dinners were arranged by reception committees and attended by many Europeans. Thus having achieved a conquest of Indian as well as

European hearts, Gokhale left South Africa on November 17, 1912. At his wish, Mr. Kallenbach and I accompanied him as far as Zanzibar. On the steamer, we had arranged to have suitable food for him. He was given an ovation at Delagoa Bay, Zanzibar and other ports.

While we were on the steamer together our talks related to India only and to the duty we owed to the motherland. Every word of Gokhale glowed with his tender feelings, truthfulness and patriotism. I observed that even in the games which he played on board the steamer Gokhale had a patriotic motive more than the mere desire to amuse himself. Excellence was his aim there also.

During the voyage we had ample time to talk to our hearts' content. In these conversations Gokhale prepared me for India. He analysed for me the characters of all the leaders in India; and his analysis was so accurate, that I have hardly perceived any difference between Gokhale's estimate and my own personal experience of them.

There are many sacred reminiscences of mine relating to Gokhale's tour in South Africa. But I must reluctantly check my pen, as they are not all relevant to a history of Satyagraha. The parting at Zanzibar was deeply painful to Kallenbach and me; but remembering that the most intimate relations of mortal men must come to an end at last, we reconciled ourselves, hoping that Gokhale's prophecy would come true and that both of us would be able to go to India in a year's time. But that was not to happen.

CHAPTER XX

THE FAMOUS MARCH

By C. F. Andrews

THE WHOLE SCENE of the passive resistance struggle after Mr. Gokhale's departure suddenly shifted from the Transvaal to Natal. This part of the conflict with the South African Union Government has already been told in full in the second volume of this series.[1] It will therefore only be necessary here for me to recapitulate the chief events in Natal during those exciting days, together with the march into the Transvaal. Then, in conclusion, it will be best to give in Mahatma Gandhi's own words the scene in the Transvaal and at the Cape, where the whole struggle was brought to an end by the signing of the Agreement between Mr. Gandhi and General Smuts.

What happened was briefly this. In the year 1913, after Mr. Gokhale had returned to India, the promise of the abolition of the £3 poll tax, levied from indentured labourers who had served their five years' indenture, was not carried out. Mr. Gokhale fully believed it to have been given, but he carried away nothing in writing.

The situation thus created was still further embittered by a judgment delivered in the Supreme Court on March 13, 1913, which treated all Hindu and Muhammadan marriages as illegal and made the children of such marriages illegitimate. When an appeal was made to the

[1] *Mahatma Gandhi: His Own Story*, pp. 192–232.

Government to amend this law no action was taken in order to do so.

In the face of these two racial injustices which affected the Indian community alone, Mr. Gandhi wrote the following letter to the Secretary for the Interior when proposing passive resistance:

I know what responsibility lies on my shoulders in advising such a momentous step, but I feel that it is not possible for me to refrain from advising a step which I consider to be necessary, to be of educational value, and, in the end, to be valuable both to the Indian community and to the State. This step consists in actively, persistently, and continuously asking those who are liable to pay the £3 tax to decline to do so and to suffer the penalties for non-payment, and, what is more important, in asking those who are now serving indenture and who will therefore be liable to pay the £3 tax upon the completion of their indenture, to strike work until the tax is withdrawn. I feel that, in view of Lord Ampthill's declaration in the House of Lords, evidently with the approval of Mr. Gokhale, as to the definite promise made by the Government and repeated to Lord Gladstone, this advice to indentured Indians would be fully justified. . . . Can I not even now, whilst in the midst of the struggle, appeal to General Smuts and ask him to reconsider his decision . . . on the question of the £3 tax?

To this letter General Smuts gave no reply. Therefore, after waiting without receiving any answer, Mr. Gandhi at last began to make preparations for re-opening the passive resistance struggle on a much wider scale than before.

The Indian women in the Transvaal anticipated his direct action by themselves seeking imprisonment as a protest against this monstrous judgment in law, which declared them to be merely concubines of their own husbands and not joined together in lawful wedlock.

Having failed to obtain the imprisonment they courted in the Transvaal, they crossed the border into Natal. There they began at once to call out, on a passive resistance strike against the hated £3 poll tax, the Indian miners who were working in the coal-fields near the border. Mine after mine was closed down, as the Indian labourers refused to work when the women pressed them to strike. A state of panic ensued among the mine-managers, who had never had a strike of coloured labourers before.

A hurried conference was held at Durban with Mr. Gandhi, who informed the mining directors of the breach of faith concerning the repeal of the £3 poll tax. The Conference telegraphed to General Smuts enquiring from him about the promise made to Mr. Gokhale. Both General Botha and General Smuts denied it: but it is significant that Mr. Fischer, who was also present with Mr. Gokhale at the interview, did not deny it. Mr. Gokhale at once cabled that the promise of repeal of the £3 tax had undoubtedly been made to him. On that point he had no doubt at all.

Then Mr. Gandhi determined to uphold the strike which the indentured labourers had already begun of their own accord. Albert Christopher, an Indian Christian, was placed in charge of the commissariat organization and a camp was formed at Newcastle, Natal, where the indentured labourers who had struck work flocked in large masses. Soon their number increased to between three and four thousand. The weather was bad and the hardships endured were at times almost unbearable All except the sick and infirm slept out on the bare veldt. Their ration of food was rice and bread and sugar. But so long as Mr. Gandhi was seen each day sharing every hardship with them there was no murmuring or discontent. The women at this time were the leaders in every heroic endeavour. One mother, whose little child died of exposure on the road to Newcastle, said: "We must not pine for the dead, but work for the living." Another mother lost her child through exposure on the high veldt, but went on with the march. No one turned back, and the courage of the women very often sustained and heartened the men.

At last the order came from Mr. Gandhi himself that the whole body of the strikers should march forward into the Transvaal in order to court arrest and imprisonment. On October 30, 1913, at the head of his tattered army he began his famous march. The first centre where all were to be gathered together was Charlestown. This small town stands near to the Transvaal border. Every day hundreds pressed forward into Charlestown, where a vast camp was organized. The Indian merchants in Durban supplied large stores of rice. Mr. Gandhi telegraphed to the Government his intention of crossing the border when his whole force had been collected. Meanwhile attempts were made both by the Government and by the employers to force the indentured labourers back to work in the mines and plantations, but these efforts were altogether unavailing. Forcible acts of this kind on the part of the employers soon led to serious assaults, in which many Indians were injured.

At the border of the Transvaal, Mr. Gandhi came forward to interview the police officer who was on duty at the gate of entry. An eye-witness describes the scene thus: "Whilst these official preliminaries were in train, the main body became impatient, and a mass of cheering, shouting Indians, clad in ragged clothes, and bearing their pitifully small belongings upon their heads, swarmed through the streets of Volksrust, determined to do or die, brushing the handful of police aside like so many helpless and insignificant atoms. They encamped on the farther side of the town, and the great march had commenced. The programme was to march at the rate of some twenty-five miles a day, until either the men were arrested or Tolstoy Farm, at Lawley, near Johannesburg, was reached. The Government were informed of each stopping-place. Eight days were set aside to reach their destination, unless they were earlier arrested, and from the swing and energy of their marching it was plain that a phenomenal feat was being performed by men, many of them heavily burdened, unused to conditions of 'war,' but accustomed to a hard and simple life, and on a meagre and unusual diet. That night they reached Palmford, where special accommodation was offered to Mr. Gandhi, who, however, refused to accept hospitality which his humbler countrymen could not share."

At this point a warrant was issued for the arrest of the Indian leader. Mr. Gandhi had been expecting this from the very first and quietly surrendered to the officials. He was tried at Volksrust for a breach of the Immigration Act and then applied for bail, which was granted. Thereupon he despatched the following telegram to General Smuts:

Whilst I appreciate the fact of Government having at last arrested prime mover in passive resistance struggle, I cannot help remarking that from point view humanity the moment chosen must be considered unfortunate. Government probably know that marchers include 122 women, 50 tender children, all voluntarily marching on starvation rations without provision for shelter during stages. Tearing me away under such circumstances from them is violation all considerations of justice. When arrested last night, I left men without informing them. They might become infuriated. I, therefore, ask either that I may be allowed continue the march with the men, or Government send them by rail to Tolstoy Farm and provide full rations for them. Leaving them without one in whom they have confidence, and without Government making provision for them, is, in my opinion, an act from which I hope on reconsideration Government will recoil. If untoward incidents happen during further progress of the march, or if deaths occur, especially amongst women with babies in arms, the responsibility will be Government's.

No reply was given to this appeal, and Mr. Gandhi hurried back to his followers, rejoining them on the march when they had reached as far as Paardeberg. There the women and children, who had still kept up with the army, were now at last left behind in charge of a few men, whose own feet had become so sore that they could walk no further. The army itself reached Standerton on November 8th and here Mr. Gandhi was arrested for a second time, but was again released on bail because he alone could completely control his followers at this critical juncture. Meanwhile the Government was completing its own arrangements.

On Sunday, November 9th, the passive resistance army marched forward in the direction of Greylingstad. Mr. Polak had come up from Durban and had joined the column on the march. Mr. Gandhi greeted his friend as the army moved on, and it was arranged that if Mr. Gandhi should be imprisoned Mr. Polak should take his place till he was arrested also. Mr. Kallenbach had been

THE FAMOUS MARCH

left behind with Miss Schlesin at Charlestown in charge of the women and children and infirm people.

Mr. Kachhalia, along with leading Indians of the Transvaal, had meanwhile started to join the invading army of passive resisters. He had also fully prepared for all their food arrangements on their way towards Tolstoy Farm. But these special preparations were not necessary for any length of time, because on the day after Mr. Gandhi's final arrest, three long trains were drawn up by Government order at a siding on the railway, near to Balfour, and the whole army was called upon to enter the different compartments in order to be taken back and imprisoned in Natal. Mr. Polak was approached by the police officer and asked to co-operate with him in carrying out these instructions in the quietest possible manner. When he had received the assurance that they were to be sent back to Natal, to face imprisonment there, he replied that he would gladly assist them, because the whole object of Mr. Gandhi's march into the Transvaal would thus be fulfilled. At the same time he offered himself for arrest along with Mr. Gandhi and Mr. Kallenbach.

This arrest of Mr. Polak and Mr. Kallenbach came later; but at the time of entraining so many hundreds of passive resisters every moral assistance of leaders was required to prevent a breaking up of the previous discipline, such as might have led to untoward results. As it happened, the resisters were entrained without much commotion and sent southward into Natal, where the prisons soon became overcrowded and other forms of imprisonment had to be adopted.

Seeing that it was impossible to break the resolution of

the Indian community by a policy of force, General Smuts released Mr. Gandhi in the expectation that he would be ready to negotiate and thus relieve the deadlock.

Meanwhile the Government of India had approached the South African Union Ministers through the British Cabinet at Westminster. For at that time direct negotiations between South Africa and India were hardly possible. The proposal was made that a Commission should be appointed to consider the Indian grievances. It was understood that every effort would be made to find a peaceable solution of all the points at issue.

But a question of honour immediately arose concerning the choice of the names of the Commissioners. Mr. Gandhi claimed that the Indian community should be consulted before the Commission was appointed and that one member should be chosen to represent Indian interests. This request was refused, though it had been granted only a short time before to the Europeans who had been on strike. It was impossible for the Indian leader to accept a lower status.

From this point forward the story may be resumed in Mr. Gandhi's own words.

CHAPTER XXI

THE END OF THE STRUGGLE

OUR FIRMNESS WAS very disconcerting and distressing to General Smuts, coupled as it was with our determination to keep the peace, and he even said as much. How long can you harass a man of peace? How can you kill the voluntarily dead? There is no zest in killing one who welcomes death, and therefore soldiers are keen upon attacking the enemy while he answers blow with blow and violence by violence. Great hunters would give up lion-hunting if the lion took to non-resistance. Our victory was implicit in our combination of the two qualities of non-violence and determination.

Among the Satyagrahi prisoners of note there was one old man, named Harbatsingh, who was about seventy-five years of age. He had completed his indenture many years ago and he was therefore not one of those who had struck work on the plantations. But the Indians had grown far more enthusiastic after my arrest on the march into the Transvaal and many of them got arrested by crossing from Natal into the Transvaal. Harbatsingh was one of these enthusiasts. I met him in Volksrust jail.

"Why are you in jail?" I asked Harbatsingh. "I have not invited old men like yourself to court jail."

"How could I help it," he replied, "when you, your wife and even your boys went to jail for our sake?"

"But you will not be able to endure the hardships of jail life," said I. "I would advise you to leave jail. Shall I arrange for your release?"

"No, please," said Harbatsingh. "I will never leave jail. I must die one of these days and how happy I should be to die in prison!"

It was not for me to try to shake such determination, which would not have been shaken even if I had tried. My head bent in reverence before this illiterate sage. Harbatsingh had his wish and he died in jail on January 5, 1914. His body was cremated with great honour according to the Hindu rites in the presence of hundreds of Indians. There were many like him in the Satyagraha struggle who had risked life itself for the cause. But the great good fortune of dying in jail was reserved for Harbatsingh alone, and hence he is entitled to this honourable mention in the history of the Satyagraha struggle in South Africa.

Pain is often the precursor of pleasure; the pain of the Indians in South Africa made itself heard everywhere, and reached other parts of the world. As every part has its place in a machine, every feature has its place in the movement of men. As a machine is clogged by rust, dirt and the like, so is a movement hampered by a number of hindering factors. We are merely the instruments of the Almighty Will and are therefore often ignorant of what helps us forward and what acts as an impediment. We must thus rest satisfied with the knowledge only of the means we ought to use; and if these are pure, we can fearlessly leave the end to take care of itself.

I observed in the Satyagraha struggle that its end drew nearer as the distress of the fighters became more intense, and the innocence of the distressed grew clearer. I also saw that in such a pure non-violent struggle, the material required for its prosecution, be it men or money, is always forthcoming. Volunteers rendered help whose names even I do not know to this day. Such workers are generally selfless and put in a sort of invisible service. No one takes note of them; no one awards them a certificate of merit. Some of them hardly know that their nameless but priceless unremembered acts of love do not escape the sleepless vigilance of the recording angel.

Indians of South Africa successfully passed the test to which they were subjected. They entered the fire and emerged out of it unscathed. In the end, they exerted as much quiet strength as they could and more than might have been expected from them. The large majority of these passive resisters were poor down-trodden men of whom no great expectations could possibly be entertained. All the responsible workers of the Phoenix settlement, with the exception of two or three, were now in jail. Of the workers outside Phoenix, Kachhalia Sheth was still at large, and so were Mr. West, Miss West, and Maganlal Gandhi in Phoenix.

Kachhalia Sheth exercised a general supervision. Miss Schlesin kept all the Transvaal accounts and looked after the Indians who crossed the border. Mr. West was in charge of the British section of *Indian Opinion* and of a cable correspondence with Gokhale. At a time like this crisis, when the situation assumed a new aspect every moment, correspondence by post was quite out of the question. Cablegrams had to be dispatched, hardly shorter than letters in length, and the delicate responsibility regarding them was shouldered by Mr. West.

Like Newcastle in the mine area, Phoenix now became the centre of the strikers on the north coast and was visited by hundreds of them who came to seek advice as well as shelter. It therefore naturally attracted the attention of the Government, and the angry looks of the Europeans thereabouts. It became somewhat risky to live in Phoenix, and yet even children there accomplished dangerous tasks with courage. West was arrested in the meanwhile, though as a matter of fact there was no reason for arresting him. Our understanding was, that West and Maganlal Gandhi should not only not try to be arrested, but on the other hand should, as far as possible, avoid any occasion for arrest. West had not therefore allowed any ground to arise for the Government to arrest him.

My first interview with General Smuts was short, but I saw at once that the General did not ride the same high horse as he did before, when the Great March began. At that earlier date the General would not so much as talk with me. The threat of Satyagraha was the same then as it was now. Yet, before, he had declined to enter into negotiations, while now he was ready to confer with me.

The Indians had demanded that a member should be co-opted to the Commission to represent the Indian interests. But on this point General Smuts would not give in. "That cannot be done," he said, "as it would be derogatory to the Government's prestige and I should be unable to carry out the desired reforms. You must understand that Mr. Esselen is our man, and he would fall in with the Government's wishes as regards reform. Colonel Wylie is a man of position in Natal and might even be considered anti-Indian. If therefore even he agrees to a repeal of the £3 tax the Government will have an easy task before them. Our troubles are manifold: we have not a moment to spare and therefore wish to set the Indian question at rest. We have decided to grant your demands, but for this we must have a recommendation from the Commission.

"I understand your position, too. You have solemnly declared that you will not lead evidence before it so long as there is no representative of the Indians sitting on the Commission. I do not mind if you do not tender evidence, but you should not organize any active propaganda to prevent anyone who wishes to give evidence from doing so, and you should suspend Satyagraha in the interval. I believe that in this way you will be serving your own interests as well as giving me a respite. As you will not tender evidence you will not be able to prove your allegations as regards ill-treatment accorded to the Indian strikers. But that is for you to think over."

Such were the suggestions of General Smuts, which on the whole I was inclined to receive favourably. We had made many complaints about ill-treatment of strikers by soldiers and warders, but the difficulty was that we were precluded by a boycott of the Commission from proving our allegations. There was a difference of opinion among the Indians on this point. Some held that the charges levelled by the Indians against the soldiers must be proved, and therefore suggested that if the evidence could not be placed before the Commission we must challenge libel proceedings by publishing the authentic evidence in our possession. I disagreed with these friends. There was little likelihood of the Commission giving a decision unfavourable to the Government. Libel proceedings would land the community in endless trouble, and the net result would be the barren satisfaction of having proved charges of ill-treatment. As a barrister, I was well aware of the difficulties of proving the truth of statements which gave rise to libel proceedings.

But my weightiest argument was, that the Satyagrahi is out to suffer. Even before Satyagraha was started, the Satyagrahis knew that they would have to suffer unto death, and were also ready to undergo such suffering. Such being the case, there was no sense in proving now that they did suffer. A spirit of revenge being alien to Satyagraha, it was best for a Satyagrahi to hold his peace when he encountered extraordinary difficulties in proving the fact of his suffering.

A Satyagrahi fights for essentials alone. The essential thing was that the obnoxious laws should be repealed or suitably amended, and when this was fairly within his grasp, he would not bother himself with other things. Again, a Satyagrahi's silence would at the time of settlement stand him in good stead in his resistance to unjust laws. With arguments like these I was able to win over most of the friends who differed from me, and we decided to drop the idea of proving our allegations of ill-treatment.

Correspondence passed between General Smuts and myself, placing on record the agreement arrived at as a result of a number of interviews. My letter dated January 21, 1914, may be thus summarized:

> We have conscientious scruples with regard to leading evidence before the Commission as constituted at present. You appreciate these scruples and regard them as honourable, but are unable to alter your decision. As, however, you have accepted the principle of consultation with Indians, I will advise my countrymen not to hamper the labours of the Commission by any active propaganda,

and not to render the position of the Government difficult by reviving passive resistance, pending the result of the Commission and the introduction of legislation during the forthcoming session. It will further be possible for us to assist Sir Benjamin Robertson, who has been deputed by the Viceroy.

As to our allegations of ill-treatment during the progress of the Indian strike in Natal, the avenue of proving them through the Commission is closed to us by our solemn declaration to have nothing to do with it. As Satyagrahis we endeavour to avoid, as far as possible, any resentment of personal wrongs. But in order that our silence may not be mistaken, may I ask you to recognize our motive and reciprocate by not leading evidence of a negative character before the Commission on the allegation in question?

Suspension of Satyagraha, moreover, carries with it a prayer for the release of Satyagrahi prisoners.

It might not be out of place here to recapitulate the points on which relief has been sought:

(1) Repeal of the £3 tax.

(2) Legalization of the marriages celebrated according to the rites of Hinduism, Islam, etc.

(3) The entry of educated Indians.

(4) Alteration in the assurance as regards the Orange Free State.

(5) An assurance that the existing laws especially affecting Indians will be administered justly, with due regard to vested rights.

If you view my submission with favour I should be prepared to advise my countrymen in accordance with the tenor of this letter.

General Smuts' reply of the same date was to this effect:

I regret but understand your inability to appear before the Commission. I also recognize the motive which makes you unwilling to revive old scores by courting libel proceedings before another tribunal. The Government repudiates the charge of harsh action against the Indian strikers. But as you will not lead evidence in support of these allegations, it would be futile for the Government to lead rebutting evidence in vindication of the conduct of its officers. As regards the release of Satyagrahi prisoners, the Government had already issued the necessary orders before your letter arrived. In regard to the grievances submitted at the end of your letter, the Government will await the recommendation of the Commission before any action is taken.

Andrews and I had frequently interviewed General Smuts before these letters were exchanged. But meanwhile Sir Benjamin Robertson, too, arrived at Pretoria. Sir Benjamin was looked upon as a popular official, and he brought a letter of recommendation from Gokhale, but I observed that he was not quite free from the usual weakness of English officials. He had no sooner come than he began to create factions among the Indians and to press the Satyagrahis to give way. My first meeting with him in Pretoria did not prepossess me in his favour. I told him about the telegrams I had received informing me of his peremptory procedure. I dealt with him, as indeed with everyone else, in a frank, straightforward manner, and we therefore became friends. But I have often seen that officials are apt to bully those who will tamely submit to them, and will be correct with those who will not be cowed down.

We thus reached a provisional agreement, and Satyagraha was suspended for the last time. Many English friends were glad of this, and promised their assistance in the final settlement. It was rather difficult to get the Indians to endorse this agreement. No one would like the enthusiasm which had arisen to be allowed to subside.

No matter how often a Satyagrahi is betrayed, he will repose his trust in the adversary so long as there are not cogent grounds for distrust. Pain to a Satyagrahi is pleasure. He will not therefore be misled by the mere fear of suffering into groundless distrust. On the other hand, relying as he does upon his own strength, he will not mind being betrayed by the adversary and will continue to trust in spite of frequent betrayals, and will believe that he thereby strengthens the forces of Truth and brings victory nearer.

Meetings were therefore held in various places, and I was able to persuade the Indians to approve of the terms of the agreement. The Indians came to a better understanding of Satyagraha. Andrews was the mediator and the witness in the present agreement, and then there was Sir Benjamin Robertson as representing the Government of India. There was therefore the least possible likelihood of the agreement being subsequently repudiated.

If I had obstinately refused to accept the agreement it would have become a count of indictment against the Indians, and the victory which was achieved in the next six months would have been beset with various obstacles. The author of the Sanskrit saying, "Forgiveness is an ornament of the brave," drew upon his rich experience of Satyagrahis who never give anyone the least opportunity of finding fault with them. Distrust is a sign of weakness, and Satyagraha implies the banishment of all weakness, and therefore of distrust, which is clearly out of place when the adversary is not to be destroyed but to be won over.

When the agreement was thus endorsed by the Indians, we had only to wait for the next session of the Union Parliament. Meanwhile, the Commission set to work. Only a very few witnesses appeared before it on behalf of the Indians, furnishing striking evidence of the great hold which Satyagraha had acquired over the community. Sir Benjamin Robertson tried to induce many to tender evidence, but failed except in the case of a few who were strongly opposed to Satyagraha.

The boycott of the Commission did not produce any bad effect. Its work was shortened and its report was published at once. The Commission strongly criticized the Indians for withholding their assistance and dismissed the charge of misbehaviour against the soldiers, but recommended that there should be compliance without delay with all the demands of the Indian community, such as for instance the repeal of £3 tax and the validation of Indian marriages, and the grant of some trifling concessions in addition. Thus the report of the Commission was favourable to the Indians as predicted by General Smuts. Andrews left for England on his way to India. He was to meet Gokhale in London, where he was under medical treatment, and explain what had happened. We received an assurance that the requisite legislation would be undertaken with a view to implementing the recommendation of the Commission.

Within a short time of the issue of the Commission report the Government published in the official Gazette of the Union the Indians' Relief Bill, which was to effect a settlement of their long-standing dispute with the Indians; and I went at once to Cape Town, where the Union Parliament sits. The Bill contained nine sections and would take up only two columns of a paper like *Indian Opinion*. One part of it dealt with the question of Indian marriages and validated in South Africa such marriages as were held legal in India, except that if a man had more wives than one, only one of them would at any time be recognized as legal in South Africa. The second part abolished the annual licence of £3 to be taken out by every indentured Indian labourer who failed to return to India and settled in the country as a free man on the completion of his indenture. The third part provided that the domicile certificates issued by the Government to Indians in Natal and bearing the thumb impression of the holder of the permit should be recognized as conclusive evidence of the right of the holder to enter the Union as soon as his identity was established. There was a long and pleasant debate over the Bill in the Union Parliament.

Administrative matters which did not come under the Indians' Relief Bill were settled by correspondence between General Smuts and myself, as, for example, safeguarding the educated Indian's right of entry into the Cape Colony, allowing "specially exempted" educated Indians to enter South Africa, the status of educated Indians who entered South Africa within the last three years, and permitting existing plural wives to join their husbands in South Africa. After dealing with all these points, General Smuts, in his letter of June 30, 1914, added:

With regard to the administration of existing laws, it had always been and will continue to be the desire of the Government to see that they are administered in a just manner with due regard to vested rights.

I replied to the above letter to this effect:

I beg to acknowledge the receipt of your letter of even date. I feel deeply grateful for the patience and courtesy which you showed during the discussions.

The passing of the Indians' Relief Bill and this correspondence finally close the Satyagraha struggle which commenced in the September of 1906 and which to the Indian community cost much physical suffering and pecuniary loss and to the Government much anxious thought and consideration.

As you are aware, some of my countrymen have wished me to go further. They are dissatisfied that the Trade Licence Laws of the different provinces, the Transvaal Gold Law, and the Transvaal Townships Act and Transvaal Law No. 3 of 1885 have not been altered so as to give them full rights of residence, trade and ownership of land. Some of them are dissatisfied that full inter-provincial migration is not permitted, and some are dissatisfied that on the marriage question the Relief Bill does not go further than it does. They have asked me that all the above matters might be included in the Satyagraha struggle. I have been unable to comply with their wishes. Whilst, therefore they have not been included in the programme of Satyagraha, it will not be denied that some day or other these matters will require further and sympathetic consideration by the Government. Complete satisfaction cannot be expected until full civic rights have been conceded to the resident Indians.

I have told my countrymen that they will have to exercise patience, and by all honourable means at their disposal educate public opinion so as to enable the Government of the day to go further than the present correspondence does. I shall hope, when the Europeans of South Africa fully appreciate the fact that now the importation of indentured labourers from India is prohibited, and the Immigrants' Regulation Act of last year has in practice all but stopped further free Indian immigration, and that my countrymen do not entertain any political ambition, they, the Europeans, will see the justice and indeed the necessity of my countrymen being granted the rights I have just referred to.

Meanwhile, if the generous spirit that the Government has applied to the treatment of the problem during the past few months continues to be applied, as promised in your letter, in the administration of the existing laws, I am quite certain that the Indian community throughout the Union will be able to enjoy some measure of peace and never be a source of trouble to the Government.

THE END OF THE STRUGGLE

Thus the great Satyagraha struggle closed after eight years, and it appeared that the Indians of South Africa were now at peace. On July 18, 1914, I sailed for England, to meet Gokhale, on my way back to India, with mixed feelings of pleasure and regret—pleasure because I was returning home after many years and eagerly looked forward to serving the country under Gokhale's guidance, regret because it was a great wrench for me to leave South Africa, where I had passed twenty years of my life sharing to the full the sweets and bitters of human experience, and where I had realized my vocation in life.

When one considers the painful contrast between the happy ending of the Satyagraha struggle and the present condition of Indians in South Africa, one feels for a moment as if all this suffering had gone for nothing, or is inclined to question the efficacy of Satyagraha as a solvent of the problems of mankind. But let us consider this point for a little while.

There is a law of nature that a thing can be retained by the same means by which it has been acquired. A thing acquired by violence can be retained by violence alone, while one acquired by truth can be retained by truth alone. The Indians in South Africa, therefore, can ensure their safety to-day if they can wield the weapon of Satyagraha. There are no such miraculous properties in Satyagraha that a thing acquired by truth could be retained even if truth were given up. It would not be desirable even if it were possible. If therefore the position of the Indians in South Africa has now suffered deterioration, this argues that there is an absence of Satyagraha amongst them. There is no question here of finding fault with the present generation of South African Indians, but of merely stating the facts of the case. Individuals or bodies of individuals cannot borrow from others qualities which they themselves do not possess. The Satyagrahi veterans passed away one after another. Sorabji, Kachhalia, Parsi Rustomji and others being no more, there are but very few now who passed through the fire of Satyagraha. The few that remain are still in the fighting line, and I have not a shadow of doubt that they will be the saviours of the community on the day of its trial if the light of Satyagraha is burning bright within them.

Had it not been for this great struggle and for the untold sufferings which many Indians invited upon their devoted heads, the Indians to-day would have been hounded out of South Africa. Nay, the victory achieved by Indians in South Africa more or less served as a shield for Indian emigrants in other parts of the British Empire, who, if they are suppressed, will be suppressed owing to the absence of Satyagraha among themselves and to India's inability to protect them, and not because of any flaw in the weapon of Satyagraha. I shall consider myself amply repaid if I have demonstrated with some success that Satyagraha is a priceless and matchless weapon, and those who wield it are strangers to disappointment or defeat.

APPENDIX I

FIRST DAYS IN SOUTH AFRICA

THE FOLLOWING STORY is given by the Rev. J. J. Doke of Mr. Gandhi's first experiences in South Africa and his Christian contacts:

In 1893 Mr. Gandhi made his first acquaintance with South Africa. It was not altogether happy, but it accurately foreshadowed what has been his experience ever since. His first day in Natal disillusioned him. He said, "I have made a mistake in coming. My clients have misled me." The country was beautiful. The waving banana leaves, the vast fields of sugar-cane, the date bushes springing from a tangle of tropical growth, reminded him of his native land. The white English faces suggested pleasant reminiscences of the little Island across the sea. It would be difficult to imagine a more lovely spot than Durban, or more hospitable people than its citizens. But, apparently, there was no welcome for an Indian. Evidences of a radical difference of treatment between white and coloured people startled the new arrival, and cut him to the quick.

He himself was a high-caste Hindu, the child of an ancient and noble race. His father, grandfather, and uncle had been Prime Ministers of their respective Courts. His childhood and youth had been spent in India, familiar with all the splendour of an Eastern palace. In manhood he had known nothing of colour-prejudice, but had been granted free access to polite English society. Prince Ranjitsinhji was his friend. By profession he was a barrister, trained in the fine old English Law Schools of the Inner Temple, and called to the Bar in London—a cultured gentleman in every sense of the term. Hitherto he had looked upon a white face as the face of a friend. He had been taught from childhood to admire the justice of British law and the purity of British honour. It is true, that, now and then, some British official had shown himself brusque or overbearing, but nothing, so far, had happened to chill his loyalty.

Here, in Natal, it was all changed. When, on the day following his advent, according to Eastern habits of respect, he wore his barrister's turban in Court, sitting beside his client's solicitor at the horse-shoe, and was rudely ordered to remove his hat, he left the building smarting under a sense of insult. It was a feeling frequently to be aroused.

The case for which he was engaged needed his presence in Pretoria. The train could only take him as far as Charlestown. His clients had advised him to take a bed-ticket for the journey. This he neglected to do, having his own rugs with him. At Pietermaritzburg, before starting, a fellow-passenger called the guard and, to his surprise, Mr. Gandhi was ordered to "come out and go into the van-compartment." As he held a first-class ticket, and knew that the carriage went through to Charlestown, he refused. The guard insisted. The train was ready to start. He refused again. A constable was brought, and the Indian stranger was forcibly ejected, his bundles pitched out after him, and with the train gone, he was left to shiver in the waiting-room all night.

When at length he reached the Transvaal, and began his coach-journey, he again felt the disadvantage of being an Indian. The coach was about to leave Paardeberg with Mr. Gandhi seated on the box, when the guard, a big Dutchman, wishing to smoke, laid claim to this place, telling the Indian passenger to sit down at his feet. "No," said Mr. Gandhi, quietly, "I shall not do so." The result was a brutal blow in the face. The victim held on to the rail, when another blow nearly knocked him down. Then the passengers "interfered, much to the guard's disgust." "Let the poor beggar alone," they said, and the man, threatening to "do for him" at the next stage, desisted. But at Standerton the coach was changed, and the rest of the journey was accomplished without incident.

It is almost amusing now, to anyone acquainted with Colonial prejudice, if it were not so pitiful, to note how utterly ignorant the newcomer was of it all. He even drove to the Grand National Hotel on reaching Johannesburg, where, of course, there was "no room" for him. Everywhere it was the same. The colour bar was a terrible disadvantage, and experiences like these so disheartened and disgusted him that, but for his contract with the Indians, he would have left South Africa at once.

As it was, the contract held him, and the twelve months spent in Pretoria was a distinct gain. He learned self-restraint. Even when the sentry kicked him off the foot-path in front of President Kruger's house, and his European friends wished to test the legality of the act, he refused to retaliate. He learned to bear the insults which attached to his race and colour, until, for the sake of his people, he almost gloried in them, and gradually pride of birth and education gave way before the humility of sacrifice.

During this period Mr. Gandhi attended Bible classes conducted by a prominent solicitor in Pretoria, and studied the characters of Christian people with a keenness of vision which they seldom suspected. Having plenty of time, he read widely, "quite eighty" books within this year; among them, Butler's *Analogy*; Tolstoi's works; *The Six Systems*, by a Jain philosopher; and a great deal of Dr. Parker's *Commentaries*. He also read the whole Bible for the first time. When, in his consecutive study, he reached the "Sermon on the Mount," he began to realize the full charm of Scriptures. "Surely," he said, "there is no distinction between Hinduism, as represented in the Bhagavad-Gita, and this revelation of Christ; both must be from the same source."

In order to clear his thought or confirm his conviction, Mr. Gandhi consulted his friend Dr. Oldfield, and a learned Jain teacher in Bombay. He also corresponded on the subject with Edward Maitland, an exponent of Estoric Christianity. Mrs. Anna Kingsford's book entitled *The Perfect Way* had greatly impressed him. He was slowly feeling his way to some definite religious faith. Not least among the formative influences of that year was a visit to the Wellington Convention, and his contact with Dr. Andrew Murray, the veteran Dutch Reformed Minister, Mr. Spencer Walton, and other leaders of the Keswick school. Speaking with appreciation of this experience, he said, with an amused smile: "These people loved me so well, that if it would have influenced me to become a Christian, they would have become vegetarians themselves!" So this memorable year passed.

APPENDIX II

THE ORIGIN OF SATYAGRAHA

THE FOLLOWING ACCOUNT is given by the Rev. J. J. Doke of the origin of Satyagraha in Mr. Gandhi's own mind:

"I remember," he said, "how one verse of a Gujarati poem, which, as a child, I learned at school, clung to me. In substance it was this:
'If a man gives you a drink of water and you give him a drink in return, that is nothing.
Real beauty consists in doing good against evil.'
"As a child, this verse had a powerful influence over me, and I tried to carry it into practice. Then came the 'Sermon on the Mount.'"

"But," said I, "surely the Bhagavad-Gita came first?"

"No," he replied, "of course I knew the Bhagavad-Gita in Sanskrit tolerably well, but I had not made its teaching in that particular a study. It was the New Testament which really awakened me to the rightness and value of Passive Resistance. When I read in the 'Sermon on the Mount' such passages as 'Resist not him that is evil but whosoever smiteth thee on thy right cheek turn to him the other also,' and 'Love your enemies and pray for them that persecute you, that ye may be sons of your Father which is in heaven,' I was simply overjoyed, and found my own opinion confirmed where I least expected it. The Bhagavad-Gita deepened the impression, and Tolstoy's *The Kingdom of God is Within You* gave it permanent form."

Undoubtedly Count Tolstoy has profoundly influenced him. The old Russian reformer, in the simplicity of his life, the fearlessness of his utterances, and the nature of his teaching on war and work, has found a warm-hearted disciple in Mr. Gandhi. I think, too, very probably, the Count's representation of the Christian Church has had its weight with him, and his own experience of

Christian Churches has not been sufficiently happy to withstand it. But Tolstoy's teaching on some questions, notably on governments, has not won his assent. Ruskin and Thoreau have both had some share in forming his opinions, Ruskin's *Crown of Wild Olive* being an especial favourite. Last, but not least, the Passive Resistance movement in England with regard to education has proved an object-lesson, not only to him, but to his people, of singular force and interest.

Some months ago a prize was offered by *Indian Opinion* to competitors in South Africa for the best essay on "The Ethics of Passive Resistance." I was invited to act as judge. What surprised me most of all in the essays by Indians was the familiarity which the essayists showed with the education controversy in England. Dr. Clifford's name was as familiar to them as to me.

But, as may be imagined from the seed-thought planted by the Gujarati verse in Mr. Gandhi's mind, his ideal is not so much to resist evil passively; it has its active complement—to do good in reply to evil. "I do not like the term 'passive resistance,'" he said; "it fails to convey all I mean. It describes a method, but gives no hint of the system of which it is only part. Real beauty, and that is my aim, is in doing good against evil. Still, I adopt the phrase because it is well known, and easily understood, and because, at present, the great majority of my people can only grasp that idea. To me, the ideas which underlie the Gujarati hymn and the 'Sermon on the Mount' should revolutionize the whole of life."

APPENDIX III

PRISON DAYS: MR. DOKE'S DIARY

THE FOLLOWING ACCOUNT is given by the Rev. J. J. Doke of Mr. Gandhi's prison days:

October 27th.—When he reached Johannesburg, dressed in convict clothes, marked all over with the broad arrow, he was marched under guard through the streets, before sundown, carrying his bundles as any convict would.

It makes one ashamed of the British rule under which such insults are possible. Of course, it is simply a result of the prison system. The governors of these gaols are gentlemanly and courteous; the warders, with one exception, have been most kind, but an Indian is classed as a Native; and a Passive Resister as a criminal; while a criminal native must suffer the utmost degradation that the law provides. So the batteries of the Reef crush criminal savage and conscientious Indian without distinction. We have heard that Mr. Gandhi's experiences during that night were extremely shocking. Again the cast-iron regulations were at fault. As a native prisoner of the criminal class, he was locked into a cell with native and Chinese convicts, men more degraded than it is easy to imagine, accustomed to vices which cannot be named. This refined Indian gentleman was obliged to keep himself awake all night to resist possible assaults upon himself, such as he saw perpetrated around him. That night can never be forgotten.

October 28th.—Once more we have seen him. The Crown required Mr. Gandhi yesterday and to-day at the Court as a witness in some trial and we saw and spoke to him. He looks thin and unkempt. The wretched food, and his gaol experiences, have told sensibly on his health. But his soul is calm and his mind clear. "It is all well," he said, in his quick incisive way.

Two children, greatly attached to him, accompanied their friend on his return march to the Fort. They walked in line with him, for a long distance up the dusty road, in hope of attracting his attention, and of throwing him a word of cheer. But they failed. His face was "steadfastly set to go to Jerusalem," and he saw nothing but that.

I wonder what he saw in that long march. Not the immediate Jerusalem, I imagine—the place of crucifixion. I know of no vision more terrible than that. The Fort, with its cells and its hateful associations. Those long files of prisoners. The white-clad, brutal native warders, swaggering along with their naked assegais. The lash for the obdurate, and the criminal taint for all. A city whose secrets may not be told; from whose dens children emerge criminals, and criminals infinitely worse than when they entered.

No, not that; it is another Jerusalem which he faces steadfastly. It is such a city as all inspired men see, and to build whose walls they still "endure the Cross, despising shame." A holy City, already come down from God out of Heaven, forming, unrecognized, unseen by worldly souls, amid the squalor of to-day, wherever God's children are. A new Jerusalem, whose beautiful gates are ever open to all nations; where no "colour bar" is permitted to challenge the Indian, and no racial prejudice to daunt the Chinese; into whose walls even an Asiatic may build those precious stones which, one day, will startle us with their glory.

APPENDIX IV

THE ASSAULT ON MR. GANDHI

IN THE *Life of the Rev. J. J. Doke*, by W. E. Cursons, the incident of the assault is thus related:

It was at this juncture that Mr. Gandhi's life was endangered by a savage assault. Doke gives the following account of the occurrence: "Registration was to begin (in Johannesburg) on Von Brandis Square, on Monday, February 10th. Mr. Gandhi said he intended to be the first to register with all his digit impressions. His aim was to set a good example, that the rank and file might be influenced to meet the desire of the Government voluntarily. At nine o'clock I was on my way to town and passed the registration office. Near by, Mr. Leung Quinn (the leader of the Chinese Passive Resisters) stopped me to say that Mr. Gandhi had not yet appeared, and that he was going to do some business, but would be back presently.

"I remember particularly that morning being led to pray as I went through the streets, especially that I might be guided completely to do God's will, but I little thought what the answer would be.

"As I passed the office, Mr. Polak came out and held me a little while talking in the Square. Suddenly a young Indian ran up in a very excited manner and cried out: 'Coolie he hit Mr. Gandhi; come quick!' and with that he ran off in the direction of Von Brandis Square. We naturally followed him as quickly as possible, and I remember noticing several other people running. As we turned into Von Brandis Street we could see that below President Street it was literally crammed with Indians. There must have been five or six hundred there in front of Mr. Gibson's office. Policemen were guarding the door and everybody was full of excitement. I speedily reached the office and, as no one objected, pushed my way in. I found Mr. Gandhi lying on the floor, looking half-dead, while the doctor was cleaning wounds on his face and lips. Mr. Thambi Naidoo, with a severe scalp wound and blood all over his collar and coat, was describing the assault to some policemen. Mr. Essop Mia, with a gash across his head, was also there. When the doctor had finished with Mr. Gandhi, I went over and he recognized me. Then the question was mooted: where should he be taken? He was badly knocked about, his face cut right open through the lip, an ugly swelling over the eye, and his side so bruised that he could hardly move; there might be complications. Some said: 'Take him to the Hospital.' I had hardly time to think, but it seemed as though God had led me there for a purpose and possibly for this purpose. So I said: 'If he would like to come home with me, we shall be glad to have him.' The doctor asked where that was, and hardly seemed able to grasp my meaning. Then he asked Mr. Gandhi where he would like to go; but the sick man seemed perfectly indifferent; so the question was thrown back again on us. Then I stooped down and said: 'Mr. Gandhi, you must decide; shall it be the Hospital or would you like to come home with me?'"

At this point Doke's diary ceases; so the narrative must be concluded without his help. Mr. Gandhi was taken to the temporary Manse on Hospital Hill, which the Doke family were then occupying, and was tended with every care by Mr. and Mrs. Doke and their children. Many messages of sympathy and inquiry were received, including kind ones from Lord Selborne and General Smuts. By careful attention, and an insistence on his own method of treatment—semi-starvation and earth-plasters—Mr. Gandhi regained his health. It appears that the assault was delivered by some dissatisfied Pathans. "They thought they were doing right," the sufferer said, "and I have no desire to prosecute them." They were punished, but Mr. Gandhi took no part in it.

APPENDIX V

THOUGHTS ON THE GITA

[The following were written by Mahatma Gandhi from Yeravada Jail during his last imprisonment.]

IF WE TRY to understand from all possible points of view, and so continuously meditate on the Gita, we must become one with it. As for myself, I run to my Mother Gita whenever I find myself in difficulties, and up to now she has never failed to comfort me. It is possible that those who are getting comfort from the Gita may get greater help, and see something altogether new, if they come to know the way in which I understand it from day to day.

The Twelfth chapter of the Gita tells of Bhaktiyoga—realization of God through Devotion.[1] At the time of marriage we ask the bridal couple to learn this chapter by heart and meditate upon it, as one of the five sacrifices to be performed. Apart from Devotion, Action and Knowledge are cold and dry, and may even become shackles. So with the heart full of love, let us approach this meditation on the Gita. Arjuna asks of the Lord: "Which is the better of the two, the devotee who worships the Manifest, or the one who worships the Unmanifest?" The Lord says in reply: "Those who meditate upon the Manifest in full faith, and lose themselves in Me, those faithful ones are My devotees. But those

---

[1] In Hinduism there are three pathways of union with God. Bhakti (Devotion), Karma (Action) and Jnana (Spiritual learning). The last is sometimes translated Knowledge, but it implies much more than this English word.

who worship the Unmanifest, and in order to do so restrain all their senses, looking upon and serving all alike, regarding none as high or low, those also realize Me."

So it cannot be affirmed that one way is superior to the other. But it may be regarded as impossible for an embodied being fully to comprehend and adore the Unmanifest. The Unmanifest is without attributes and beyond the reach of human vision. Therefore all embodied beings consciously or unconsciously are devotees of the Manifest.

"So," saith the Lord, "let thy mind be merged in My Universal Body, which has form. Offer thy all at His feet. But if thou canst not do this, practise the restraint of passions of thy mind. By observing *Yama* and *Niyama*,[1] with the help of *Pranayama*, *Asan*[2] and other practices, bring the mind under control. If thou canst do thus, then perform all thy works with this in mind; that whatever work thou undertakest, thou doest it all for My sake. Thus thy worldly infatuations and attachments will fade away, and Love will rise in thee.

"But if thou canst not do even this, then renounce the fruit of all thy actions; yearn no more after the fruit of thy work. Ever do that work which falls to thy lot. Man cannot be master over the fruit of his work. The fruit of work appears only after causes have combined to form it. Therefore be thou only the instrument. Do not regard as superior or inferior any of these four

---

[1] Yama and Niyama represent the things to be done and the things to be avoided in order to lead a moral life.
[2] Pranayama means regulation of one's breathing. Certain breathing exercises are regarded as helpful in restoring health and bringing the passions under control. Asan means the mode of sitting while engaged in meditation.

methods which I have shown unto thee. Whatever in them is suitable for thee, that make use of in the practice of devotion."

It seems that the path of hearing, meditating and comprehending may be easier than the path of *Yama, Niyama, Pranayama* and *Asan*. Easier than this may be concentration and worship. Again, easier than concentration may be renunciation of the fruit of works. The same method cannot be equally easy for everyone; some may have to turn for help to all these methods. They are certainly intermingled.

In any case, the Lord says, "Thou wishest to be a devotee. Achieve that goal by whatever method thou canst. My part is simply to tell thee whom to count a true devotee. A devotee hates no one; bears no grudge against anyone; befriends all creatures; is merciful to all. To accomplish this, he eliminates all personal attachments; his selfishness is dissolved and he becomes as nothing; for him grief and happiness are one. He forgives those who trespass against himself, as he hungers for forgiveness from the world for his own faults. He dwells in contentment; and is firm in his good resolves. He surrenders to Me his mind, his intellect, his all. He never causes in other beings trouble or fear, himself knowing no trouble or fear through others. My devotee is free from joy and sorrow, pleasure and pain. He has no desires, but is pure, skilful and wise. He has renounced all ambitious undertakings. He stands by his resolves, renouncing their good or bad fruit and he remaining unconcerned. Such an one knows not enemies and is beyond honour or disgrace.

"In peace and silence, contented with whatever may

come his way, he lives inwardly as if alone and always remains calm, no matter what may be going on around him. One who lives in this manner, full of faith, he is My 'Beloved devotee.' "

Fearlessness is an essential for the growth of other noble qualities. How can one seek Truth or cherish Love without fearlessness? As Pritam has it, "the path of Hari (the Lord) is the path of the brave and not of cowards." Hari here means Truth, and the brave are those armed with fearlessness, not with the sword, the rifle and other carnal weapons, which are affected only by cowards.

Fearlessness connotes freedom from all external fear —fear of disease, bodily injury and death, of dispossession, of losing one's nearest and dearest, of losing reputation or giving offence, and so on. One who overcomes the fear of death does not surmount all other fears, as is commonly but erroneously supposed.

Some of us do not fear death, but flee from the minor ills of life. Some are ready to die themselves, but cannot bear their loved ones to be taken away from them. Some misers will put up with all this, will part even with their lives, but not with their property; others will do any number of black deeds in order to uphold their supposed prestige. Some will swerve from the straight and narrow path, which lies clear before them, simply because they are afraid of incurring the world's odium.

The seeker after Truth must conquer all these fears. He should be ready to sacrifice his all in the quest of Truth even as Harischandra did. The story of Harischandra may be only a parable; but every seeker will bear witness to its truth for his personal experience, and therefore that story is infinitely more precious than any historical fact whatever, and we would do well to ponder over its moral.

Perfect fearlessness can be attained only by him who has realized the Supreme, as it implies the height of freedom from delusions. But one can always progress towards this goal by determined and constant endeavour and by increasing confidence in oneself. As I have stated at the very outset, we must give up external fears.

As for the internal foes, we must ever walk in their fear. We are rightly afraid of animal passion, anger, and the like. External fears cease of their own accord, when once we have conquered these traitors within the camp. All fears revolve round the body as the centre, and would therefore disappear as soon as one got rid of the attachment of the body.

We thus find that all fear is the baseless fabric of our own vision. Fear has no place in our hearts when we have shaken off the attachment for wealth, for family, and for the body. Wealth, the family, and the body will be there, just the same; we have only to change our attitude to them. All these are not ours but God's. Nothing whatever in this world is ours. Even we ourselves are His. Why, then, should we entertain any fears?

The Upanishad, therefore, directs us "to give up attachment for things while we enjoy them." That is to say, we must be interested in them not as proprietors, but as only trustees. He, on whose behalf we hold them, will give us strength and the weapons requisite for defending them against all comers. When we thus cease to be masters and reduce ourselves to the rank of servants, humbler than the very dust under our feet, all fears will roll away like mists; we shall attain ineffable peace and see Satyanarayan (the God of Truth) face to face.

Man's delight in renunciation differentiates him from the beasts. Some demur that life thus understood becomes dull and devoid of art, and leaves no room for the householder.[1] But these critics fail to grasp the true meaning of renunciation, which does not mean abandoning the world and retiring into the forest, but rather the infusion of the spirit of self-sacrifice into all the activities of life.

The life of a householder may take the colour either of indulgence or renunciation. A merchant who does his work in a sacrificial spirit will have large sums of money passing through his hands every day, but his thoughts will be entirely devoted to service. He will not cheat or speculate, but will lead a simple life. He will not injure a living soul, but will lose millions rather than do any harm.

Let no one run away with the idea that this type of merchant only exists in my imagination. Fortunately for the world, it is represented in the West as well as in the East. It is true, such merchants may be counted on one's fingers, but the type ceases to be imaginary as long as even one living specimen can be found to answer to it.

If we go deeply into the matter, we shall come across men in every walk of life who lead dedicated lives. No doubt these men of sacrifice obtain their livelihood by their work. But livelihood is not their objective, it is only the by-product of their vocation. Motilal was a tailor at first and continued as a tailor afterwards. But his spirit

[1] Referring to the four Ashrams or stages of the complete human life in Hinduism. The second stage is that of the householder who lives in the world, enjoys the married life and has children. The third and fourth stages imply renunciation.

was changed and his work was transmuted into worship. He began to think about the welfare of others, and his life became artistic in the highest sense of the term.

A life of sacrifice is a pinnacle of art, and is full of true joy which ever renews itself. A man is never surfeited with it, and the spring of interest is inexhaustible. Indulgences lead to destruction. Renunciation leads to immortality. Enjoyment has no independent existence. It depends upon our attitude towards life. One man will enjoy theatrical scenery, another the ever-new scenes which unfold themselves in the sky. Enjoyment, therefore, is a matter of individual and national education. We enjoy things which we have been taught to enjoy as children.

Again, many self-sacrificing people imagine that they are free to receive in return everything they need and many things they do not need, because they are rendering disinterested service. Directly this idea sways a man, he ceases to be a servant and becomes a tyrant over the people.

One who would serve will not waste a thought upon his own comforts, which he leaves to be attended to or neglected by his Master on high. He will not therefore encumber himself with everything that comes his way; he will take only what he strictly needs and leave the rest. He will be calm, free from anger, and unruffled in mind, even if he finds himself put to great difficulty. His service, like virtue, is its own reward, and he will rest content.

Again, one dare not be neglectful in service or be behindhand with it. He who thinks that one must be diligent only in one's personal business, and that unpaid public business may be done in any way and at any time, has still to learn the rudiments of renunciation. Voluntary service, where others demand the best, must take precedence over service of self. In fact, the pure devotee consecrates himself to the service of humanity without any reservation whatever.

APPENDIX VI

THE CLOSING EVENTS

IN THE *Life of the Rev. J. J. Doke*, by W. E. Cursons, a chapter giving a brief account of the closing events of the passive resistance struggle was contributed by Mr. Gandhi. It runs as follows:

"Mr. Doke, who played an important part in the Indian Passive Resistance Movement, did not live to see the final stages. He has described the struggle in his own graphic style in his Monograph on me, 'Gandhi.'

"This chapter is intended to take a brief survey of the Movement from where Mr. Doke left it. No Englishman had such a keen grasp of the subject as he, by patient study, had acquired. Busy though he was with the work of his own flock, if a man of his breadth of vision and his all-round humanity could be said to have had a special flock, he made this Indian Question as much his own as the work of the pastorate. He collected and tabulated every scrap of paper upon the subject. He wrote much upon it. He saw the authorities and spoke to them with the certainty of the knowledge of an expert. He took charge of the editorial work of the Passive Resistance Organ, *Indian Opinion*, during our absence from South Africa. The leading articles he wrote for the journal during the period are literary monuments. His anxiety to keep up the traditions of the journal was so great that, in matters of policy, he took the advice of, and allowed himself to be guided by, those whom he was not bound to consult. He came in contact with the best and the worst of Indians. All his study was not merely to bring to a close a Passive Resistance Movement, however great it may have been. He had dreams about the future of South Africa, the part that Indians were to play in it, the part that Christianity had to play in the great drama that was being enacted before him. His Indian work was taken up in answer to the question of his soul: 'What am I to do in South Africa in the midst of many races?'

"Mr. Doke had intended, if he lived, to take part in the constructive programme of the Indian community after the struggle was finished. He had intended, too, to write a volume on the lessons of the struggle. But that was not to be.

"The readers of these pages will be glad to know the final result of the historical struggle which attracted world-wide attention. Only a bird's-eye view is possible in a single chapter of a book, when a full description would require several volumes. During the last stages it took a most unexpected and brilliant turn. Every act of repression by the authorities only heartened the resisters. The refusal of the Government to recognize the legal status of Indian miners and to abolish the poll-tax on indentured Indians, which it was claimed on their behalf the Government had promised the late Mr. Gokhale to do, brought thousands of Indians to the Passive Resistance fold. Indentured Indians, working in the Natal mines and in the sugar fields, struck work and sought imprisonment. This strike must be distinguished from ordinary strikes. It was undertaken, not to usurp the functions of the Government, or to paralyse the industries concerned. It was declared simply as a protest against the £3 tax. It was an assertion on the part of the strikers, men and women, of their self-respect. They were no longer content to pay a tax, which not only told heavily upon their slender purses, but which was a mark of their degradation and a cause of terror to the women-folk. At one time nearly 30,000 men were on strike. The Government and the planters tried every means to bend the strikers, but without avail. They had but one purpose in life: these strikers refused to be left alone. They wanted to fill the prisons. After due notice to the Government, nearly two thousand of them, men, women and children, marched into the Transvaal. They had no legal right to cross the border; their destination was Tolstoy Farm, established by Mr. Kallenbach for Passive Resisters; the distance to be covered was 150 miles. No army ever marched with so little burden. No waggons or mules accompanied the party. Each one carried his own blankets and daily rations, consisting of one pound of bread and one ounce of sugar. This meagre ration was supplemented by what Indian merchants gave them on their way. The Government imprisoned the leaders, i.e. those whom they thought were leaders. But they soon found that all were leaders. So when they were nearly within reach of their destination the whole party was arrested. Thus their object (to get arrested) was accomplished. That extreme reasonableness was mixed with such an unbending spirit was shown, when the Indian strikers voluntarily stayed their activity during the strike of the Government railwaymen, which was certainly not a Passive Resistance Movement.

"The Indian strikers at once stood aloof, and their

self-restraint was much appreciated throughout the Empire; whilst it had not a little to do with the final settlement, for which negotiations were opened.

"It will be easily imagined that India would not remain supine when a mighty effort was being made by her sons in this far-off Continent. Under the splendid leadership of the late Honourable Mr. Gokhale, meetings of protest were held all over the country, and thousands of pounds were collected to aid the Resisters. Lord Hardinge, the Viceroy, who strongly protested in a public speech at Madras against what was transpiring in South Africa, sent a Commission to investigate the cause of the upheaval. A local Commission was appointed. Though for high political reasons the Indian community as a whole refused to give evidence before it, the Commissioners completely vindicated the Resisters by declaring in favour of every one of the main contentions of the aggrieved Indians. And so at last legislation was passed repealing the poll-tax, restoring racial equality in law, and recognizing the status of Indian wives. Thus ended the great struggle in 1914, after having lasted nearly eight years.

"Mr. Doke, along with many, considered it to be a religious or an ethical struggle. It was not undertaken in order to gain individual rights but to gain national dignity. The methods adopted were not those of brute force or violence, but those of self-sacrifice and suffering. Repeal of obnoxious legislation was an embodiment of the vital principles that Indian sentiment must not be flouted on Indian matters. It was an admission of the right of the Indians to be consulted in everything affecting their status and intimate well-being. And it was for such an achievement that Mr. Doke laboured during his lifetime. Who knows how important a part he would have played in the more difficult work of reconstruction? Certainly the Indian community misses the guiding hand."

APPENDIX VII

MR. POLAK'S VISIT TO INDIA

WHEN MR. GANDHI and Seth Haji Habib left for England in 1909, Mr. H. S. L. Polak was sent by the Transvaal Indian Community to India in order to tell the story of Satyagraha in South Africa. Mr. Gokhale and the Servants of India Society arranged his itinerary, and a thirteen months' campaign followed with striking results. In December, 1909, at Lahore, the Indian National Congress for the first time made the South African Indian grievances the central feature of the session. Gokhale's speech deeply moved the large audience. He then proposed in the Viceroy's Council and the Government adopted a resolution to stop recruitment of indentured labour for Natal unless the Indian grievances were remedied. Thus public attention was focussed on this question, and Gokhale's later visit to South Africa was partly due to this campaign.

APPENDIX VIII

THE INDIAN WOMEN'S PART

THE FOLLOWING WAS written by Mrs. Polak for the Golden Number of *Indian Opinion* immediately after the struggle was over:

Ruskin has said: "A woman's duty is twofold, her duty to her home and her duty to the State." Scarcely an Indian woman in South Africa has read Ruskin's words, probably they have never heard of them, but the spirit of truth manifests itself in many ways, and the Indian women of South Africa intuitively know this as one of the true laws of life, and their work showed that they performed their greater duty accordingly. These women, without any training for public life, accustomed to the retirement of women in India, not versed or read in the science of sociology, just patient, dutiful wives, mothers, and daughters of a struggling class of workers, in an hour of need, moved by the spirit of a larger life, took up their duty to their country, and served it with that heroism of which such women alone are capable.

It is often said that woman does not reason, and perhaps it is a charge largely true, but where the elementary laws of being are concerned, woman follows a surer path than any dictated by reason, and sooner or later gets to her goal. Every reform movement has shown that from the moment women stand side by side with men in the maintenance of a principle, however dimly understood by them, the spirit of the movement grows, is crystallized, and success to the movement is assured.

The Westerner is so accustomed to think of the Indian woman as one living in retirement, without any broad thought and without any interest in public affairs, that it must have come with a shock of surprise to learn that many Indian women, some of them with babies in their arms, some expecting babies to be born to them and some quite young girls, were leaving their homes and taking part in all the hardships of the Passive Resistance campaign.

The last phase of the struggle, and the one through which to-day we rejoice in peace, was practically led in the early stages by a small band of women from Natal, who challenged prison to vindicate their right to the legal recognition of their wifehood, and a similar small band of women from Johannesburg.

The women from Natal, all of them wives of well-known members of the Indian community, travelled up to Volksrust, were arrested and sentenced to three months' hard labour, and were the first of hundreds to go to jail. The women from the Transvaal travelled down the line, taking in the mines on their way, holding meetings and calling upon the men to refuse to work and to die rather than live as slaves; and at the call of these women, thousands laid down their tools and went on strike. I think it may safely be said that, but for the early work of these brave women, the wonderful response to the call of honour and country might never have taken place. About six weeks after the Transvaal women left, they also were arrested, and a similar sentence to that passed upon the women of Natal was passed upon them, and they were forcibly vaccinated. So these brave women were shut away from life, but the struggle now so splendidly begun went on.

A few days after the release of these last women, two gave birth to children, and another, a young girl of about twenty, passed away, and a fourth hovered between life and death for months, but the victory was won. To-day, all these women are back in their homes and are busy in the usual routine of an Indian woman's life.

There is absolutely none of the pride of heroism about them. They are the same patient, dutiful women that India has produced for centuries; yet they endured the publicity of being in the open glare of all that was going on. No one who does not know India can understand how terrible to the Indian woman such publicity is. They endured the physical hardship, the mental sorrow, the heartache of absence from all they loved most in the world; for nearly all who did not take young children with them left young ones at home. They endured hunger-strikes without hardness or bitterness. India has many things to be proud of, but of none more than the part the Indian women of South Africa took in the uplifting of a people here despised

APPENDIX IX

MR. GANDHI'S FAREWELL

THE FOLLOWING REPORT of the farewell speech of Mr. Gandhi at Johannesburg on the eve of his departure from South Africa gives his own considered view of the struggle. It is reported in the Golden Number of *Indian Opinion* thus:

Mr. Gandhi said that they or circumstances had placed him that evening in a most embarrassing position. Hitherto those who had known him in Johannesburg had known him in the capacity of one of many hosts at gatherings of that kind, but that evening they had placed him in the unfortunate position of being a guest, and he did not know how he would be able to discharge that duty. For the other, he thought long experience had fitted him, if he might say so with due humility, most admirably; but the present position was entirely new to him and Mrs. Gandhi, and he was exceedingly diffident as to how he was going to discharge this new duty that had been imposed upon him. So much had been said about Mrs. Gandhi and himself, their so-called devotion, their so-called self-sacrifice, and many other things. There was one injunction of his religion, and he thought it was true of all religions, that when one's own praises were sung one should fly from those praises; and, if one could not do that, one should stop one's ears; and if one could not do either of these things, one should dedicate everything that was said in connection with one to the Almighty, the Divine Essence, which pervaded everyone and everything in the Universe, and he hoped that Mrs. Gandhi and he would have the strength to dedicate all that had been said that evening to that Divine Essence.

Of all the precious gifts that had been given to them, those four boys were the most precious, and probably Mr. Chamney could tell them something of the law of adoption in India, and what Mr. and Mrs. Naidoo had done. They had gone through the ceremony of adoption, and they had surrendered their right to their four children and given them (Mr. and Mrs. Gandhi) the charge. He did not know that they were worthy to take charge of those children. He could only assure them that they would try to do their best. The four boys had been his pupils when he had been conducting a school for Passive Resisters at Tolstoy Farm and later on at Phoenix. Then when Mrs. Naidoo had sought imprisonment, the boys had been taken over to Johannesburg, and he thought that he had lost those four pearls, but the pearls had returned to him. He only hoped that Mrs. Gandhi and he would be able to take charge of the gift.

Johannesburg was not a new place to him. He saw many friendly faces there, many who had worked with him in many struggles in Johannesburg. He had gone through much in life. A great deal of depression and sorrow had been his lot, but he had also learnt during all those years to love Johannesburg even though it was a Mining Camp. It was in Johannesburg that he had found his most precious friends. It was in Johannesburg that the foundation for the great struggle of Passive Resistance was laid in the September of 1906. It was in Johannesburg that he had found a friend, a guide, and a biographer in the late Mr. Doke. It was in Johannesburg that he had found in Mrs. Doke a loving sister, who had nursed him back to life when he had been assaulted by a countryman who had misunderstood his mission and who had misunderstood what he had done. In Johannesburg he had found a Kallenbach, a Polak, a Miss Schlesin and many another who had always helped him, and had alway cheered him and his countrymen. Johannesburg, therefore, had the holiest associations that Mrs. Gandhi and he would carry back to India, and, as he had already said on many another platform, South Africa, next to India, would be the holiest land to him and Mrs. Gandhi and to his children; for, in spite of all the bitterness, it had given them those life-long companions.

It was in Johannesburg again that the European Committee had been formed, when Indians were going through the darkest stages in their history, presided over then, as it still was, by Mr. Hosken. It was last, but not least, Johannesburg that had given that young girl, Valiamma, whose picture arose before him even as he spoke, who had died in the cause of truth. Simple-minded in faith—she has not the knowledge that he had, she did not know what Passive Resistance was, she did not know what it was the community would gain, but she was simply taken up with unbounded enthusiasm for her people. She was sent to jail, came out of it a wreck, and within a few days died.

It was Johannesburg again that produced a Nagappan, and Naryansamy, two lovely youths hardly out of their teens, who also died. But both Mrs. Gandhi and he stood living before them. He and Mrs. Gandhi had worked in the limelight; those others had worked behind the scenes, not knowing where they were going, except this, that what they were doing was right and proper. If any praise was due anywhere at all, it was due to those three who died.

They had had the name of Harbatsingh given them. He (the speaker) had had the privilege of serving imprisonment with him. Harbatsingh was seventy-five years old. He was an ex-indentured Indian, and when he (the speaker) asked him why he had come there, telling him that he had gone there to seek his grave, the brave man replied, "What does it matter? I know what you are fighting for. You have not to pay the £3 tax, but my fellow ex-indentured Indians have to pay that tax, and what more glorious death could I meet?"

He had met that death in the jail at Durban. No wonder if Passive Resistance had fired and quickened the conscience of South Africa! Therefore, whenever he had spoken, he had said that, if the Indian community had gained anything through this settlement, it was certainly due to Passive Resistance. But it was not due to Passive Resistance alone. He thought that the cablegrams read that evening showed that they had to thank that noble Viceroy, Lord Hardinge, for his great effort. He thought, too, that they had to thank the Imperial Government, who, during the past few years, in season and out of season, had been sending dispatch after dispatch to General Botha and asking him to consider their standpoint—the Imperial standpoint. They had also to thank the Union Government for the spirit of justice they had adopted that time. They had, too, to thank the noble members of both Houses of the Legislature, who had made those historic speeches and brought about the settlement; and, lastly, they had to thank the Opposition also for their co-operation with the Government in bringing about the passage of the Bill, in spite of the jarring note produced by the Natal Members.

When one considered all these things, the service that he and Mrs. Gandhi had rendered could be only very little. They were but two of many instruments that had gone to make this settlement. And what was that settlement? In his humble opinion, the value of the settlement, if they were to examine it, would consist not in the intrinsic things they had received, but in the sufferings and the sorrows long drawn out that were necessary in order to achieve those things. If an outsider were to come there and find that there was a banquet given to two humble individuals for the humble part they played in a settlement which freed indentured Indians from a tax which they should never have been called upon to pay, and if he were told also that some redress were given in connection with their marriages, and that their wives who were lawfully married to them according to their own religions had not hitherto been recognized as their wives, but by this settlement those wives were recognized as their valid wives according to the law of South Africa, that outsider would laugh and consider that those Indians or those Europeans who had joined them in having a banquet, and giving all those praises and so on, must be a parcel of fools. What was there to gloat over in having an intolerable burden removed which might have been removed years ago? What was there in a lawful wife being recognized in a place like South Africa?

But, proceeded Mr. Gandhi, he concurred with Mr. Duncan in an article he wrote some years ago, when he truly analysed the struggle, and said that behind that struggle for concrete rights lay the great spirit which asked for an abstract principle and the fight which was undertaken in 1906, although it was a fight against a particular law, was a fight undertaken in order to combat the spirit that was seen about to overshadow the whole of South Africa, and to undermine the glorious British Constitution, of which the Chairman had spoken so loftily that evening and about which he (the speaker) shared his views.

It was his knowledge, right or wrong, of the British Constitution which bound him to the Empire. Tear that Constitution to shreds and his loyalty also would be torn to shreds. Keep that Constitution intact, and they held him bound a slave to that Constitution. He had felt that the choice lay for himself and his countrymen between two courses, when this spirit was brooding over South Africa, either to sunder themselves from the British Constitution, or to fight in order that the ideals of that Constitution might be preserved—but only the ideals. Lord Ampthill had said, in the preface to Mr. Doke's book, that the theory of the British Constitution must be preserved at any cost if the British Empire was to be saved from the mistakes that all the previous Empires had made. Practice might bend towards the temporary aberration through which local circumstances might compel them to pass; it might bend before unreasoning or unreasonable prejudice; but theory once recognized could never be departed from, and this principle must be maintained at any cost. It was that spirit which had been acknowledged now by the Union Government and acknowledged nobly and loftily.

The words that General Smuts so often emphasized still rang in his ears. "Gandhi," he had said, "this time we want no misunderstanding, we want no mental or other reservations. Let all the cards be on the table. I want you to tell me wherever you think that a particular passage or word does not read in accordance with your own reading."

That was what happened. That was the spirit in which he approached the negotiations. When he remembered General Smuts of a few years ago, telling Lord Crewe that South Africa would not depart from its policy of racial distinction, that it was bound to retain that distinction, and that, therefore, the sting which lay in this Immigration Law would not be removed, many friends, including Lord Ampthill, asked whether they could not for the time being suspend their activity. He said "No." If they did that it would undermine his loyalty, and even though he might be the only person he would still fight on. Lord Ampthill had congratulated him, and that great nobleman had never deserted the cause even when it was at its lowest ebb, and they saw the result that day. They had not by any means to congratulate themselves on the victory gained. There was no question of a victory gained, but the question of the establishment of the principle that, so far as the Union of South Africa at least was concerned, its legislation would never contain the racial taint, would never contain the colour disability. The practice would certainly be different. There was the Immigration Law—it recognized no racial distinctions, but in practice they had arranged, they had given a promise that there should be no undue influx from India as to immigration. That was a concession to present prejudice. Whether it was right or wrong was not for him to discuss then. But it was the establishment of that principle which had made the struggle so important in the British Empire and the establishment of that principle which had made those sufferings perfectly justifiable and perfectly honourable, and he thought that, when they considered the struggle from that standpoint, it was a perfectly dignified thing for any gathering to congratulate itself upon such a vindication of the principles of the British Constitution.

One word of caution he wished to utter regarding the settlement. The settlement was honourable to both parties. He did not think there was any room left for misunderstanding, and whilst it was final in the sense that it closed the great struggle, it was not final in the sense that it gave to Indians all that they were entitled to. There was still the Gold Law,[1] which had many a sting in it. There was still the Licensing Laws throughout the Union, which also contained many a sting. There was still a matter which the Colonial-born Indians especially could not understand or appreciate, namely, the water-tight compartments in which they had to live; while there was absolutely free inter-communication and inter-migration between the Provinces for Europeans, Indians had to be cooped up in their respective Provinces. Then there was undue restraint on their trading activities. There was the prohibition as to holding landed property in the Transvaal, which was degrading, and all these things took Indians into all kinds of undesirable channels. These restrictions would have to be removed, but for that, he thought, sufficient patience would have to be exercised. Time was now at their disposal, and how wonderfully the tone had

[1] This was a racial law going back to the times of the Boer Republic; its object was to prevent any coloured person obtaining any land rights in the mining areas except in locations.

been changed! And here he had been told in Cape Town, and he believed it implicitly, the spirit of Mr. Andrews had pervaded all those statesmen and leading men whom he saw. He came and went away after a brief period, but he certainly fired those whom he saw with a sense of their duty to the Empire, of which they were members.

To whatever favouring circumstances that healthy tone was due, it had not escaped him. He had seen it amongst Europeans whom he met at Cape Town; he had seen it more fully in Durban, and this time it had been his privilege to meet many Europeans who were perfect strangers to him, even on board train, who had come smilingly forward to congratulate him on what they had called a great victory. Everywhere he had noticed that healthy tone. He asked European friends to continue that activity, either through the European Committee or through other channels, and to give his fellow-countrymen their help and extend that fellow-feeling to them also, so that they might be able to work out their own salvation.

To his countrymen he would say that they should wait and nurse the settlement, which he considered was all that they could possibly and reasonably have expected, and that they would now live to see, with the co-operation of their European friends, that what was promised was fulfilled, that the administration of the existing laws was just, and that vested rights were respected in the administration; that after they had nursed these things, if they cultivated European public opinion, making it possible for the Government of the day to grant a restoration of the other rights of which they had been deprived, he did not think that there need be any fear about the future. He thought that, with mutual goodwill, the Indian community need never be a source of weakness to that Government or to any Government. On the contrary, he had full faith in his countrymen that, if they were well treated, they would always rise to the occasion and help the Government of the day. If they had insisted on their rights on many an occasion, he hoped that the European friends who were there would remember that they had also discharged the responsibilities which had faced them.

And now it was time for him to close his remarks and say a

few words of farewell. He did not know how he could express those words. The best years of his life had been passed in South Africa. India, as his distinguished countryman, Mr. Gokhale, had reminded him, had become a strange land to him. South Africa he knew, but not India. He did not know what impelled him to go to India, but he did know that the parting from them all, the parting from the European friends who had helped him through thick and thin, was a heavy blow, and one he was least able to bear; yet he knew he had to part from them. He could only say farewell and ask them to give him their blessing and to pray for them that their heads might not be turned by the praise they had received, that they might still know how to do their duty to the best of their ability, that they might still learn that the first, second, and last thing should be the approbation of their own conscience.

BIBLIOGRAPHY

(A)

Mahatma Gandhi. By Romain Rolland. Published by George Allen & Unwin Ltd., London.
> (By far the best sketch of his life and thoughts. A work of supreme genius. The book was published in French and has been well translated.)

Mahatma Gandhi's Ideas, including selections from his writings. By C. F. Andrews. Published by George Allen & Unwin Ltd., London, and Macmillan Company, New York.

Mahatma Gandhi: His Own Story. Edited by C. F. Andrews. Published by George Allen & Unwin Ltd., London, and Macmillan Company, New York.

An Indian Patriot in South Africa. By the Rev. J. J. Doke. Published by the *London Indian Chronicle*. Reprinted by G. A. Natesan, Madras.
> (An invaluable account of Mahatma Gandhi's early days in South Africa.)

My Experiments with Truth: An Autobiography. Published by Navajivan Press, Ahmedabad.
> (This is the standard work.)

Satyagraha in South Africa. Translated by Valji Desai. Published by S. Ganesan, Triplicane, Madras.
> (This translation has been abbreviated and edited in the present volume. It was taken from Mahatma Gandhi's original Gujarati.)

A Guide to Health. By Mahatma Gandhi. Published by S. Ganesan, Triplicane, Madras.

Hind Swaraj. By Mahatma Gandhi. Published by G. A. Natesan, Madras.

Mahatma Gandhi. By H. S. L. Polak. Published by G. A. Natesan, Madras.
> (A thoroughly accurate, well-informed, and sympathetic sketch by one of Mahatma Gandhi's closest personal friends.)

Mahatma Gandhi: An Appreciation. By R. M. Gray and Manilal C. Parekh. Published by Association Press, Calcutta.
> (Compiled with great care from a liberal Christian standpoint.)

Gandhi the Apostle. By H. M. Muzumdar. Published by Chicago University Publishing Co.
> (The work of a young and ardent admirer who has deeply appreciated Gandhi's message.)

Mahatma Gandhi: Ethical Religion, with an introduction by John Haynes Holmes. Published by S. Ganesan, Triplicane, Madras.
> (An important little book with an excellent introduction.)

Young India. Current issues. Published by Navajivan Press, Ahmedabad.
> (Mahatma Gandhi is Editor of *Young India*; therefore this is the main source from whence to discover his own ideas and life-history.)

Golden Number of *Indian Opinion.* Edited by H. S. L. Polak. Published at Phoenix, Natal, South Africa.
(A very important document for South African days, admirably edited.)
Mr. Gandhi : the Man. By Millie Graham Polak. With an introduction by C. F. Andrews. Published by Allen & Unwin.
(An intimate picture of Mr. Gandhi's personality.)
Speeches and Writings of M. K. Gandhi, with an introduction by C. F. Andrews. Published by G. A. Natesan, Madras.
(Contains many early writings not included in *Young India.*)
Economics of Khaddar. By R. B. Gregg. Published by S. Ganesan, Triplicane, Madras.
(An authoritative book on Home-Spinning in India.)
The Ethics of Non-Violence. By R. B. Gregg. Published by S. Ganesan, Triplicane, Madras.
The Indian Problem. By C. F. Andrews. Published by G. A. Natesan, Madras.
The Dawn of a New Age. By W. W. Pearson. Published by S. Ganesan, Madras.

(B)

The main supply of literature concerning Mahatma Gandhi published in India can be obtained from S. Ganesan, Publisher, Triplicane, Madras.
The following books are now in stock at this publishing house :—
Young India, Vol. I.
Young India, Vol. II.
Satyagraha in South Africa. By M. K. Gandhi.
Indian Home Rule. By M. K. Gandhi.
Ethical Religion. By M. K. Gandhi.
Gandhiji in the Villages. By Mahadev Desai.
Gandhiji in Ceylon. By Mahadev Desai.
Seven Months with Mahatma Gandhi. By Krishna Das (2 Vols.).
To the Students. By C. F. Andrews.
The current numbers of *Young India* are published by the Navajivan Press, Ahmedabad, and it may be subscribed for by writing to the Manager. Some special "Gandhi literature," including the Autobiography, may be obtained from this Navajivan office.

(C)

The *Modern Review,* 91, Upper Circular Road, Calcutta; the *Indian Review,* Georgetown, Madras; the *Indian Social Reformer,* Bombay, and the *Servant of India,* Poona, are among the most important journals which discuss the problems in India connected with this book. The *Modern Review* also publishes from time to time translations from Rabindranath Tagore's writings. All this literature may be obtained from India. British Postal Orders are current in India, and form a useful means for the payment of small amounts, but cheques for larger amounts can also be sent. A rupee in India should be reckoned at 1s. 6d.

INDEX

Abdullah Dada, 62
Abdurrahman, Dr., 30
Abubakr, 42, 53
Aiman, J. and Maud, 12
Akho, Poet, 118
Alexander, H. and O., 12
Ali, 174, 175
Ali, H. O., 12
Ampthill, Lord, 301, 302
Andrews, C. F., 1, 365, 366, etc.
Arjuna, 380
Aryas, 56
Asiatic Department, 82

Bantu, 25, 26, etc.
Baptist, 236
Bawazir, 25, 26
Bhandarkar, 73
Bhowanagree, 77
Bloemfontein, 24
Boers, 32, 33
Bombay, 79
Borah, 43
Boston, 274
Botha, General, 15, 331, 349, etc.
Brahmachari, 104, etc.
Brahmacharya, 20, 100, 104, etc.
Buddhist, 9

Calcutta, 40
Campbell-Bannerman, 35, 38
Capetown, 11
Carlyle, 202
Cartwright, A., 218, 219
Chamberlain, J., 79, 82
Chamneys, 232
Chesney, 73
Christopher, A., 12
Clifford, Dr., 152
Colonial Office, 47, 48
Crewe, Lord, 298, 399
Cursons, W. E., 13, 378
Curtis, Lionel, 132, 134

Dadabhai, 69
Damania, 306

Delagoa, 60
Desai, P. K., 12, 284, 306
Desai, Valji, 12
De Wet, General, 33
Dick, Miss, 244
Doke, Rev. J. J., 13, 16, 232, etc.
Doke, Olive, 235
Doukhobors, 154
Duncan, P., 148, 149
Durban, 13, 16, 232, etc.
Dutch, 30

Elgin, Lord, 48, 157, 160, etc.
Escombe, 41, 68
Esselen, 360
Essop Mia, 221, 379
European, 45, 46, 47, etc.

Farrar, Sir G., 161
Fox, G., 9

Gandhi, Maganlal, 5, 150, 359
Gandhi, Mahatma, 7, 8, 9, etc.
Ganesan, S., 12
Ganges, 15, 276
Gani, 42
Gita, 16, 20, 166
Gladstone, 59, 99
Godfrey, Dr., 85
Gokhale, G. K., 15, 60, 92, 336
Gool, Mrs., 12
Griffin, Sir Lepel, 157
Gujarati, 42

Habib Haji, 12, 143, 144, etc.
Hajura Singh, 208
Harbatsingh, 357, 358, 397
Harrison, Agatha, 12
Hertzog, General, 33, 297
Hobhouse, Miss, 247
Hosken, 151, 152
Hottentot, 31
Howard, Rev. J., 246
Hoyland, J., 12
Hunter, Sir W. W., 41, 76
Huxley, 202

Indian Opinion, 13, 137
Indus, 25
Ismail, Yusuf, 171

Jain, 373
James, W., 8
Jews, 56
Jinnabhai, 204, 205
Jiva, 198
Johannesburg, 11
Joshi, 136

Kacchhalia, 172, 173, etc.
Kadva, 198
Kallenbach, 12, 107, 305, 332, etc.
Kathiawar, 43
Khan, Advocate, 78
Khan, Samundar, 195, 201
Kimberley, 24
Kingsford, Anna, 373
Kitchener, Lord, 34, 36
Kitchin, H., 183
Konkani, 345
Kotwal, P. K., 327
Kruger, President, 33, 54, etc.
Kuhne, 90, 331

Lansdowne, Lord, 53, 79
Lichtenstein, 213
Lutavan, 331, 332

Madanjit, 24, 183, 240
Madeira, 160, 165
Madras, 40
Maharasthra, 20
Majuba, 31
Mansukhlal, 77, 78, 183
Marian Hill, 319
Maritzburg, 65
Mauritius, 42
Mazzini, 216
Medh, S. B., 11, 136, 284, etc.
Mehta, Dr., 279
Mehta, Sir P., 73
Meman, 42, 43, etc.
Mercury, Natal, 66
Merriman, J. X., 59, 218
Mian, K., 72
Milner, Lord, 35, 38, 125
Mir Alam, 231

Molteno, Miss, 59, 248
Morley, Lord, 53, 157
Motilal, 385
Murray, Dr. A., 373

Nagappan, 294, 295
Naidoo, P. K., 292, 293
Naidoo, Thambi, 12, 188, 189, etc.
Natal, 12
Natesan, G. A., 293

Oldfield, Dr., 373
Orange Free State, 24, 31

Pathan, 136, 225
Phillips, Rev. C., 246
Phoenix, 28, etc.
Pillay, 214
Pioneer, 73
Playford, 199
Polak, Henry S. L., 12, 89, 90, 354, etc.
Polak, Millie, 12, 88, 393
Porbandar, 43, 63
Pretoria, 11

Quinn, 187
Quran, 202

Ramayana, 20
Ramazan, 109
Ramdas Gandhi, 86, 87
Ranade, 73, 92
Raychand, 99, 100
Redmond, 157
Ripon, Lord, 50
Ritch, L. W., 158, 160, 272, etc.
Roberts, Lord, 31
Robertson, Sir B., 363, 364, 365
Royappen, 288
Ruskin, 88, 202
Rustomji, Parsi, 118, 119, etc.

Sankarananda, 216
Satyagraha, 15, 19, 23, etc.
Savage, Dr., 136
Schreiner, Olive, 59, 248
Schreiner, W. P., 59, 340
Sclesin, Sonya, 12, 245
Selborne, Lord, 53, 79

INDEX

Shelat, 136
Smuts, General, 33, 220, 264, 265, etc.
Sodha, 284
Solomon, Sir R., 163, 164
Sorabji, 11, 207
Stead, W. T., 37
Stent, Vere, 247
Sundara, Rama, 178, 179, etc.
Symonds, 161, 162

Tagore, Rabindranath, 13
Times, The, 76, 77
Tolstoy, 154, 202, 374, 375
Tolstoy Farm, 15, 93
Transvaal, 20, 23, 34, etc.
Trappist, 319
Tribhuvandas, 98
Tulsidas, 20, 178
Tyabji, Justice, 73
Tyeb Haji, 62

Upanishad, 20

Vaishnava, 108, 109
Valiamma, 11, 398
Vedas, 20
Vereeninging, 35
Vernon, 220, 283
Vogl, Mr. and Mrs., 246
Volksrust, 206
Von Brandis, 11, 231, 378

Washington, Booker, 131
Wedderburn, Sir W., 75, 157
West, Ada, 359
West, Mr., 232, 240, 359
Whyte, Mrs., 12
Wylie, Colonel, 360

Yajnik, Indulal, 12

Zanzibar, 248
Zealand, New, 235
Zulus, 25, 27, etc.

GEORGE ALLEN & UNWIN LTD
LONDON: 40 MUSEUM STREET, W.C.1
CAPE TOWN: 73 ST. GEORGE'S STREET
SYDNEY, N.S.W.: WYNYARD SQUARE
AUCKLAND, N.Z.: 41 ALBERT STREET
TORONTO: 77 WELLINGTON STREET, WEST

For Product Safety Concerns and Information please contact our EU representative GPSR@taylorandfrancis.com
Taylor & Francis Verlag GmbH, Kaufingerstraße 24, 80331 München, Germany

www.ingramcontent.com/pod-product-compliance
Lightning Source LLC
Chambersburg PA
CBHW071236300426
44116CB00008B/1060